SEX RESEARCH

SEX RESEARCH
Studies from the Kinsey Institute

edited by
Martin S. Weinberg

New York
Oxford University Press
London   1976   Toronto

Dedicated to the memory of
Alfred C. Kinsey
1894–1956

Pioneer in studies of human sexual behavior
Founder of the Institute for Sex Research

CONTENTS

SEX RESEARCH

INTRODUCTION

1

The Institute for Sex Research, founded on the campus of Indiana University by Alfred C. Kinsey, was first catapulted to national prominence with the publication of the famous "Kinsey Reports." Since that time, the Institute has continued to publish many interesting and informative, though less celebrated, works dealing with a wide range of sexual topics. The purpose of this book is to bring together, for the first time, a history of the Institute and selections from its various publications.

Upon joining the Institute in 1968, I felt obliged to become familiar with all of its previous publications. At that time, in book form alone, this amounted to some 3500 pages (a figure that has since nearly doubled). Even after I had been at the Institute for a number of years, however, I still had not read every book, let alone the plethora of journal articles. Frustrated over this failure to do my "homework," I finally worked out and followed a systematic program of reading. All the while, I was wishing that a survey of these works were available.

During the course of my reading, I thought that other people might also be interested in a survey of the work of the Institute for Sex Research. Consequently, I began pulling together selections that I thought would best provide such an overview. This book is the result.

As is evident in this survey, a prominent thread running through the Institute's works is its sociological perspective. Alfred Kinsey and his associates, for example, compared the sexual patterns found in different segments of society. Thus, in *Sexual Behavior in the Human Male* and *Sexual Behavior in the Human Female*, they describe, among other things, the different sexual patterns of men and women, of people belonging to different social classes, and of people with different educational, geographic, and religious backgrounds.

After Kinsey's death, Paul Gebhard and his associates continued to work in the Kinsey tradition, developing social/sexual typologies. In *Sex Offenders*, they discuss different types of rapists, child molesters, Peeping Toms, and other sex offenders, and they provide social explanations for these behaviors. In *Pregnancy, Birth and Abortion*, they describe and analyze the differences among women of different classes and races with regard to pregnancy and its outcomes.

John Gagnon, who collaborated on *Sex Offenders*, and William

Simon, who later joined the Institute, provided additional socio-logical insights with regard to sexual development and the character of different sexual patterns. One of their central themes is that sex is not Freud's programmed, raging tiger as much as it is simply another form of scripted social behavior. That is, sex is elicited and organized by socially acquired conceptions of appropriate desires, partners, settings, sequences of behaviors, and so forth. This model of human sexuality is implicit in all the Institute's studies. During the 1960's, it was made explicit and was developed by various Institute members with regard to a variety of realms of human sexuality—for example, homosexuality, premarital sex, fetishism, and sadomasochism.

Within such a sociological framework, sex is approached by the Institute in a matter-of-fact way. It is not seen as anything exotic, even in its unusual or diverse forms, and people with unconventional sexual habits are not seen as fundamentally different from other people. The Institute works treat sex, like other behaviors, as something that is molded in an understandable way by social experiences.

Alan Bell, a psychologist at the Institute, has given attention to the psychological element in this developmental process. He is interested in the psychological consequences of social experiences and how these psychological factors in turn affect one's sexuality. This is illustrated in his book, *The Personality of a Child Molester*, which is an in-depth study of how one man became a child molester. Bell has also continued the Institute's tradition of describing social/sexual typologies. At present, he is especially interested in delineating a variety of types of homosexuals and the developmental patterns that produce each type.

My own interests, and those of my colleague Colin Williams, include social reactions to sexuality. What are the reactions that surround various facets and forms of human sexuality? How do people deal with these reactions? And what are their consequences? Questions such as these have been the focus of my work on nudists and our joint work on homosexuality.

In addition to the work of Institute staff, there is a monograph series composed of books appearing under the auspices of the Institute but written by authors who are not employed by the Institute. This series shows the range of meanings that sex has in human life. It deals with the spectrum of human sexuality in other societies and in earlier times, and with sexual expression in various media such as art and literature.

This book condenses the above works, providing a survey of the history, ideas, and findings of the Institute for Sex Research. Hopefully, it will inform the reader about the social factors that influence human sexuality. For the whole purpose behind the Institute for Sex Research is to dispel the myths and lack of knowledge that have far too long surrounded this elusive subject.

OUR HISTORY
How It All Began

2

Most Americans have heard of Alfred Kinsey and the famous "Kinsey Reports." Yet few people know much about Kinsey or the Institute for Sex Research, which he founded. For example, how did Kinsey come to embark on his unprecedented course of research; how did the Institute for Sex Research develop; and how has its research been carried out?

This chapter, which includes writings by three of Kinsey's closest colleagues, provides an historical backdrop with which to begin. It starts with a description of the Institute by Paul Gebhard. Gebhard, an anthropologist, joined Kinsey's research team in 1946. He is coauthor of a number of Institute books and has been director of the Institute since Kinsey's death in 1956.

Cornelia Christenson's absorbing biography of Kinsey provides the second selection. Christenson, who has degrees in English and psychology, has been affiliated with the Institute since 1950. She is coauthor of a number of Institute works and is presently writing the biography of an elderly homosexual male.

The chapter ends with Wardell Pomeroy's fond recollections of Kinsey and their association, as described in his book *Dr. Kinsey and the Institute for Sex Research*. Pomeroy, a psychologist who joined the Institute in 1943, is coauthor of its first four books. He is now a practicing psychotherapist in New York City and has recently published a number of books for sex education.[1]

---

[1] These include: *Boys and Sex* (New York: Delacorte Press, 1968); *Girls and Sex* (New York: Delacorte Press, 1970); and *Your Child and Sex* (New York: Delacorte Press, 1974).

THE INSTITUTE

Paul H. Gebhard

While the name of the "Kinsey Institute" has circulated widely, relatively few persons have a clear image of the Institute for Sex Research or any adequate idea as to its purposes. Indeed, an occasional individual is under the impression that the Institute died with its founder, Dr. Alfred Charles Kinsey. . . . [Thus, I would like] to outline the history of the Institute and describe its content, goals, policies, and functions.

THE BEGINNINGS, 1938–1947

In 1938 the Association of Women Students petitioned Indiana University to inaugurate a course for students who contemplated marriage soon or were already married, and it was decided that the course be taught by a group of faculty. One of the group, it was felt, should be Dr. Kinsey, since he was not only a biologist, but had encouraged the student petition. At that time he was a professor best known for his evolutionary studies of a species of wasp and for his biology textbooks. He was more knowledgeable about human sexuality than the average educated person, having studied many of the scientific and medical books on the topic. He continued delving into the literature and ultimately came to the painful realization that very little reliable scientific data existed for this vital subject. After the classroom lectures, the students sometimes came to Kin-

From "Institute for Sex Research." Copyright © 1970, Indiana University Publications.

sey privately to ask questions or engage in further discussion. Kinsey began questioning these students as to their opinions and experiences. Gradually he extended his inquiries to other students and, ultimately, to off-campus groups as well. Meanwhile he developed a standard interview, recording the answers in a code which only he could read.

As news of Dr. Kinsey's endeavors spread, a substantial amount of opposition arose, chiefly from conservative faculty members. A number of his friends and colleagues tried to persuade him to abandon such controversial research before he destroyed his own reputation and tarnished that of the University. The power of the reaction was such that the research might well have been suppressed had Kinsey not been staunchly defended by the University President, Dr. Herman B Wells, and by his Department Chairman, Dr. Fernandus Payne, both of whom considered that academic freedom was at stake.

In addition to students, Kinsey in the beginning interviewed almost anyone whom he could persuade: colleagues, visitors, friends, and others. He soon became aware that sexual behavior and attitudes varied markedly according to socioeconomic class. Consequently, he began traveling on his own time and at his own expense to midwestern cities such as Indianapolis, Gary, and Chicago in order to interview nonstudent populations of various occupational groups.

News of Kinsey's efforts reached the National Research Council's Committee for Research on Problems of Sex when he applied for a grant. This led to his meeting with one of the Committee in late 1940. Being favorably impressed, the National Research Council awarded Kinsey his first grant in 1941—$1,600, the monies being provided by the Medical Division of the Rockefeller Foundation. Some of this grant went toward the salary of Mr. (later Dr.) Clyde Martin, a student assistant who had been employed by Kinsey in other research. In 1942, following a visit by three Committee members, the grant increased to $7,500, and Kinsey was able to enlarge the scope of his operations. The year 1943 marked the beginning of large grants which, by 1946, reached $35,000. This infusion of money permitted the enlargement of the staff and a great increase in interviewing. Mr. (later Dr.) Wardell Pomeroy joined Kinsey in 1943, and from then until 1945 a large number of case histories were collected, chiefly in colleges, medical schools, hospitals, prisons, and other institutions in the midwestern and northeastern states. In 1946, a year when emphasis shifted from data gathering to analysis

1. Kinsey interviewing. 1953. *Dellenback*

and writing of the first "Kinsey Report," Dr. Paul Gebhard was added to the staff. In 1947, in order to clear up ambiguity as to ownership of the interview records, possession of anticipated royalties, and to make it possible to guarantee confidentiality of the records, the Institute for Sex Research was established as an Indiana non-profit corporation. . . .

FAME, 1948–1953

In 1948 the first "Kinsey Report," *Sexual Behavior in the Human Male*, was published and met with an unexpected reception. The publisher, W. B. Saunders, had felt that the first printing of 20,000 volumes was optimistic, yet this was quickly exhausted as the book went on to make the best seller lists. Dr. Kinsey's name became a household word, and an enormous amount of controversy and attendant publicity developed. On one hand were those who hailed the work as a long overdue break through the barriers of ignorance, and on the other were those who construed it as an attack on Judeo-Christian sexual morality.

In the midst of this, interviewing on an extensive scale was resumed despite the fact that the demands on Kinsey's time had multiplied. In addition to the innumerable requests for lectures, the expansion of the Institute, made possible in large part by book royalties, brought increased administrative obligations. The staff grew from six to nearly twenty, and the library proliferated from a few hundred to thousands of volumes. . . . To add to the complexity, data analyses and writings were begun for a book on females, a long-planned companion to the "male" volume. Fortunately, by this time Dr. Kinsey had been allowed to relinquish teaching and devote himself full time to his research. Kinsey's concept of full-time employment for Institute staff was 8 a.m. to 5 p.m. weekdays and 8 a.m. to 12 p.m. Saturdays; on field trips the standard was generally 9 a.m. to 11 p.m. every day except Sunday. It was difficult to complain of this schedule since Kinsey himself invariably put in a thirteen- to fourteen-hour day. This grinding pace took its inevitable toll, and as the writing of the "female" volume neared completion, Kinsey was in a state of chronic fatigue.

The publication, in 1953, of *Sexual Behavior in the Human Female* was preceded and accompanied by enormous publicity. Numerous reporters for magazines and newspapers requested access to the data. In order to

2. Kinsey, Martin, and Pomeroy. Circa 1947. *Dellenback*

3. Institute staff, 1953. Standing, left to right: Jean Brown, William Dellenback, Pomeroy, Ritchie Davis, Eleanor Roehr, Dorothy Collins; seated, center: Gebhard, Kinsey; seated, front row: Christenson, Hedwig Leser, Martin. *Dellenback*

be scrupulously fair to journalists and to check on the factual accuracy of their reports, Kinsey had arranged that they visit the Institute for several days and read copies of the page proof after signing agreements not to publish before a specified date. The unintended result was a synchronizing of publicity: there was a period of about a month when virtually every popular magazine and newspaper contained a leading article on Kinsey and his research. This unprecedented flood of attention was by no means wholly to the advantage of the Institute. Some persons considered it a carefully contrived publicity campaign done for financial gain; others simply found the amount of publicity somehow unseemly and offensive. The mail achieved proportions which made form-letter responses a necessity.

While the scientific community in general received the new volume as a large and worthwhile contribution to knowledge, there were, in addition to those who voiced legitimate criticism in moderate tones, a small highly vocal minority who attacked both Kinsey and the research with what can only be described as passion. The research was so much a part of Kinsey's life that he construed an attack on it, or even a well-intended criticism, as being directed toward him personally. Consequently he suffered more stress and wounds than a person less deeply involved in his work. The emotional stresses, the excessive demands he made upon himself, and the inability to delegate responsibility or to reduce his sphere of obligations all combined to seriously erode his previously remarkable health, and he developed symptoms of cardiovascular trouble.

Meanwhile the two "Reports" continued to spread literally around the world, being translated into almost a dozen languages and meeting acceptance everywhere except in the Iron Curtain countries, South Africa, and Ireland, where they were banned.

TROUBLE, 1954–1956

While crank mail was commonplace, organized efforts to halt or restrict the research were fortunately few. One or two lay religious organizations officially protested to the University, and the governor became perturbed on at least one occasion, but difficulties at this local level were handled sagaciously and effectively by President Wells and were never allowed to assume critical proportions. At the federal level, however, the Institute was vulnerable.

As early as 1950 the U.S. Customs had begun confiscating shipments of erotic materials addressed to the Institute. For several years it seemed that the matter might be settled out of court, but by 1954 it was evident that a major court case was inevitable and that it would be most expensive in terms of time and money. This inconvenience and worry was to seem almost insignificant compared to a direct assault on the Institute which nearly proved fatal.

Senator Joseph McCarthy had begun attacking foundations on the grounds that they were providing funds to persons or organizations who had communist sympathies or who were unknowingly assisting in the achievement of communist goals. In this battle the Senator and those aiding him were willing to use any weapon available, and the great publicity and controversy surrounding the Institute made it an ideal means of discomfiting the Rockefeller Foundation in 1954. Indeed, a member of the House of Representatives had already advocated that the "Kinsey Reports" be barred from the mails, and the books were kept out of or removed from some military libraries and post exchanges. A professor highly critical of the Institute's work was found to testify before a Special House Committee. Armed with testimony which cast the Institute and its works in a most unfavorable light, the Committee then interrogated the Rockefeller Foundation as to its support. From the formal hearings and from statements made to the press, it became clear that, without calling in additional scientists or consulting published reviews, the Committee had decided that the Institute's research was unscientific, its findings constituted an insult to the population, and its effect would be to weaken American morality and render the nation more susceptible to a communist takeover.

Rockefeller support terminated that year, and from 1954 through 1956 no foundation or individual could be found who would compensate for this financial loss. The sole grant was an annual $3,000 to $5,400 from the National Research Council—a token of their belief in the value of the research and a stamp of scientific approval. The situation was ironic: Dr. Kinsey was at the height of his fame, his books were acclaimed throughout the world, and the grant-giving organizations gave him either sympathy without money or treated him as though he were dangerously radioactive—which, indeed, he was from a political viewpoint. Fortunately the Institute was able to subsist on its savings from book royalties while Kinsey exhausted himself in a fruitless search for funds.

This crisis and Kinsey's failing health did not halt Institute research. Intensive interviewing, especially in California prisons, was resumed after the publication of the "female" volume, and there were various other ventures, including an expedition to Orange Park, Florida, to investigate the sexual behavior of the chimpanzees kept there and an expedition to Peru to study and photograph the erotic prehistoric materials in both public and private museums. All of these projects were financed from Institute savings. . . .

"Indeed, an occasional individual is under the impression that the Institute died with its founder, Dr. Alfred Charles Kinsey."

Kinsey's weakened and enlarged heart was by this time seriously interfering with the work schedule he insisted on trying to maintain. His concerned family and colleagues finally persuaded him to take a vacation trip to Europe in 1955, but this "vacation" soon became an arduous business trip. Exhausted by the demands upon his time, still deeply wounded by what he deemed unjustified attacks upon the research, and continually weighted down by the knowledge that Institute savings were rapidly eroding, Kinsey's health deteriorated rapidly. In August, 1956, while convalescent, he insisted on honoring a lecture engagement made months previously, caught a cold which developed into pneumonia, and died of cardiac failure at the age of sixty-two.

RENAISSANCE, 1957–

Deprived of the man who had exclusively directed it and beset by the still unsolved problems as well as new ones emerging from Kinsey's death, the Institute was in critical condition. Fortunately, the University provided encouragement and increased support. Administrative reorganization was soon undertaken. . . . Dr. Gebhard was made head of the Institute. Dr. Pomeroy, who was put in charge of field work, and Gebhard addressed themselves to the most immediate problems: getting money and dealing with the legal case against U.S. Customs. In the latter, the Institute was immeasurably aided by the University entering the case as *amicus curiae.*

Fortunately, both pressing problems were satisfactorily solved during 1957. With McCarthy discredited and dead, and recognizing the importance of sex in matters of emotional well-being, the National Institute of Mental Health awarded the Institute the first in a series of grants which were destined to continue for years and to constitute the major financial support of the research. In the Customs case a federal district court ruled in favor of the Institute, empowering it to import for research purpose any sort of erotic material and allowing such materials to be sent through the mails. . . .

The Institute inaugurated a number of important new policies periodically during the following decade. First, it was decided to temporarily forego gathering new data by interviewing and to concentrate on analyzing and publishing the large amount already accumulated. . . . A second and more far-reaching innovation was making the Institute library and collections, hitherto used almost exclusively by staff members, available to qualified scholars with demonstrable research needs.

In later years still other changes were made. Instead of a monolithic structure acting as a unit, the Institute became more diversified with several projects headed by different individuals, or combinations of individuals, going on simultaneously. As projects became more specialized, the old-style general interview schedule with its code was replaced by printed questionnaires to be verbally administered by interviewers. The interviewers themselves were no longer only senior staff. Graduate students were trained to interview, and also contracts were let to professional interviewing and polling organizations. The senior staff was thereby largely freed to concentrate on research design, supervision, and analysis. In these later studies the Institute, having progressed beyond the necessity for simple pioneering description, began emphasizing the social and psychological elements of sexual behavior and was less concerned with details of techniques and frequencies. While some measure of accurate description must remain the foundation upon which any study is based, the Institute has now matured to the point where it can and must investigate the more complex and intangible factors which give sex its meaning and importance.

The founding of the Monograph Series was an outgrowth of having made the Institute library and collections available to other scientists and scholars. Originally the Series, entitled *Studies in Sex and Society* and sponsored by the Institute, was intended for books whose authors had obtained most of their material from the Institute. However, others who had worthwhile contributions to make to scholarship wished to publish under the aegis of the Institute, and so provision was made for this as well.

"In 1948 the first 'Kinsey Report,' *Sexual Behavior in the Human Male*, was published and met with an unexpected reception. The publisher, W. B. Saunders, had felt that the first printing of 20,000 volumes was optimistic, yet this was quickly exhausted as the book went on to make the best seller lists."

Lastly, one important innovation concerned teaching. . . . The Institute began in 1962 a seminar for psychiatrists at the Indiana University School of Medicine. In addition to this, the Institute now assists in a general sex education course for medical students and in 1970 began a seminar on human sexuality for graduate students in the behavioral sciences on the Bloomington campus. In that same year a special two-week summer program for clinicians, scientists, and educators was inaugurated. [This program is now given annually with over 100 professionals and laymen attending each year.]

Despite the magnitude of these changes and innovations, most basic policies of the Institute have remained unchanged: the care in maintaining the secrecy of confidential materials, the avoidance of commercialism and politics, and an objective nonjudgmental approach to the study of sex in all its manifestations.

During all of this time the Institute steadily increased in size and productivity. Its third volume, *Pregnancy, Birth and Abortion*, was produced in 1958 by the Institute's new publishers, Harper & Row. Intensive work was then concentrated upon the large amount of data previously collected from prison inmates, and in 1965 a fourth volume, *Sex Offenders: An Analysis of Types*, was published. . . . In keeping with its plan to diversify, the Institute entered in 1966 the period of multiple simultaneous projects: a national sample of college students, a study of a sex education program, and a study of a homosexual community in a large metropolis. In 1968–69 other projects were added as the earlier ones neared completion: a much larger study of homosexuality, a national sample of public opinion as to forms of sexual behavior, a study of sex education in high school and the degree to which the students were exposed to what is considered pornography, a comparative study of certain aspects of homosexuality in the U.S.A., . . . [the Netherlands], and Denmark, and a number of other projects. All of these have resulted in a large number of journal articles and book chapters. In fact, in the last three years of the 1960's, more of those were published than in the entire preceding history of the Institute. In addition, a number of books are in progress.

The funding for these endeavors was chiefly federal—the National Institute of Mental Health and, to a lesser extent, the National Institute of Child Health and Human Development. Two private foundations, the H. M. Hefner Foundation and the Ledler Foundation, have also subsidized some research. Lastly, the University steadily assumed a greater share of the staff salaries and general support. . . .

There was the inevitable turnover in staff. In 1960, Clyde Martin, Kinsey's earliest assistant, resigned in order to devote himself to earning an advanced degree. Dr. Pomeroy, long desirous of following the profession for which he had trained, clinical psychology, left the Institute in 1963 for private practice in New York. These losses were partially offset by the presence of Mr. John Gagnon, who joined the Institute in 1959 and served it for nearly ten years before leaving to teach and complete his doctoral dissertation. A number of research persons in charge of projects were associated with the Institute for much briefer periods: Mrs. Alice Field, Dr. Ritchie Davis, Dr. William Simon, and Mr. James Elias. . . .

In 1966, Dr. Alan Bell joined the Institute, becoming Senior Research Psychologist the following year. Mr. Albert Klassen came to the staff in 1967 as a specialist in survey research, and Dr. Martin Weinberg, Senior Research Sociologist, joined the staff in 1968. [Dr. Colin Williams was appointed Research Sociologist in 1970, after having joined the staff in 1968 as a research assistant.]

[THE] LIBRARY
_____

Anything which has been written and which has some value in the understanding of human sexuality is considered for inclusion in the [Institute's] library. With such a vast scope the library collects a great diversity of items: scientific books, fiction, learned journals, pornography, religious essays, etc., *ad infinitum*. Presently the library has over 20,000 bound volumes and uncounted reprints, pamphlets, and separate items. . . . The Institute library is the largest of its kind in the world. . . . It is unique in a number of respects, not only because it collects erotica, but also because of its ephemeral sexual materials: pamphlets, magazines, clippings, advertisements, and similar items which are rarely, if ever, preserved in libraries.

[THE] ARCHIVAL COLLECTIONS

Since the projects of a society give one insights into that society's interests and values, the Institute acquires and preserves sexual materials of all sorts from a diversity of cultures, past and present.

The photograph collection consists of approximately 50,000 photographs. Most are erotic, ranging from art photography to pornography. Included are a number of scientific documentary photographs. . . .

The film collection consists of several subdivisions. First, there are scientific documentary films, such as those depicting sexual behavior in mammals or physiologic responses in humans. Secondly, the Institute has a large sample of commercial pornographic films which reflect changes in attitudes and in censorship. Thirdly, there is a small sample of experimental avant-garde films, many of which have been publicly exhibited, generally with ensuing legal troubles, so that they are of value in terms of censorship studies as well as art studies.

The Institute has long been interested in the erotic element in art and consequently has amassed a collection of drawings, prints, paintings, and other graphic art forms. . . . Europe, the United States, and Japan are well represented in our archives. . . . The art runs the gamut from works of the famous to the efforts of untalented amateurs. One unique section consists of the sexual art produced by prison inmates. . . .

A collection of objects has also been made. Many of these are classified as objets d'art; other cruder examples are folk art, and still other objects are not art at all, but consist of implements, devices, and humorous trinkets. For example, on one hand we have beautiful, small wooden panels from China inlaid with ivory, semiprecious stones, and mother-of-pearl; on the other hand we have "joke" items such as might be purchased at a modern amusement park booth.

Many persons have contributed biographical materials: diaries, love letters, records of sexual activity, personal essays, and similar data. . . . These materials give us information and insights which cannot be obtained through conventional interviews.

Lastly, we maintain a small audio collection, consisting of phonograph records and tapes representing both commercial and scientific recordings.

SERVICES

Members of the Institute have been in great demand to deliver lectures, serve on panels, and act as consultants. . . . Institute members have lectured to and worked with a wide diversity of organizations such as service clubs, governmental agencies, scientific associations, education groups, law enforcement bodies, churches, and medical groups. [Also, an Information Service was established in 1971 which answers approximately 400 queries each month.]

In many instances individuals and groups visit the Institute to confer and obtain information. . . . [For example,] the Congressionally appointed Committee on Obscenity and Pornography or a committee of the Group for the Advancement of Psychiatry. . . . Other individuals visit the Institute primarily for access to the Institute library or collections. . . .

KINSEY'S LIFE

Cornelia V. Christenson

YOUTH

In his mid-fifties, Alfred C. Kinsey was suddenly catapulted into world-wide fame and notoriety by the publication of his sensational findings on sexual behavior. The social and scientific impact of his two controversial volumes, *Sexual Behavior in the Human Male* (1948) and *Sexual Behavior in the Human Female* (1953), may never be fully measured or documented. That they had a profound effect on the life of our time is certain. To measure the influence of his work and to attempt to disentangle it from the other important currents of change contemporary with it would be a social historian's nightmare. I tend to share the view that the sexual revolution which has brought us franker, more realistic attitudes toward sex and a greater tolerance of variant behavior was inevitable and that Kinsey's work only helped to hasten these inevitable changes.

What kind of man was Kinsey, and what impelled him to enter on, and persevere in, a course of research that entailed so many obstacles and frustrations? . . .

[Kinsey's father] . . . was a self-made man who had finished only the eighth grade at Cooper Union night school. He was not one to easily tolerate differing points of view. His strong drive and his determination to accomplish what he set out to do were clearly mirrored in his first-born, Alfred Charles Kinsey. There was an inevitable clash of wills between the two as the son grew toward adulthood.

From *Kinsey: A Biography*. Copyright © 1971, Indiana University Press. Reprinted by permission of the publisher.

Kinsey's mother, Sarah Ann Charles, a carpenter's daughter, had only four years of schooling. This minimal education betrayed itself only in her letter writing, not in her manner of speaking, Clara Kinsey, her daughter-in-law, recalls. Clara calls her mother-in-law "the sweetest person I have ever known." With this disposition it is no wonder that she submitted readily to the domination of her disciplinarian husband. . . .

Both of his parents were deeply religious during Kinsey's youth, and the family were members of a nearby Methodist church. Sunday observance was so strict that father Kinsey forbade his family to ride to church on Sunday, even with the minister. Nor was the milkman permitted to make Sunday deliveries. A neighborhood boy remembers that all the family was permitted to do on Sunday was "to go to church and eat." The head of the house also taught in the Sunday school and set an example by taking his family to triple Sabbath services—Sunday school, church, and evening prayer meeting. Later Kinsey also taught a Sunday school class at the behest of his father. . . .

Alfred's family life might be described as unduly restrictive during his boyhood and adolescent years, but he was already reaching outside of his home into the beginnings of his lifelong romance with nature and the out-of-doors. . . . Ever since Alfred had been in the seventh grade, he had ranged the countryside on Saturdays to collect botanical specimens. This hobby continued all through high school. . . . Alfred joined the Boy Scouts soon after their founding in 1910 and, with his strong bent for nature craft and the outdoors, worked energetically and persistently on the many tests and badges. He progressed through the necessary qualifications and became an Eagle Scout, one of the earliest in the country to gain this rank. . . .

"Both of his parents were deeply religious during Kinsey's youth, and the family were members of a nearby Methodist church. Sunday observance was so strict that father Kinsey forbade his family to ride to church on Sunday, even with the minister."

He did not date or show any interest in girls. In fact, in his senior year the South Orange High School yearbook placed under his picture a quotation from *Hamlet:* "Man delights not me; no, nor woman neither." A classmate recalls that he was "the shyest guy around girls you could think of." Kinsey senior did not approve of dating in any case, so socializing on young Alfred's part would have undoubtedly led to increased friction at home. . . .

Alfred's father was determined that his son should be trained as a mechanical engineer, which led to increasing conflict between them. . . . After graduating from high school, he did attend . . . [Stevens] Institute from 1912 through 1914, including some summer periods. There he was enrolled in courses in German, mathematics, physics, chemistry, and mechanical drawing. Years later he ruefully recounted his painstaking and laborious efforts to complete a detailed drawing of a steam engine in the mechanical drawing course. At one point he was close to failing in physics, but a compromise was reached with the professor, who agreed to pass him if he would not attempt any advanced work in the field! By this time it was apparently clear to him that he had given it a fair try but that his gifts were not in the field of engineering.

Robert Kinsey, Alfred's brother, remembers clearly a dramatic family scene he witnessed one evening as a child of six or seven. It took place after the family had returned to their home in South Orange from a graduation program at Stevens Institute in nearby Hoboken. Alfred, who was now twenty years old, took this occasion at the close of the school year to announce formally to his parents that he was making a drastic change in plans. Up to now, he said, he had done what his father had wanted him to do, and from now on he was going to do what he wanted to do. His career in engineering was certainly cut short at this point, probably not without some harsh words between a determined father and an even more determined son. . . .

In the fall of 1914 Alfred Kinsey enrolled as a junior in Bowdoin College, Brunswick, Maine, headed for study in biology. . . . Following this change of career plans, the young student was thrown largely upon his own financial resources. . . . According to Kinsey's account, a single suit of clothes costing $25.00 was the only help he received from home from this point on.

STUDENT YEARS

Kinsey's two years at Bowdoin (1914–1916) were busy but not eventful. He came to the campus as an upper classman, obtaining junior status as the result of his two previous years at Stevens Institute. He was able to enroll at once in the biology courses he had looked forward to. . . .

Most of his days and many of his evenings were spent in the college laboratories and classrooms, withdrawn from the social affairs of campus life. He was generally considered shy and scholarly and somewhat of a "loner." . . .

His biological interests were versatile. Birds, flowers, and particularly snakes fascinated him. The college yearbook remarked that "on entering his room one never knows whether Mr. Kinsey or a large, able-bodied snake is going to greet him!" . . .

Kinsey was graduated *magna cum laude* from Bowdoin in June of 1916 with a B.S. degree. . . .

The summer following graduation he spent working in summer camps, by now a well-established pattern for his summer vacations. With the closing of camp he set his face toward Harvard University, which had awarded him a scholarship, and in the fall of 1916 he started his postgraduate studies at the Bussey Institution on the campus there. . . .

Kinsey at this time was already outstanding in more ways than one. His active outdoor life more than compensated for his physical disability, the spine curvature which had kept him out of the army. He is recalled as "a lithe, slender, almost athletic young man more often in field khaki than in tweeds, with an engaging smile, a twinkle in the eye, and an enthusiastic earnestness about his research."

His interest had already been drawn to the study of gall wasps, more particularly, the American Cynipidae. These are insects about the size of a small ant which produce an abnormal growth or gall on a plant, most commonly on oaks, by laying their eggs deep inside the plant tissue. . . .

Although well started on his research and serving as assistant in the laboratories of Radcliffe for the Zoology I courses (1917–18) and in those of Harvard for the Botany I courses (1918–19), he still found time for another project not associated with work toward his degree. This involved compiling a book on edible wild plants under the direction of Professor Merritt Lyndon Fernald at the Gray Herbarium. . . .

This definitive work, *Edible Wild Plants of Eastern North America*, . . . was not actually published until 1943, when the conditions of World War II developed the concept of survival training, which led to sudden interest in how man could live off the countryside. . . .

After the completion of his graduate work he spent the better part of a year traveling to the South and to the West Coast and back on a Sheldon Travelling Fellowship, collecting gall wasps and getting a better understanding of the continent in which he lived and the kinds of people in it. He went on foot with a rucksack, using trains and buses to get from one collecting spot to another, sending his collections back to Harvard by mail and express. . . .

Many days were spent on foot, and he often camped comfortably all alone for a week or so at a time in the deserts and forests of the West. He noted many things besides insects, and was immensely curious about how people spent their lives and what they did and why. . . .

"A classmate recalls that he was 'the shyest guy around girls you could think of.' "

THE FIRST YEAR AT INDIANA

. . . When he was invited . . . to come to Bloomington in April, 1920, to be interviewed for a teaching job at Indiana University, he was unenthusiastic about the prospect of taking his first job in a spot where he felt the summer months would be so unpleasant. . . . After being assured . . . that the terrain around Bloomington was hilly, in contrast to the flat country . . . [further north], he decided, in spite of his doubts, to make the trip to southern Indiana to be looked over and to see the Bloomington campus. On one of the first evenings of his visit Dr. Fernandus Payne invited the young job candidate to attend a Sigma Xi lecture as his guest. It was here, in the entrance to the lecture room and just before the program, that Kinsey was first introduced to Clara Bracken McMillen, later to be his wife. The result of his trip was that he accepted a position as Assistant Professor of Zoology to start the following fall. . . .

Thus it was with a department with a high reputation for scholarship and research, but with a comparatively small faculty . . . that Kinsey cast his lot in 1920. He brought with him the prestige of his Harvard degree, and this, plus his inquiring mind, driving ambition, and unrelenting hard work, brought him rapid academic advancement. He came as an assistant professor, was given the associate professor rank in 1923—three years after his arrival—and was promoted to full professorship in 1929. . . .

It is generally agreed that Alfred Kinsey was an excellent teacher and lecturer, and he enjoyed the expository discourse of undergraduate teaching. . . . .

Later in the fall of 1920 Clara McMillen and Alfred Kinsey met . . . [again]. The occasion was a Zoology Department picnic. . . .

Most of the young couple's six months of courting was within the framework of their second love, outdoor life. On Sundays Alfred felt free to take the day off, and he and Clara would hike out to a nearby scenic area, sometimes with other couples, taking along a campfire lunch. . . .

The Kinseys were married on June 3, 1921, at the home of Clara's grandparents in Brookville [Indiana]. The ceremony was in the parlor with only relatives and a few close friends present. . . .

THE NEW HOUSEHOLD, TEACHING, AND WRITING

The Kinsey children were born in fairly rapid succession. Donald came in mid-1922, Anne followed on January 1, 1924, Joan was born on October 16, 1925, and the fourth child, Bruce, . . . in November of 1928. . . .

Music was already playing an important role in the new household. The Kinseys have always had a piano in their home. Kinsey played regularly for the children while they were growing up and gave his two daughters, Anne and Joan, piano lessons. When he played informally for the family, Chopin and Beethoven were his favorites. . . .

By the Christmas vacation period of 1921, the first year of his marriage, Kinsey had started to draw together material for a high school introductory biology textbook intended for the ninth and tenth grades. . . . He was aiming at an age group he had worked with successfully in his many summers of camp experience. . . . Tutoring youngsters in nature's exciting, intricate lessons was one of his real pleasures. . . .

Lippincott published the first edition of *An Introduction to Biology* in October of 1926, providing strong promotion and advertising. Most reviews were enthusiastic, even in British journals, and adoptions began to flow in. One of the book's chief merits was that it insisted that fancy equipment was not needed to teach biology and that a thoughtful teacher could demonstrate some of the most fundamental problems on almost any vacant lot in the city or the suburbs. . . .

Donald's illness and death at the age of three years and nine months was the family's first tragedy. His was an exophthalmic case, not recognized at first. In June, 1925, his parents took him to the Mayo Clinic, where his case was given intensive study. A successful operation on the thyroid was performed in September, and Kinsey left Clara in Rochester with Donald and returned home with twenty-month-old Anne to meet his classes and keep the household running. . . . Although the operation on Donald had been successful, after the return to Bloomington he became seriously ill again. By the time his illness was diagnosed as diabetes, he had gone into a coma. . . .

The first edition of Kinsey's high school biology text was published the year of Donald's death. . . .

Meanwhile Kinsey was vigorously pursuing the field of research which he had set for himself, the systematic classification of the many species of Cynipidae or gall wasps. He spent long days at the desk and in his laboratory classifying and studying his thousands of specimens. The field work necessary to collect adequate specimens was completely to his liking. . . .

Just before Christmas of his first year at Indiana the findings of his graduate research appeared under three successive titles in the *Bulletin of the American Museum of Natural History*. . . .

His next four major articles appeared during 1922 and 1923 . . . and all dealt with the specimens he had gathered in the West during his year of travel on the Sheldon Fellowship. . . .

In 1930 the first major study of his mature years appeared, ten years after his arrival on the Indiana University campus. It was entitled *The Gall Wasp Genus Cynips: A Study in the Origin of Species*. This weighty volume of over 500 pages with an almost equal number of illustrations appeared in the University series. Six years later, in 1936, he was to publish his second major work, *The Origin of High Categories in Cynips*.

These two volumes . . . which he published during his second decade at Indiana University, firmly established his reputation both here and abroad as one of the leading authorities in his field; they are contributions not only to the taxonomy of the gall wasp but to genetic theory.

They were the culmination of his earlier years of field work and study, painstakingly done and just as carefully seen into printed form. Kinsey's personal, bound copies of these two studies reveal, in their carefully inked marginal corrections and annotations, his straining for the unattainable goals of completeness and total accuracy. . . .

THE EARLY THIRTIES

The question naturally arises whether Kinsey was on . . . comfortable terms with his colleagues. . . . Some accounts [1] make the intra-faculty relationships sound almost ideal, but Kinsey's strongly independent streak actually stood in the way of his working as smoothly with equals or superiors as he did with those under him. When Kinsey was first on campus his youthful arrogance and frankly critical attitude of anyone who he felt did not measure up to his professional standards was the subject of comment. . . .

In the following decades Kinsey certainly mellowed in many ways. For one thing, he became increasingly urbane in his relationships with his peers. This probably developed from a wider experience with problems of interpersonal contact at many levels, as well as from the growing awareness of his own desperate need for public support from his colleagues and the University administration for his work in sex research. . . .

Various honors came to Kinsey during . . . [the 1930's]. In the fall of 1937 he became a "starred scientist"; his name in *American Men of Science* would be starred to indicate this coveted distinction. Such names were chosen by a vote of the outstanding biologists in the country. In April of 1938 he was elected to the executive committee of the American Association for the Advancement of Science at their meeting at Columbus, Ohio. One of the duties of this committee was to survey contributions of science to college cultural programs and to evaluate methods of college teaching. . . .

Kinsey took his last real field trip to collect gall wasp specimens during the summer of 1939. . . .

Although the material was successfully gathered it was never fully studied. Other interests and new responsibilities were by now absorbing more and more of Kinsey's time, and his hope of finding a competent technician to whom he could relegate the task of making twenty pains-taking measurements on each of the tiny insects failed to materialize. . . . Commitment to research in human sex behavior would soon de-mand a very different kind of field work.

THE PIVOTAL YEARS (1938–41)

Kinsey came to the study of human sex behavior as a biologist, not a social reformer. Essentially a taxonomist, he gradually became aware of a new, little cultivated field that lent itself perfectly to taxonomic explora-tion. Eventually this new field absorbed his entire interest, and his gall wasps were neglected. But though primarily a scientist, he was well aware of the human, social, and educational implications of his new sci-entific labors. . . .

In the summer of 1938 a noncredit marriage course, at that time a pioneering venture, was introduced at Indiana University. . . . Its con-tent, method, and material were to be placed in the hands of a seven-member faculty committee, of which Dr. Kinsey was asked to serve as chairman. Three important recommendations had been included . . . They were that it should be a noncredit course for seniors only; that it should cover a wide range of topics, including legal, economic, biologi-cal, sociological, and psychological aspects of marriage; and that men and women should attend the lectures, together. . . . The final provision, . . . that all material in individual conferences "is to be considered con-fidential, and that it is not to be available to the disciplinary deans," is of special significance. It may have slightly tilted open the lid of Pandora's box. . . .

Just when Kinsey grew to realize the real long-range potential of the research material which these individual conferences produced is dif-ficult to pinpoint. The shift of viewpoint from seeing the conferences in the light of information and counseling sessions to considering them primarily as a source of research data was probably gradual. . . . Kinsey was well aware of the lack of scientific information on sex questions, and there were earlier instances of his graduate students asking him questions that he could not answer. The original aim in the interview was certainly a combination of giving out information or advice and factfinding which would aid him in furnishing valid answers to further questions. In order to furnish such answers he discovered that he usually needed to ask the student further questions to gain insight into the real dynamics of individual sexual behavior. Even though his findings were based on very small samples at this early point, he soon started summarizing the results in his marriage course lectures. Thus he achieved an immediacy and significance which he felt added greatly to his presentation. . . .

It was clearly during [1939] . . . that Kinsey developed and put into execution his idea of incorporating a larger and more varied sample of subjects. . . . His first out-of-town trips for the histories appear to have been to Chicago, beginning in June, 1939. . . . He was now working in a community where he had few contacts and it was an uphill job at the start to establish himself. . . .

Some of these interviews were primarily for homosexual histories, but along with them was a mixture of divorce cases made available to him by an investigator for a state committee, and also histories of big-city prostitutes. . . . By this time his enthusiasm was unbounded and he describes his work as a "research project that is growing constantly more exciting." . . .

It was this spill-over into off-campus interviewing that made it feasible for Kinsey's taxonomic approach to be applied to his new field of investigation. . . .

Kinsey's concept of wide variation and extreme range in individual sexual patterns, all to be tabulated in great number and to be sheltered under the label of a biological norm, was his first major contribution. To this he added an analysis of the social factors that operated in part to create these differences: education, religious devoutness, and decade of birth. These items could never have been envisaged or developed without wider sampling than the campus provided. . . .

The marriage course was clearly successful with the majority of students who attended the noncredit lectures. . . . But during the second year there was growing criticism from other sources. Some conservative faculty members felt it was an inappropriate program at the University for various reasons. . . .

Matters came to a head in the summer of 1940, after the project had completed its second year. Following complaints from the local ministerial association, President Wells called Kinsey to his office and placed a choice before him. He could continue either with the marriage course or with his research project of collecting the case history studies in human sex behavior, but not with both. . . .

A month later Kinsey had made up his mind. He wrote Wells that he must "as a research scientist, choose to continue with the case history studies," and he submitted his resignation as chairman and lecturer in the marriage course. . . .

With the decision regarding withdrawal from the marriage course behind him and thus freed from its restrictions, Kinsey started in the fall of 1940 to pour his tremendous drive and energy into furthering his off-campus field work. . . .

Through the period from 1939 on, one can trace the gradual move away from gall wasp research on Kinsey's part. It was with great reluctance that he gave it up; his hopes of keeping both fields active finally faded as he saw the immensity of the new project he had become involved with. . . .

One seeks the reasons why the study of human sex behavior won out over the study of gall wasps during these pivotal years in Kinsey's life. In part it was doubtless the freshness of a different field and the excitement of new, vital discoveries that tilted the balance in favor of sex research. . . .

Most important, however, was his realization of the need which people, especially young people, had for the sex information he was collecting. . . . He saw that there was a problem to solve and a job that needed to be done. . . .

NOTES

1. Notably that by Louise Rosenzweig and Saul Rosenzweig, "Notes on Alfred C. Kinsey's Pre-Sexual Scientific Work and Transition," *Journal of the History of the Behavioral Sciences,* 1969, V, 175–76.

KINSEY AND THE INSTITUTE

Wardell B. Pomeroy

When I walked into Alfred C. Kinsey's office at Indiana University on my first day of work in 1943, I had a somewhat let-down feeling. I had seen it before, but not as a place where my life would be centered. It was a typically drab office in a typical gray-stone Middle-Western university building left over from the last century. The office was large, but it was designed for utility, not comfort, about which Kinsey cared little. It had a musty, institutional air, and it was still cluttered with the remains of his gall-wasp collection.

I was impressed from the beginning with Kinsey's supreme dedication. He was fired-up with a driving resolution that he communicated to me and to the other staff members. He spent most of the first day talking to me about future research, and how he would train me in two-hour sessions every day.

My job was to be chiefly interviewing, and he was extremely careful about those he chose for that work. There were only nine interviewers over the years, and three stayed only a short time. Kinsey and I took about 85 percent of the ultimate 18,000 histories, dividing them almost equally between us. This was of course a vital part of the project, and Kinsey was never more arbitrary than when he was hiring interviewers.

. . . He sought in each instance an interviewer who embodied three paradoxes: he must be happily married, but be able to travel about half the time; he should have an M.D. or a Ph.D. in some related science, yet he must like and get along with people from low social levels; and he must have been born and raised in this country and exposed to our mores and customs, yet must never evaluate what others did sexually. That third point was the largest stumbling block, and Kinsey was ruthless about it.

He had sound reasons for his paradoxical demands. He wanted interviewers who were happily married because people who had never been married were suspect to a good many Americans. It was necessary for them, obviously, to be able to work with lower socioeconomic groups, and he wanted to avoid ivory-tower academic types who could not do so. Finally, it was important for an interviewer to be familiar with our culture, but not prone to moral evaluations, as far as humanly possible, because there were few areas of research where the investigator's own system of morals was so challenged and so crucial as in the study of human sexual behavior.

It was suggested to us at various times that he ought to have women interviewers to interview women, and black interviewers for blacks. But by that logic, Kinsey pointed out, he would have to have prostitutes for prostitutes, drug addicts for drug addicts and so on.

"At the beginning Kinsey was so naive that everything was a revelation to him."

. . . In hiring me, the objections were my lack of a doctorate, which Kinsey insisted I remedy as soon as possible, and my age (29), about which nothing could be done. For a while, considerable attention was given to ways of "making Pomeroy look older," until Kinsey saw that it did not help. In any case he was overjoyed to get a qualified full-time staff member now that he could afford one. He turned to me in one of his infrequent outpourings of feeling and said, like a boy, "Gee, I'm glad you're going to be on the staff." He always treated me as a colleague, never as an inferior.

More and more as I began to work with him, I came to esteem his total dedication. We rarely talked about anything but sex research in general and the project in particular. Like many scientists, he was largely incapable of dealing with the commonplace preoccupations and amusements of other people. I could never forget how one day as we lunched together . . . he announced he had heard a sexy joke he wanted to tell me. I waited with some anticipation, wondering what kind of smoking-car story the authority on sex would produce. He told it straight-forwardly, without a hint of humor. It was a terrible joke, badly related. I tried to laugh, but my polite appreciation was as grim as the joke. Kinsey didn't appear to notice, and laughed at his own humor with the heartiness that always sounded so convincingly Midwestern, even though it came from a former New Jersey boy. It was the only time that I heard him try to tell such a story—mercifully, I might add.

. . . Kinsey found an office across the hall from his own and divided it into three parts, for me, for Clyde Martin, who also was doing interviews, and for a secretary who would work for both of us. So that we could take histories in them, our offices, like his, were soundproofed, and that had not been easy to accomplish, but Kinsey was adamant. His insistence was characteristic; he was a perfectionist.

I may have had a little anxiety at first about doing interviews. At least two psychology departments had dismissed researchers in the early 1930s because the administrators were not yet ready to look at sex objectively. Before 1940, only five psychologists had published anything approaching good statistical data on sexual behavior, and consequently, in spite of my tremendous confidence in Kinsey, I ventured into the deep water with some initial, and concealed, reservation. It was only momentary.

Kinsey was concerned that I be drawn into the project gradually. The first history I took was that of a male college student. Kinsey called these "baby histories," because the young men were like lambs jumping after each other and their histories were innocuous by comparison with, say, those of inmates he had interviewed in prisons. Consequently this first history made little impression on me.

Before I could begin, of course, he had to teach me the code. I was so anxious to get started that I learned it in a little less than two months—a phenomenal time, and possible only because I worked at it night and day. This was the code used in taking the histories. There was another code, involving a rearrangement of the symbols, that was the key to identifying histories in the files. I was so wrapped up in my work that I cracked this second code by myself, and soon, examining the files, to which of course I had access, I was able to identify Kinsey's own history, that of his wife and his daughter and those of about six other persons.

I told him at once what I had done. At first he appeared irritated, but then, quickly, he was pleased because I had shown myself so anxious to absorb everything as rapidly as possible. Nevertheless, he prudently changed the coding of the names so that no new person coming to the project could crack the code so easily. He took every conceivable precaution to protect the identities of the persons who had given histories. The codes were not on paper; they were taught by rote, verbally, to those few who had to know them.

. . . Since so many of the interviews at first had come from the campus itself, a primary consideration from the beginning was the necessity to keep the identity of the people and the facts related to them absolutely secret. No one was more insistent on this point than Kinsey himself, who recognized that it was his guarantee of absolute confidence to those who gave histories that made the research possible. He drilled it into everyone who came to work for him.

I believe there was something more to this than Kinsey's basic rocklike integrity. I think he liked secrets, that their possession gave him a sense of power. And there was no question that the histories did give him a unique potential power. They included political, social and business leaders of the first rank, and with his intimate knowledge of their lives Kinsey figuratively could have blown up the United States. On the Indiana campus alone, as would be true of any campus, there were at least 20 professors with homosexual histories unknown to anyone else, not to mention the professors whose numerous extramarital experiences were recorded.

. . . Martin thought that Kinsey never ceased to be amazed that people, especially in high places, would tell him the things they did. At the beginning Kinsey was so naive that everything was a revelation to him. He came to believe, however, that people would tell him anything about themselves if the circumstances were right, and the way the research was conducted gave them the proper circumstances. Nevertheless, at the start, he was constantly astonished by the difference between public behavior and private acts.

I wondered how he could have taken his own history, but he told me that he had given it to himself just as Freud had analyzed himself. After I joined the project, I took his history about every two years, and he

4. Kinsey writing. 1953. *Dellenback*

5. Kinsey, Pomeroy, and Martin, working with an IBM sorting machine. 1947. *Dellenback*

6. Kinsey with an overflow crowd at the University of California gymnasium, Berkeley. 1952.

took mine. This was good practice at the beginning, to perfect techniques and discover possible inadequacies, and it helped to measure error in recall.

. . . The staff discovered that we could converse with each other in the same shorthand we used in taking histories. We did it in ordinary conversation in private, and of course it permitted us to speak much more openly in public. I might say to Kinsey while we were going up in a public elevator, "My last history liked Z better than Cm, although Go in Cx made him very er." Translated: "My last history liked intercourse with animals better than with his wife, but mouth-genital contact with an extramarital partner was very arousing."

There was, I am sure, a tremendous amount of public curiosity about exactly what questions we asked in taking a history. People viewed the idea sometimes with horror, sometimes with fear or distaste, often with anticipation of various kinds. But in reality there was nothing mysterious or frightening about the interview, as nearly all of our 18,000 subjects discovered. In that number we found only six persons who were visibly upset in the course of history-taking. Three of them were psychiatrists, one of whom was asked to rate himself on the zero-to-six homosexual scale. On the basis of the history he had given, he was obviously a four, and when he was compelled to face this fact, he rushed to the bathroom to vomit.

But time after time people would say, "This has been one of the most therapeutic experiences I've ever had," or, "We should be *paying* you," or commonly, "I've told you things I never thought I'd tell anybody." One psychiatrist told us, "I've been in therapy for three years, and this is the first time I've ever put it all together."

. . . The interview was, of course, at the core of the project, and Kinsey's success must be attributed in large part to his complete mastery of the interviewing art, applied to this most difficult of topics. For *Sexual Behavior in the Human Male* he wrote a truly extraordinary chapter describing the techniques we used. It remains, in my opinion, one of the best accounts in the literature of how to interview.

In each history, there was systematic coverage of a basic minimum of about 350 items. A maximum history covered 521 items. However, whenever there was any indication of sexual activity beyond what the questions covered, we would go as far beyond the basic interview as we thought necessary to get the additional material. "As scientific explorers," Kinsey wrote, "we . . . have been unlimited in our search to find out what people do sexually."

If a subject found it hard to estimate the frequency with which he had engaged in some activity, we were careful not to give him any idea of what the frequencies might be in the general population, or what he himself could be expected to have. Instead we suggested that his activity might average once a week, three or four times a week, three times a day, or once a year—indicating the widest possible range. We were also on guard against people who were obviously very suggestible; we took care to avoid implying an answer and to check the answers for consistency.

. . . We asked our questions directly, without hesitance or apology. Kinsey correctly pointed out that if we were uncertain or embarrassed in our questioning we could not expect to get anything but a corresponding response. Unlike previous researchers, we did not say "touching yourself" when we meant masturbation, or "relations with other persons" when we meant "sexual intercourse." We also never asked *whether* a subject had ever engaged in a particular activity; we assumed that everyone had engaged in everything, and so we began by asking *when* he had first done it. Thus the subject who might want to deny an experience had a heavier burden placed on him, and since he knew from the way we asked the question that it would not surprise us if he had done it, there seemed little reason to deny it.

Since there were so many questions to be asked, the questioning went as rapidly as the subject could comprehend. But there was a better reason for doing this. Under the rapid fire, the subject was much more likely to answer spontaneously, and so it would be virtually impossible for him to fabricate answers. We looked our subjects squarely in the eye and fired the questions at them as fast as we could. These were two of our best guarantees against falsifying.

In making cross-checks on accuracy, we used interlocking questions. Before we ever asked direct questions about homosexuality, for instance, there were 12 preliminary inquiries, whose significance only a psychiatrist would have recognized; and it would have been hard for anyone with more than incidental homosexual experience to deny it after he had answered them.

If we thought a subject's answer was wrong or incomplete, we tried to rephrase the question so that he would have to prove his answer or expose its falsity. If a subject was of low mentality we might pretend that we had misunderstood his negative reply, and ask another question as though he had answered affirmatively. To make it as easy as possible for subjects to correct their answers, we ignored contradictions, accepting the correction as though it were a first reply. On a few occasions, as Kinsey recalled in the *Male* volume, we took a complete history even though we were convinced from the outset that it was going to be a fraud, then put it aside and told the subject, "Now give it to us straight." Naturally, we had to be sure of our ground in such cases. Kinsey pointed out that the false record, viewed against the corrected record, gave us valuable insights into an individual's public admissions compared with his actual behavior.

There were times, too, when we did not recognize the falsity of an interview until after it had been given, and in each of those cases we went back to the subject and demanded that he correct the record. These cases included feeble-minded subjects, prison inmates and even clergymen. We did not lose a single history by taking such action. It was Kinsey's firm belief that giving a history was voluntary, but once the commitment was made, the subject assumed responsibility for its accuracy.

. . . A way of reassuring our subjects was to make it clear that we had no desire to have the names of persons with whom they had been involved sexually. If names were given anyway, we let the subject know that they were not being recorded. Even so, it was obviously impossible to avoid identifications in many instances, and that was why we found it hard to get histories from some married persons, or from those who had had sexual relations with relatives or persons prominent in their communities. It was also difficult with those who were involved in deeply emotional love affairs and consequently might find it hard to avoid identifications.

. . . It was particularly important that we know the sexual viewpoint of the cultures from which our subjects came. Kinsey illustrated this point with the case of an older black male who at first was wary and evasive in his answers. From the fact that he listed a number of minor jobs when asked about his occupation and seemed reluctant to go into any of them, Kinsey deduced that he might have been active in the underworld, so he began to follow up by asking the man whether he had ever been married. He denied it, at which Kinsey resorted to the vernacular and inquired if he had ever "lived common law." The man admitted he had, and that it had first happened when he was 14.

"How old was the woman?" Kinsey asked.

"Thirty-five," he admitted, smiling.

Kinsey showed no surprise. "She was a hustler, wasn't she," he said flatly.

At this the subject's eyes opened wide. Then he smiled in a friendly way for the first time, and said, "Well, sir, since you appear to know something about these things, I'll tell you straight."

After that, Kinsey got an extraordinary record of this man's history as a pimp, which would not have been possible without his understanding that Kinsey knew all about his world.

Again, we would ask a prostitute when she "turned her first trick," not "how old were you when you were first paid as a prostitute." Then we might ask her how many of her tricks returned after their first contact, and much later in the interview we would inquire how often she "rolled her tricks," that is, robbed them. If she had reported that few of the men ever returned, and then later said that she never robbed any of the men, we would tell her that we knew it didn't work that way. If she didn't roll them, why didn't they return? Very often that question would produce a smile and the admission that, since we seemed to know how the business operated, she would tell us the whole story—and it was usually that she robbed every time she thought she could get away with it.

. . . If, at this point, there is any further curiosity about the questions we actually asked, let me give you a guided tour through the interview, which has been so much debated and discussed.

When the subject arrived, we began with some general conversation, thanking him for coming, perhaps explaining the value of the contribution he was making if we had not discussed that before. There would even be desultory chat about the weather.

Then we asked, "Do you have any questions?" Usually the subject did not, but occasionally there were casual inquiries, and sometimes he would ask a question about his sexual problems. We had a standard answer for that contingency: "Well, we need to get your history first. When I have more information about you, we'll come back to that."

There were routine questions about age, birthplace, place of residence. We were establishing bench marks with the early questions. For example, a subject might say he had lived in Connecticut until he was 14, then had moved to California. Then later, when we asked such questions as "How old were you when you first masturbated?" if the subject said "Fourteen," we could say, "Oh, that was after you went to California?" to which he might respond, "No, it was before," and thus we could tell whether he was older or younger than 14 when he first masturbated.

. . . Next we took a religious history, both the subject's present status and his relationships with religion from his early days onward. That would give us some idea of what his particular frustrations might be and where blocks might occur. Then came his health, his hobbies, and his interests. Obviously all of this was nonthreatening material. People concentrated so much on answering these questions that they began to forget they were giving a sex history at all.

We moved on to the subject's non-sexual activities in high school or college, if he had attended, and went on from that point chronologically to his marriage; how long the marriage had lasted, how long he had known his wife, and so on. From that series we went to family background—the relationships with brothers and sisters, occupations of father and mother, and similar questions.

It took about 15 or 20 minutes to answer all these, and not one of them had been about sex. Thus usually it was easy at that juncture to go on to early sex education. Again the subjects did not feel threatened, because these things had happened when they were little children and they did not feel responsible for them. Here, too, we began using sexual terms for the first time, asking questions about how and where the subject got his first knowledge of sexual matters. We asked, for instance, how old he was when he first learned that babies grow inside mothers, how old he was when he first learned there was such a thing as intercourse, how he acquired a knowledge of such things as condoms and how he found out about homosexuality. We asked males when they first ejaculated, females when they first menstruated. That led naturally to questions about when pubic hair developed, when the voice changed in males, how quickly or how slowly growth occurred. When this series had been answered, our bench marks were firmly established.

. . . Now we could go directly to early sex experiences. It was still fairly easy going for the subject, because again it had all happened when he was small and he was not responsible.

From this point, the order of the questions varied. For example, with upper-level males we could go next to masturbation, a natural consequence of the question about first ejaculation, and then we got a history of the subject's masturbation, the fantasies accompanying it and his reaction to it. This would be followed by questions about nocturnal emissions, the subject's petting experience and his premarital intercourse, if any, his extramarital intercourse, and his use of contraceptives.

In the questions about masturbation, we would ask about his use of the basic techniques. If we found a man who had used all or most of them, this would open the way to pursue with other questions what further techniques he might have used, and the frequency as well. Specifically, we asked male subjects about techniques, including manual masturbation, making coital movements against a bed or some other object, self-fellation (possible for only a few men, but attempted by most), insertion of various objects in the urethra and anus, and the use of melons or similar objects to masturbate in. We asked about any unusual position that the subject might have employed, the use of ropes to tie up the penis, or the use of toilet paper tubes, bottles and condoms as aids. We were quick to explore any lead the subject gave us into any rare or unusual masturbatory activity, because the purpose was to record the whole range of human sexual behavior.

. . . If the subject were a female, the masturbation questions naturally were a little different. Routinely we asked about the subject's use of clitoral friction, about bed masturbation (that is, lying on her stomach and making coital movements), crossing the legs and using thigh pressure, stimulation of breasts and insertion of objects into the vagina. If it became obvious that she was using a wide variety of techniques, that would open the way to such questions as whether she used a vibrator, or whether she practiced anal stimulation.

With both men and women, we routinely asked about erotic fantasies during masturbation, and if these were elaborate we might spend several minutes eliciting further details. In this as in other types of behavior, answers to questions about one kind of activity would tell us whether nothing more was to be learned, or whether we could further explore a subject with additional questioning.

We asked how subjects responded sexually to reading about sex, or seeing it, or hearing music that might excite them, or whether they were excited sexually by traveling in vehicles. From such questions we could get clues to the homosexual content of a subject's history. His erotic response to dreams, for example, might be greater, he would say, if he dreamed about masculine figures, and that might be supplemented with similar images when he masturbated. It was possible, then, to build up a picture of the relative components of the individual's sex life. Another clue to homosexuality might be a subject's desire to look at his penis while masturbating.

. . . Now we were at the core of perhaps the deepest and strongest of the taboos—that against homosexuality—in persons who had no idea they had such feelings, or who were aware of them and had tried to suppress them. If there was any resistance to be encountered, this was where we would find it.

There followed the details, if any, of the subject's sadomasochistic feelings. Did he bite when he was having intercourse? Did he enjoy being bitten? Similar questions completed this aspect, if it existed. We asked if the subject was aroused by seeing animals copulating, and this would lead to queries relating to his own sexual activity with animals, if any. We asked about the individual's anatomy—the size of his penis, whether he was circumcised and the angle of the penis in erection.

With lower-level males, we could go directly from here to intercourse, then back to masturbation, petting, wet dreams and homosexuality. It was the same with lower-level females. If an individual had an extensive homosexual history, from the point at which we discovered it we could go into 250 more questions. The two major extensions from the questions were in homosexuality and prostitution.

. . . Though the average interview ran from an hour and a half to two hours, college students did it usually in an hour, partly because they were so quick and precise in their answers, having more rapid mental reflexes and less to remember. Older persons might take three hours to work their way through. Those with multiple marriages quite naturally took more time. The 350 questions, which had to be memorized, were in one order for females and in another for males, and there were other variations.

How do you know people are telling you the truth? I am confident that those who hated the whole idea of the research, or were skeptical of it for other reasons, would never believe any answer Kinsey or I or any-

7. Jordan Hall on the Indiana University campus, where the Institute for Sex Research was once housed. Circa 1956. *Dellenback*

8. Staff conference: Christenson, Kinsey, Pomeroy, Gebhard. 1953. *Dellenback*

9. Martin, Gebhard, Kinsey, and Pomeroy consulting the male interview files. 1953. *Dellenback*

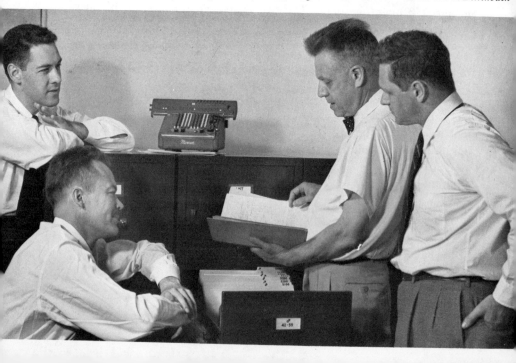

one else might give to that question. Yet the answer is a simple one. There are only three possible ways of not telling the truth: by denying or covering up, by exaggerating, or by remembering incorrectly. Exaggeration was almost impossible with the system we used for asking questions rapidly and in detail. Persons who later told us they had tried deliberately to exaggerate reported little success. Not remembering accurately could be dealt with statistically; the errors one person might make were offset by errors another one made in the opposite direction.

. . . Covering up was the most serious problem, since there were so many taboo items in most histories. But there were numerous cross-checks, so that an answer at one point actually gave us a clue to an answer elsewhere. We took histories of husbands and wives and could cross-check certain parts of their backgrounds. We made some retakes after a minimum interval of two years, and an average interval of four years, to see how well people could reproduce the same material. In most cases, the cover-up factor was very slight, although some leeway had to be made for it.

We added questions as the project developed. For example, it was not until 1948 that we started asking about extramarital petting. We were late in getting to this area primarily because Kinsey was still a little naive on the subject and because he resisted changing the interview questions. The later histories, then, were better and more productive. Yet there were few changes. Of the 350 questions in the basic interview, only about 10 were changed.

It was possible to get the equivalent of 25 typewritten pages on one page by using our code.

. . . The recording of a history was a sensitive process because we were taking down not only the answer but also the tonal inflection. The answer might be "YES," "*Yes!*" or simply "Yes," or perhaps a very hesitant "Ye-e-e-s." We would record these answers four different ways. To be sure that we were setting down the inflections in the same way, it was necessary sometimes for Kinsey and me (or any other combination of interviewers) to record simultaneously, which also gave us an opportunity to criticize each other's techniques.

Understandably, it was an anxiety-producing situation the first time "the master" sat in while I took a history, but I got used to this, as did the others. When we observed Kinsey taking a history, we tended to be a little deferential, partly for the obvious reason and partly because he was quite defensive; he had an explanation for everything he did. We found that we were able to record an individual's history simultaneously with about 98 percent accuracy.

. . . The longest history we ever took was done jointly by Kinsey and me. We had heard of a man who had kept an accurate record of a lifetime's sexual behavior. When we got the record after a long drive to take his history, it astounded even us, who had heard everything. This man had had homosexual relations with 600 preadolescent males, heterosexual relations with 200 preadolescent females, and intercourse with countless adults of both sexes and animals of many species; he also had used elaborate techniques of masturbation. He had set down a family tree going back to his grandparents; of 33 family members, he had had sexual contact with 17. His grandmother introduced him to heterosexual intercourse, and his first homosexual experience was with his father. If that sounds like *God's Little Acre*, I will add that he was a college graduate who held a responsible government job. We traveled from Indiana to the Southwest to get this single extraordinary history, and felt that it had been worth every mile. At the time we saw him, this man was 63 years old, quiet, soft-spoken, self-effacing—a rather unobtrusive fellow. It took us 17 hours to get his history, which was the basis for a fair part of Chapter Five in the *Male* volume, concerning child sexuality. Because of these elaborate records, we were able to get data on the behavior of many children, as well as of our subject.

At one point in his history-taking, he said he was able to masturbate to ejaculation in 10 seconds from a flaccid start. Kinsey and I, knowing how much longer it took everyone else, expressed our disbelief, whereupon our subject calmly demonstrated it to us. I might add, in case this story confirms the worst fears of any surviving critics, that it was the only sexual demonstration among the 18,000 subjects who gave their histories.

. . . Few interviews were anything more than routine—or seemed so, after the first few thousand—but some responses were memorable. Early in the interviewing we learned that the most embarrassing question we asked, particularly for women, was "How much do you weigh?" I remember, too, the female psychiatrist, quick and sharp in her answers, who said, when I asked how she found out about masturbation: "I invented it, and if I could have patented it, I'd have made a million dollars." Memorable, too, was the female gynecologist, an inhibited old maid, who told us she thought masturbation was normal unless it was excessive. When we asked her what "excessive" meant, she said, "Anything over once a month." Not surprisingly, her own masturbation occurred once a month.

Always in the interviewing we had the example of Kinsey before us, and it was inspiring, to say the least. He was never the rigid, academic college professor, but a scientist whose pragmatism and willingness, even urge, to experiment at any time gave him the flexibility to handle any kind of problem that arose.

He was inflexible about one thing, though. He was determined to get sex information from people, and he intended to get it no matter what obstacle might intervene. If he went into a house and found every room occupied, so that it seemed impossible to find a place for confidential interviewing, Kinsey would nevertheless find one. Sometimes it was a bathroom, more than once an attic. If there was no room inside, he would take a history sitting out on a lawn under a tree. Often he used his car, if nothing else was available.

. . . For Martin, as he recalled later, interviewing meant shedding some cherished preconceptions. He found, for example, that there was no relationship between the sexy appearance of a girl and her actual sexual experience.

As soon as Martin had learned the code and was ready to interview, he was able to read the earlier histories that Kinsey had taken, including those of students who had been in classes with him, and whom he had heard boasting about their sexual exploits in dormitory bull sessions. Their records disclosed the truth, and Martin was astonished by the discrepancies.

. . . . In April 1943 we went with Kinsey to Nicodemus, a tiny hamlet in the northwest corner of Kansas, near Hill City. It had been an exclusively black community since its founding in 1877. Nicodemus could boast only two stores and three houses, so it was not difficult to get the histories of three quarters of the township's people over 15. Not difficult, that is, given Kinsey's powerful ability to knock on a door and persuade persons whom others would surely have thought unpersuadable.

It was in Nicodemus that I encountered my first real interviewing problem, a 35-year-old man who lived in Hill City. I met him one night at a farm where he was visiting. There was nowhere in the crowded little farmhouse where we could get any privacy, so I suggested we get into my car and do the job there.

"The interviewing trips were a grand tour through America. From Miami or Philadelphia, we might be plunged into the life of minuscule communities like Nicodemus, Kansas. Suburban matrons would be followed by prostitutes in prisons, highly placed executives by underworld characters."

We drove out a little way into the country. I stopped and turned on the dome light, then began to take his history. By this time it was near midnight, but I gave no thought to any possible difficulty until I discovered that my subject was homosexual—the first one I had encountered since I began interviewing. We had switched seats so that he sat behind the steering wheel, leaving me free to write. Fortunately that gave me freedom in both directions, since I found myself able to fend him off with my left hand and write with the other.

In the course of taking so many sexual histories over the years, it was hardly surprising that we encountered a few sexual approaches, both male and female. The men were usually more direct about it than the women. Kinsey taught us that the best way to handle this situation was to remain completely impassive, neither making any motion forward in an interested way, nor backing off in obvious disinterest. Nothing cools sexual ardor more than impassivity, he told us, and he was right.

. . . Perhaps the most difficult part of the technique for me to learn was how to control the interview. As I have said, we asked about a dozen questions indirectly related to a person's homosexual history before we came to the direct question: "How old were you the first time you had sexual contact with another person of your own sex?" By this time we would be fairly certain whether or not he had extensive homosexual experience. If at this point he denied an overt history of homosexuality but there were enough indicators in a positive direction to make us reasonably certain he was covering up, we learned to challenge his denials.

Then it became necessary to say, with firmness, even vehemence, and yet always with kindness, "Look, I don't give a damn what you've done, but if you don't tell me the straight of it, it's better that we stop this history right here. Now, how old were you the first time this happened?" Surprisingly, in not a single case did a person refuse to continue. In all of the histories we took, fewer than 10 persons refused to complete one once they started.

I remember taking the history of an Armenian scientist who spoke broken English, so that I had some trouble understanding him.

"How old were you the first time you ever ejaculated?" I asked him at one point.

"Fourteen," he answered.

"How?" I asked.

"With a horse," I thought I heard him say.

My mind went into high gear. This subject was telling me voluntarily about animal intercourse, and my instinct was to jump far ahead in the questioning and pursue the subject.

"How often were you having intercourse with animals at 14?" I inquired.

He appeared confused and taken aback, regarding me amazedly.

"Well, yes," he said, "it is true I had intercourse with a pony at 14."

Later in the interview it developed that what he had said was "whores," not "horse." He thought I was a genius to have known somehow that he had had intercourse with animals.

Since we never knew what we would get in an interview, it was necessary to ask all the questions, even when some of them did not seem applicable to the subject. Interviewing an upper-upper-level woman with an advanced degree, for example, we would nevertheless ask her, "Have you ever been paid for intercourse?" and sometimes the answers to this question were surprising. A Chicago social worker of whom I asked this question answered affirmatively and gave me a long history of prostitution before she got her job. She had had no intention of giving me this information until I asked the question.

. . . The interviews were numbered at the time they were taken, and then renumbered in Bloomington when they were filed. Paul Gebhard, the anthropologist who joined the staff in 1946 and now heads the Institute, was once taking histories in a famous music school where we knew there were a great many homosexuals. As one subject sat down, he saw Paul write "69" on the sheet, and looked up at him in amazement, thinking his sexual behavior had been categorized before he had even begun to talk.

While we encountered relatively few difficulties with the interviewing itself, there were endless problems on the road, as one might imagine from the constant traveling we did from one end of the country to the other. It tried our constitutions as much as it did our endurance. Still vivid in my mind is a trip to Miami with Kinsey and Gebhard, during which Kinsey went through one of his periodic obsessions with a certain kind of food. This time his passion was tropical fruit, and as he did when he was in this frame of mind, he saturated himself with it. We joined him on this fruit binge, and as a result I got a severe case of diarrhea.

Our suite at the hotel consisted of two bedrooms with a connecting bath. One morning I was taking histories in one of these rooms, while Paul worked in the other. About noon, having finished with his morning appointments, Paul speculated as to whether I was through or not, and whether he should wait for me to go to lunch. To see how far along I was, he tiptoed into the connecting hall and put his ear to the keyhole of my room; he would be able to tell from the questions I was asking how near I was to the end of the interview.

I was taking the history of a married woman who had been living a difficult, painful sex life, which she was trying to tell me about as best she could. Suddenly I felt a wave of diarrhea sweeping over me. Much as I hated to interrupt, I knew I must reach the bathroom with the greatest possible speed. With a muttered excuse, I rose and almost ran to the door, pulled it open and exposed Paul in the process of straightening up. When I returned, I tried to explain to the lady what had happened, but I'm sure she must have thought he was listening to her answers, not my questions.

. . . The interviewing trips were a grand tour through America. From Miami or Philadelphia, we might be plunged into the life of minuscule communities like Nicodemus, Kansas. Suburban matrons would be followed by prostitutes in prisons, highly placed executives by underworld characters. Often, in our explorations, we would plunge into a subculture that was unknown to people not only in the city where it existed, but to 90 percent of the public in general. I am thinking of the world of homosexual prostitution in the New York Times-Square area.

As early as 1942 Kinsey had heard something of this world from inmates of the Indiana State Penal Farm, and decided to explore it. He went to Times Square with no contacts whatever, and hung around the

bars on Eighth Avenue that he recognized as gay. Observing for hours at
a time on different occasions, he noticed a man who also seemed to be
constantly hanging around. Going over to him, he said, "I am Dr. Kinsey, from Indiana University, and I'm making a study of sex behavior.
Can I buy you a drink?"

That the man accepted is a testimonial to Kinsey's personality and the
persuasion he could put into the simplest statement. I suppose, too, that
such an invitation coming from someone who looked like the squarest of
the square to a Times-Square denizen had the ring of authenticity. No
one would be likely to make it up. Still, the man was skeptical until he
was having his drink and listening to Kinsey, who had turned on the full
power of his persuasion. It was impossible, one must believe, to doubt
this clear-eyed, earnest, friendly man from the Midwest. In the end, the
pickup agreed to give his history, which proved to be filled with drugs,
prostitution, and prison terms. From then on, he became a valued contact and persuaded other male prostitutes to cooperate.

. . . On one Times-Square trip we used the Lincoln Hotel as our interviewing place. The manager and his staff knew what we were doing,
but apparently the parade of prostitutes, drug addicts and other
members of the Times-Square underworld through the lobby and in the
elevators unsettled them. They told us we would have to leave. We
remonstrated that we were doing nothing illegal or immoral. The manager was adamant. "Nobody's going to undress in our hotel rooms," he
said. We protested that this was not what we were doing. "Yes, but
you're undressing their minds," he insisted. We had to go.

. . . We had much help from fellow professionals, though there was
often a problem, understandably, with other professional people, particularly psychiatrists, some of whom found it hard to accept what we were
doing. The outstanding example of this was at the Menninger Clinic. In
1943 Kinsey was invited to speak there, and the letter indicated that they
had heard of our research and wanted to know more about it. Kinsey
was quite willing to lecture to this or any other professional audience,
because close behind Kinsey the researcher came Kinsey the teacher. At
the time we had decided that we needed a good many more histories of
psychiatrists, so we resolved to combine the lecture with history taking,
as we usually did. But Kinsey accepted without telling his hosts about
his plan, fearing that they might put him off.

The lecture was held in the large board room of the Clinic. To our

10. With Institute photographer Dellenback and Dr. Fred McKenzie, head of the University of Oregon Animal Husbandry Department, investigating sexual behavior of animals.

12. Gathering data from prisoners at San Quentin. *Dellenback*

11. Kinsey and Gebhard in Peru studying pre-Columbian pottery with sexual depictions. *Dellenback*

KINSEY IN THE FIELD
1950–1955.

13. Studying animal films with Dr. McKenzie and Dr. Shadle, University of Buffalo. *Dellenback*

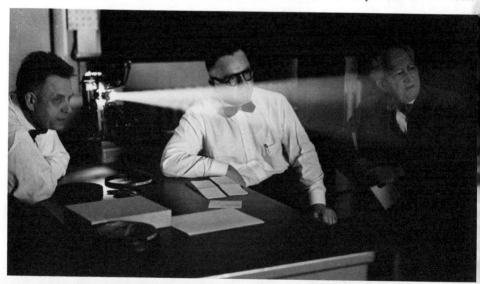

surprise, there were more than 30 psychiatrists sitting around the large boardroom table. Plainly this was not intended on their part to be a simple lecture about the research. Later we learned that at least some members of the Clinic were opposed to everything they had heard about the research, and they had set a trap for Kinsey, confronting him with a board of professional inquisitors whose intention was to show him up. The questions were biting, snide and hypercritical, and there was little warmth in the room.

But that was exactly the kind of arena in which Kinsey excelled. He fielded every question deftly, often even counterattacking. By the end of the session, respect if nothing else had been achieved. As the meeting came to an end, Kinsey said, "Just a moment, gentlemen. We are here to get your histories, and of course I expect all of you to contribute." They were set back a little by this announcement, but they had no rebuttal. As scientists they felt compelled to cooperate. We spent 10 days there collecting histories, and went away with a 100 percent sample. (Kinsey was lax about sampling techniques in the early research. But he soon developed more rigid criteria, particularly his 100 percent sampling.)

. . . What I remember most, I think, from thousands of hours of interviewing, is the driving, driving, driving under the lash of Kinsey's determination to get more and more histories. On one field trip to Chicago we were taking histories of schoolchildren and faculty members in a private school during the day, and homosexual histories from the Near North Side in the evening. Because of the hours the homosexuals kept, we often worked late into the night, but the next morning we had to start in early with the school histories. Kinsey always wanted to take "just one more."

In this homosexual community one evening, Kinsey encountered a sailor from the Great Lakes Naval Training Station, and after a brief conversation, decided it was imperative to get his history. We took him back to our hotel room, which we shared. There was no place for me to stay while Kinsey took the history, so we decided to do it jointly.

It was a long and complicated history. At 4 a.m. we were still at it, and by this time Kinsey for once was completely exhausted. There was a long pause in the questioning and I looked up to see that he had fallen asleep in the middle of a query. I went on with the questioning until Kinsey could rouse himself and take over once more. The sailor was startled at first, but he smiled and indicated he understood.

Kinsey, in fact, once feel asleep while he was lecturing at the University after a strenuous night of interviewing. I was often just as exhausted, but like Kinsey I kept going through sheer willpower. Like him, too, I could see the goal shining clearly before us in the distance—not so much the remote figure of 100,000 histories, but the opportunity to correlate everything we were taking down and to produce a book that would make a truly significant contribution to sex research.

KINSEY AND ASSOCIATES

Social Sources of Sexual Patterns

3

Kinsey and his associates gained national prominence with the publication of the famous "Kinsey Reports." Unprecedented in their scope and approach, these volumes were milestones in the study of human sexuality. Based on interviews with thousands of people, the Kinsey Reports put sex research on a firm quantitative foundation.[1]

Although himself a zoologist, Kinsey approached sex research with a distinctively sociological orientation that has continued to characterize the Institute's work. Thus, explanations offered in Institute publications tend to be more sociological than biological or psychological, and its studies have most often focused on the rates and meanings of various sexual practices in different social groups.

The Institute's first two volumes were *Sexual Behavior in the Human Male*, published in 1948, and *Sexual Behavior in the Human Female*, published in 1953. The studies are based on interviews with 5300 white males and 5940 white females. They deal with what people do sexually, how sexual experiences affect people's lives, what factors account for various patterns of sexual behavior, and the social implications of these patterns.

The effect of the Kinsey Reports was to subject human sexuality to sober and rational examination. Helping to remove sex from the realm of mystery, they educated millions of people and profoundly affected their opinions regarding sexuality.

In the following excerpts, Kinsey and his colleagues discuss the relationship between sex and social characteristics (e.g., social class), the relationship between premarital and postmarital sexual activity, and the differences between male and female sexuality.

---

[1] Edward M. Brecher, *The Sex Researchers* (Boston: Little, Brown and Co., 1969), p. 104. Brecher discusses Kinsey's place in the history of sex research.

SEXUAL BEHAVIOR
IN THE HUMAN MALE

Alfred C. Kinsey, Wardell B. Pomeroy, and Clyde E. Martin

SOCIAL LEVEL AND SEXUAL OUTLETS

Behavioral Patterns

Within any single social level there are . . . considerable differences between individuals in their choice of sexual outlets, and in the frequencies with which they engage in each type of activity. . . .

Masturbation. Ultimately, between 92 and 97 per cent of all males have masturbatory experience. . . .

The highest frequencies of masturbation among single males, in all age periods, are in the college level, . . . Between 16 and 20, for instance, masturbation among the single males of college level occurs nearly twice as frequently as it does among the boys who never go beyond grade school, and the differential is still higher in the twenties. This is the great source of pre-marital sexual outlet for the upper educational levels. For that group, masturbation provides nearly 80 per cent of the orgasms during the earlier adolescent years, as against little more than half the outlet (52%) for the lower educational level. In the late teens it still accounts for two-thirds (66%) of the college male's orgasms, while the lower level has relegated such activity to a low place that provides less than 30 per cent of the total outlet. In all later age periods the relative positions of these groups remain about the same. . . .

At lower social levels, and particularly among the older generations of the lowest levels, masturbation may be looked down upon as abnormal, a perversion, and an infantile substitute for socio-sexual contacts. Although most lower level boys masturbate during their early adolescence, many of them never have more than a few experiences or, at the most, regular masturbation for a short period of months or years, after which they rarely again depend on such self-induced outlets. Among many of these lower level males, masturbation stops abruptly and immediately after the first experiences in heterosexual coitus. The lower level boy who continues to draw any material portion of his sexual outlet from masturbation after his middle teens may be much ashamed of it, and he may become the object of community jokes and of more serious disapproval if his history becomes known. In many instances, these attitudes are bolstered by rationalizations to the effect that masturbation does physical harm; but the objections are in reality based on the idea that masturbation is either abnormal, or else an admission that one is incapable of securing heterosexual intercourse and, therefore, socially inadequate. Among some primitive peoples [1] there is a somewhat similar attitude toward masturbation—an attitude which does not involve moral evaluations as much as it involves amusement at the social incapacity of the individual who has to resort to self-stimulation for his sexual outlet. The better educated portion of the population which so largely depends upon masturbation for its pre-marital outlet, and which draws a not insignificant portion of its outlet from masturbation after marriage, will be surprised to learn what the less educated segments of the population think of one who masturbates instead of having intercourse.

The upper level more or less allows masturbation as not exactly desirable nor exactly commendable, but not as immoral as a socio-sexual contact. Older generations of the upper level were not so ready to accept masturbation. As many males were involved in the older generations, but the frequencies were definitely lower . . . , and there was considerable moral conflict over the rightness or wrongness of the "habit." . . . Upper level males have accepted masturbation more freely within the last two or three decades, and today a high proportion of the teen-age boys of the college group frankly and openly admit this form of pre-marital outlet. During their years in college about 70 per cent of these males depend upon masturbation as their chief source of outlet. . . .

The upper level's pre-marital experience leads it to include masturbation as a source of outlet after marriage. The coital adjustments of this group in marriage are frequently poor, particularly because of the low degree of erotic responsiveness which exists among many of the college-bred females. This offers some excuse for masturbation among the married males of the group; but their early acceptance of masturbation in their pre-marital histories, and their tardy acceptance of heterosexual coitus, are prime determinants in the marital patterns. There are few things in all human sexual behavior which will surprise the poorly educated groups more than this considerable utilization of masturbation by the college-bred male as an outlet after marriage. . . .

Nocturnal Emissions. . . . It is . . . interesting to find that there are still greater differences between educational levels in regard to nocturnal emissions—a type of sexual outlet which one might suppose would represent involuntary behavior.

Nocturnal emissions occur most often in that segment of the population that goes to college. . . . Among males of the college level the emissions begin at earlier ages than among males of lower educational levels. About 70 per cent of the boys who will go to college have such experience by age 15, whereas only about 25 per cent of the grade school group has started by then. Between 16 and 20 years of age, 91 per cent of the single males of the college level experience nocturnal emissions, while only 56 per cent of the lower level boys have such experience in the same period. . . . Ultimately, nearly 100 per cent of the better educated males have such experience, whereas the accumulative incidence figure is only 86 per cent for the high school group, and only 75 per cent for the grade school group.

Between adolescence and age 15, upper level males average nocturnal emissions nearly seven times as frequently as the boys of lower educational levels. Between 16 and 20 the frequencies among the upper level males are nearly three times those for the lower level, . . . About the same differences hold in the older age periods, at least up to 30 years of age. . . .

While it is clear that higher frequencies of nocturnal emissions are correlated with more extended educational histories, the explanation of this correlation is not so apparent. It is evident that nocturnal dreams are not the product of the education in itself, for two groups of boys of different social levels, working together in the same class in grade school or in high school, may have totally different histories of emissions. Is this a measure of some difference in the psychologic or physiologic capacities of the two groups which correlates in some way with factors which determine their educational careers? These are problems which the physiologist and the psychologist will want to investigate in more elaborate detail.

We do know that the frequencies of nocturnal dreams show some correlation with the level of erotic responsiveness of an individual. The boys of lower level are not so often aroused erotically, nor aroused by so many items as the boys from the upper educational levels. Nocturnal dreams may depend upon an imaginative capacity, in something of the same way that daytime eroticism is dependent upon the individual's capacity to project himself into a situation which is not a part of his immediate experience. It may be that the paucity of overt socio-sexual experience among upper level males accounts both for their daytime eroticism and for their nocturnal dreaming. . . .

"At lower social levels, and particularly among the older generations of the lowest levels, masturbation may be looked down upon as abnormal, a perversion, and an infantile substitute for socio-sexual contact. . . . The upper level more or less allows masturbation as not exactly desirable nor exactly commendable, but not as immoral as a socio-sexual contact."

Heterosexual Petting. . . . In general, males of the grade school and high school level are more restricted in their petting behavior than males of the college level. . . .

The social levels are furthest apart in their attitudes on petting and on pre-marital intercourse. The two items are related, for petting, among males of the college level, is more or less a substitute for actual coitus.

In the upper level code of sexual morality, there is nothing so important as the preservation of the virginity of the female and, to a somewhat lesser degree, the similar preservation of the virginity of the male until the time of marriage. The utilization of pre-marital petting at this level is fortified by the emphasis which the marriage manuals place upon the importance of pre-coital techniques in married relations; and the younger generation considers that its experience before marriage may contribute something to the development of satisfactory marital relations. Compared with coitus, petting has the advantage of being accessible under conditions where coitus would be impossible; it provides a simpler means of achieving both arousal and orgasm, it makes it possible to experience orgasm while avoiding the possibility of a pregnancy, and, above all, it preserves . . . "virginity." Whether consciously or unconsciously, petting is chosen by the upper level because intercourse destroys virginity and is, therefore, unacceptable. . . .

The lower educational levels see no sense in this. They have nothing like this strong taboo against pre-marital intercourse and, on the contrary, accept it as natural and inevitable and a desirable thing. Lower level taboos are more often turned against an avoidance of intercourse, and against any substitution for simple and direct coitus. Petting involves a considerable list of techniques which may be acceptable to the college group, and to some degree to the high school group, but which are quite taboo at lower levels (as discussed above). It is just because petting involves these techniques, and because it substitutes for actual intercourse, that it is considered a perversion by the lower level. . . .

Pre-marital Intercourse.   Pre-marital intercourse, whatever its source, is more abundant in the grade school and high school levels, and less common at the college level. . . . Even in the period between adolescence and 15 the active incidence includes nearly half (48% and 43%) of the lower educational groups, but only 10 per cent of the boys who will ultimately go to college. In the later teens, 85 per cent of the grade school group and 75 per cent of the high school group is having pre-marital intercourse, while the figure for the college group is still only 42 per cent. In later years the differentials are not so great but, compared with the grade school group, it is still only about two-thirds as many of the college males who have such intercourse.

The accumulative incidence figures for pre-marital intercourse show much the same differences. About 98 per cent of the grade school level has experience before marriage, while only 84 per cent of the high school level and 67 per cent of the college level is involved. . . .

The frequency figures show still greater differences between educational levels. In the age period between 16 and 20, the grade school group has 7 times as much pre-marital coitus as the college group. There is not much drop in the differential even in the older age groups. The mother who is afraid to send her boy away to college for fear that he will be morally corrupted there, is evidently unaware of the histories of the boys who stay at home. Moreover, nearly half of the males who have intercourse while in college had their first experience while they were still at home, before they started to college. . . . Varying with the age period, the college group derives 4 to 21 per cent of its pre-marital outlet from intercourse; the high school group derives 26 to 54 per cent of its outlet from that source; but the grade school group depends on coitus for 40 to 70 per cent of its total pre-marital outlet. . . .

Lower level males may have a certain respect for virginity, and this may lead them to insist (in 41 per cent of the cases) that they would not marry a girl who had had previous intercourse . . . ; but this may be more of a profession than a matter on which they will stand when it comes to the actual choice of a mate. Lower level males are likely to acquire weekly or more than weekly frequencies in intercourse soon after they start in early adolescence, or at least by the middle teens. They are often highly promiscuous in their choice of pre-marital partners, and there are many who have no interest in having intercourse with the same girl more than once. This strikingly parallels the promiscuity which is found among those homosexual males who are "oncers," as the vernacular term puts it. Some lower level males may have pre-marital intercourse with several hundred or even a thousand or more different girls before marriage, and here their behavior is most different from the behavior of the college-bred males. . . .

Marital Intercourse. . . . There are social differences . . . in regard to the percentage of the total sexual outlet which is derived from marital intercourse. In the age period between 16 and 20, among males of the grade school level, only about 80 per cent of the total sexual outlet comes from marital intercourse, while extra-marital intercourse accounts for another 11 per cent of the total outlet. . . . However, the portion of the outlet coming from marital intercourse in this grade school group rises to approximately 90 per cent in the late forties and early fifties. Among males of the high school group, marital intercourse in the early years accounts for 82 per cent, but rises to 91 per cent of the total outlet by the late forties. For the college level, marital intercourse starts out as a higher portion of the total outlet—nearly 85 per cent; but it drops steadily through the successive years until by the middle fifties it accounts for only 62 per cent of the outlet of these males. . . . In comparison with males of the college level, males of the grade school level, in their middle fifties, derive 26 per cent more of their total outlet from intercourse with their wives.

In the course of his marriage, the outlet of the married male of the college level has increasingly included masturbation and nocturnal dreams and, strikingly enough, extra-marital intercourse. On the other hand, the lower level males never have much masturbation in their marital histories, and the amount becomes less in the later years. During their teens and early twenties, lower level males find a considerable outlet in extra-marital intercourse, but with the advancing years they become increasingly faithful to their wives. In short, lower level males take 35 or 40 years to arrive at the marital ideals which the upper level begins with; or, to put it with equal accuracy, upper level males take 35 to 40 years to arrive at the sexual freedom which the lower level accepts in its teens. Some persons may interpret the data to mean that the lower level starts out by trying promiscuity and, as a result of that trial, finally decides that strict monogamy is a better policy; but it would be equally correct to say that the upper level starts out by trying monogamy and ultimately decides that variety is worth having. Of course, neither interpretation is quite correct, for the factors involve differences in sexual adjustment in marriages at the different levels, as well as the force of the mores which lie at the base of most of these class differences. . . .

Extra-marital Intercourse. In lower social levels there is a somewhat bitter acceptance of the idea that the male is basically promiscuous and that he is going to have extra-marital intercourse, whether or not his wife or society objects. There is some continuation of the group attitude on premarital intercourse into the realm of extra-marital intercourse, at least in the early years of marriage. On the other hand, the upper level male who has been heterosexually restrained for 10 or 15 years before marriage does not freely let down and start extra-marital intercourse as soon as he has learned to have coitus with his wife. As a matter of fact, a male who has been so restrained often has difficulty in working out a sexual adjustment with his wife, and it is doubtful whether very many of the upper level males would have any facility in finding extra-marital intercourse, even if they were to set out deliberately after it. The lower level's extra-marital intercourse does cause trouble, but we do not yet understand all the factors which account for the fact that with advancing age there is a steady decline and finally a near disappearance of extra-marital intercourse from lower level marital histories. . . .

The most striking thing about the occurrence of extra-marital intercourse is the fact that the highest incidences for the lower social levels occur at the younger ages, and that the number of persons involved steadily decreases with advancing age. . . . Lower level males who were married in the late teens have given a record of extra-marital intercourse in 45 per cent of the cases, whereas not more than 27 per cent is actively involved by age 40 and not more than 19 per cent by age 50. In striking contrast, the lowest incidences of extra-marital intercourse among males of the college level are to be found in the youngest age groups, where not more than 15 to 20 per cent is involved, and the incidence increases steadily until about 27 per cent is having extra-marital relations by age 50. . . .

Attitudes on Sexual Techniques

In addition to differences in frequencies and sources of sexual outlet, social levels differ in their attitudes on other matters of sex. . . .

Sources of Erotic Arousal. The upper level male is aroused by a considerable variety of sexual stimuli. He has a minimum of pre-marital or extra-marital intercourse. . . . The lower level male, on the other hand, is less often aroused by anything except physical contact in coitus; he has an abundance of pre-marital intercourse, and a considerable amount of extra-marital intercourse in the early years of his marriage. How much of this difference is simply the product of psychologic factors and how much represents a community pattern which can be properly identified as the mores, it is difficult to say. The very fact that upper level males fail to get what they want in socio-sexual relations would provide a psychologic explanation of their high degree of erotic responsiveness to stimuli which fall short of actual coitus. The fact that the lower level male comes nearer having as much coitus as he wants . . . would make him less susceptible to any stimulus except actual coitus.

The higher degree of eroticism in the upper level male may also be consequent on his greater capacity to visualize situations which are not immediately at hand. In consequence, he is affected by thinking about females and/or by seeing females or the homosexual partner, by burlesque shows, obscene stories, love stories in good literature, love stories in moving pictures, animals in coitus, and sado-masochistic literature. Upper level males are the ones who most often read erotic literature, and the ones who most often find erotic stimulation in pictures and other objects. None of these are significant sources of stimulation for most lower level males, who may look on such a thing as the use of pictures or literature to augment masturbatory fantasies as the strangest sort of perversion.

While these group differences may be primarily psychologic in origin, there is clearly an element of tradition involved. Each community more or less accepts the idea that there will be or will not be erotic arousal under particular sorts of circumstances. The college male who continuously talks about girls does so with a certain consciousness that the other persons in his group are also going to be aroused by such conversation, and that they accept such arousal as natural and desirable. The homosexual male, and the heterosexual male who does not approve of such deliberately induced eroticism, considers this public display of elation over females as a group activity which is more or less artificially encouraged. The lower level male who talks about girls quite as frequently, or even more so, is less often aroused by such talk and may be inclined to consider a listener who is so aroused as somewhat aberrant. There is an element of custom involved in these styles of erotic response.

Nudity.   In many cultures, the world around, people have been much exercised by questions of propriety in the public exposure of portions or the whole of the nude body. There are few matters on which customs are more specific, and few items of sexual behavior which bring more intense reactions when the custom is transgressed. These customs vary tremendously between cultures and nations, and even between the individual communities in particular countries. . . . There are probably no groups in the world who are free of taboos of some sort on this point. The history of the origin of clothing is more often one of taboos on nudity than a story of the utility of body coverings. . . .

Most amazing of all, customs in regard to nudity may vary between the social levels of a single community. In our American culture, there is a greater acceptance of nudity at upper social levels, and greater restraint at lower social levels. Compared with previous generations, there is a more general acceptance of nudity in the upper social level. . . . There is an increasing amount of nudity within the family circle in this upper level. There is rather free exposure in the home for both sexes, including the parents and the children of all ages, at times of dressing and at times of bathing. Still more significant, there is an increasing habit among upper level persons of sleeping in partial or complete nudity. . . . This is probably more common among males, though there is a considerable number of upper level females who also sleep nude. Among the males of the college level, nearly half (41%) frequently sleep nude, about one-third (34%) of the high school males do so, but only one-sixth (16%) of the males of the grade school level sleep that way.

Finally, the upper level considers nudity almost an essential concomitant of intercourse. About 90 per cent of the persons at this level regularly have coitus nude. . . . The upper level finds it difficult to comprehend that anyone should regularly and as a matter of preference have intercourse while clothed. This group uses clothing only under unusual circumstances, or when variety and experimentation are the desired objectives in the intercourse. On the other hand, nude coitus is regularly had by only 66 per cent of those who never go beyond high school, and by 43 per cent of those who never go beyond grade school.

This intercourse with clothing is not a product of the inconveniences of the lower level home, nor is it dependent upon the difficulties of securing privacy in a small home, as too many sociologists have gratuitously assumed. It is primarily the product of the lower level's conviction that nudity is obscene. It is obscene in the presence of strangers, and it is even obscene in the presence of one's spouse. Some of the older men and women in this group take pride in the fact that they have never seen their own spouses nude.

"Many a college male will have kissed dozens of girls, although he has had intercourse with none of them. On the other hand, the lower level male is likely to have had intercourse with hundreds of girls, but he may have kissed few of them."

Many persons at this level strictly avoid nudity while dressing or undressing. They acquire a considerable knack of removing daytime clothing and of putting on night clothing, without ever exposing any part of the body. This is less often true of the younger generation, which has been exposed to the mixture of social levels encountered in the CCC camps, the Y.M.C.A., and the Army and the Navy. Exposure of the upper half of the male body on swimming beaches started as an upper level custom, but the democracy of the public beach has fostered a much wider acceptance of nudity among lower social levels today. . . . Younger males, even of the laboring groups, are often seen at work, out of doors, in public view, while stripped to the waist; but older males of the same social level still keep their arms covered to the wrist, even on the hottest of days and while engaged in the most uncomfortable of jobs. These inroads on the traditions against nudity are reflected in the sleeping and coital customs of younger persons of these lower levels, but the older members of these groups still observe the traditions. There are some cases of lower level males who have been highly promiscuous, who have had intercourse with several hundred females, and who emphasize the fact that they have never turned down an opportunity to have intercourse except "on one occasion when the girl started to remove her clothing before coitus. She was too indecent to have intercourse with!"

Manual Manipulation. At upper social levels there may be considerable manual petting between partners, particularly on the part of the male who has been persuaded by the general talk among his companions, and by the codification of those opinions in the marriage manuals, that the female needs extended sensory stimulation if she is to be brought to simultaneous orgasm in coitus. Upper level petting involves the manual stimulation of all parts of the female body.

Manual manipulation of the female breast occurs regularly in 96 per cent of the histories of the married males of the upper level, and manual manipulation of the female genitalia is regularly found in about 90 per cent of the histories. . . . The upper level believes that this petting is necessary for successful coital adjustment; but preliminary calculations indicate that the frequency of orgasm is higher among lower level females than it is among upper level females, even though the lower level coitus involves a minimum of specific physical stimulation. . . .

The manual manipulation of the female breast occurs in only 79 per cent of the married male histories at lower levels, and the manipulation of the female genitalia occurs in only 75 per cent of the cases. . . . Even when there is such stimulation, it is usually restricted in its extent and in its duration. The lower level female agrees to manipulate the male genitalia in only 57 per cent of the cases. The record is, therefore, one of more extended pre-coital play at the upper levels, and of a minimum of play at the lower levels. Many persons at the lower level consider that intromission is the essential activity and the only justifiable activity in a "normal" sexual relation.

Oral Eroticism. Many persons in the upper levels consider a certain amount of oral eroticism as natural, desirable, and a fundamental part of love making. Simple lip kissing is so commonly accepted that it has a minimum of erotic significance at this level. The college male may expect to kiss his date the first time they go out together. Most college students understand there will be good night kisses as soon as their dating becomes regular. Many a college male will have kissed dozens of girls, although he has had intercourse with none of them. On the other hand, the lower level male is likely to have had intercourse with hundreds of girls, but he may have kissed few of them. What kissing he has done has involved simple lip contacts, for he is likely to have a considerable distaste for the deep kiss which is fairly common in upper level histories.

Deep kissing is utilized as a prime source of erotic arousal by many persons in the better educated and top social levels. A deep kiss may involve considerable tongue contacts, deep lip contacts, and extended explorations of the interior of the partner's mouth. Such behavior is, as noted before, a regular concomitant of coital activity among many of the vertebrates, and particularly among the mammals.[2] In the human mammal, at the upper level, oral eroticism may still be considered a bit sophisticated, but deep kissing is in the experience of 87 per cent of the group. . . . Its sanitary implications seem no obstacle to its acceptance. This group accepts mouth contacts in its erotic play, although it objects to the use of a common drinking glass.

On the other hand, the lower level male considers such oral contacts to be dirty, filthy, and a source of disease, although he may drink from a common cup which hangs in the water pail, and he may utilize common utensils in eating and drinking. Obviously, the arguments, at both levels, have nothing to do with the real issues. They are rationalizations of mores which place taboos upon mouth contacts for reasons which only the student of custom can explain. Once again, it is the upper level which first reverted, through a considerable sophistication, to behavior which is biologically natural and basic.

Mouth-breast contact does occur at all social levels, but it is most elaborately developed again in the upper social level. . . . Almost invariably it is a matter of the male manipulating the female breast with his mouth. It is interesting that females rarely attempt to manipulate male breasts. . . .

The upper level male considers it natural that the female breast should interest him, and that he should want to manipulate it, both by hand and by mouth. The biologic origin of this interest is, however, open to question, because many lower level males do not find the female breast similarly interesting and have little inclination to manipulate it, either by hand or by mouth. Many lower level males rate such mouth-breast contacts as perversions, and some of them dismiss the idea with considerable disgust, as something that only a baby does when nursing from the mother's breast. Considering these opposite reactions to a single type of situation, it must be apparent that a considerable psychic element is involved in the development of individual patterns on this point. The concentration of these patterns in whole social levels indicates that the mores, the long-time customs of the groups, are the fundamental factors in the picture.

Mouth-genital contacts of some sort, with the subject as either the active or the passive member in the relationship, occur at some time in the histories of nearly 60 per cent of all males. . . . As noted elsewhere . . . these are quite common in the sexual activity of many of the other mammals, particularly among the other anthropoids.[3] There have been some other human cultures which have accepted such contacts as usual behavior, and even as a part of their religious service. The suggestion that such techniques in our present-day society are a recent development among sophisticated and sexually exhausted individuals is curiously contrary to the specific record, for the figures for at least three generations do not show significant changes in this respect. . . .

Mouth-genital contacts (of any kind) occur much more often at high school and college levels . . . . , less often in the grade school group. In the histories of the college group, about 72 per cent of the males have at least experimented with such contacts, and about 65 per cent of the males who have gone into high school but not beyond. Among those males who have never gone beyond eighth grade in school the accumulative incidence figure is only 40 per cent.

The percentages for males who have made mouth contacts with female genitalia prior to marriage are 9, 10, and 18 for grade school, high school, and college levels, respectively. . . . In marriage, such contacts are in 4, 15, and 45 per cent of the histories, for the three groups. Before marriage, the percentages of males with histories which included mouth stimulation of the male genitalia during heterosexual relations were 22, 30, and 39, for the three educational levels. In marriage, such relations have been had in 7, 15, and 43 per cent of the cases, for the three levels, respectively. . . .

Positions in Intercourse. Universally, at all social levels in our Anglo-American culture, the opinion is held that there is one coital position which is biologically natural, and that all others are man-devised variants which become perversions when regularly engaged in. However, the one position which might be defended as natural because it is usual throughout the Class Mammalia, is not the one commonly used in our culture. The usual mammalian position involves, of course, rear entrance, with the female more or less prone, face down, with her legs flexed under her body, while the male is above or to the rear. Among the anthropoids this mammalian position is still the most common, but some variety of positions also occurs.[4]

Most persons will be surprised to learn that positions in intercourse are as much a product of human cultures as languages and clothing, and that the common English-American position is rare in some other cultures. Among the several thousand portrayals of human coitus in the art left by ancient civilizations, there is hardly a single portrayal of the English-American position. It will be recalled that Malinowski [5] records the nearly universal use of a totally different position among the Trobrianders in the Southwestern Pacific; and that he notes that caricatures of the English-American position are performed around the communal campfires, to the great amusement of the natives who refer to the position as the "missionary position."

The origin of our present custom is involved in early and later Church history, and needs clarification before it can be presented with any authority; but certain it is that there was a time in the history of the Christian Church when the utilization of any other except the present-day position was made a matter for confession. What has been taken to be a question of biologic normality proves, once again, to be a matter of cultural development.

"Each social level is convinced that its pattern is the best of all patterns; but each level rationalizes its behaviors in its own way. The upper level rationalizes on the basis of what is right or wrong. . . . Lower social levels, on the contrary, rationalize their patterns of sexual behavior on the basis of what is natural or unnatural."

Since this is so, it is not surprising to find that within our American culture there is some variation in coital positions among the social levels. Throughout the population as a whole, a high proportion of all the intercourse is had in a position with the female supine, on her back, with the male above and facing the female. Only a part of the intercourse is had with the female above the male. This occurs in about 35 per cent of the college level histories, in 28 per cent of the high school histories, but in only 17 per cent of the grade school histories. . . .

It should be emphasized that the most common variant position is the one with the female above. It is used, at least occasionally, by more than a third (34.6%) of the upper level males. The position was more nearly universal in Ancient Greece and Rome (vide the art objects and materials, as well as the literature from that period). It is shown in the oldest known depiction of human coitus, dating between 3200 and 3000 B.C., from the Ur excavations in Mesopotamia.[6] The position with the female above is similarly the commonest in the ancient art of Peru, India, China, Japan, and other civilizations. In spite of its ancient history, many persons at lower social levels consider the position a considerable perversion. It is associated in their rationalizations with the idea that the female becomes masculine while the male becomes effeminate in assuming such a position, and that it destroys the dignity of the male and his authority in the family relationship. There may be a feeling that a male who accepts this position shows homosexual tendencies. One of the older psychiatrists goes so far as to insist that the assumption of such a dominating position by the female in coitus may lead to neurotic disturbances and, in many cases, to divorce. Even the scientifically trained person is inclined to use such rationalizations to defend his custom. . . .

Each social level is convinced that its pattern is the best of all patterns; but each level rationalizes its behavior in its own way.

The upper level rationalizes on the basis of what is right or wrong. For this group, all socio-sexual behavior becomes a moral issue. Morality and sexual morality become more or less synonymous terms. Many persons at this level believe that there are few types of immorality which are more enormous than sexual immorality. Proper, straight, upright, honorable, clean, fine, wholesome, manly, and pure refer primarily to abstinence from socio-sexual relations. Their opposites refer to participation in non-marital sexual relations. Honor, fidelity, and success in marriage are understood to involve the complete absorption of the individual's sexual urge in coitus with his wife. There is nothing of which persons at this level are more afraid than a charge of immorality, as immorality is defined by the group. There is no disgrace that is more feared than that which may result from sexual scandal. Sex is so clearly a moral issue that many persons in the group consider it a religious obligation to impose their code upon all other segments of the population.

Lower social levels, on the contrary, rationalize their patterns of sexual behavior on the basis of what is natural or unnatural. Pre-marital intercourse is natural, and it is, in consequence, acceptable. Masturbation is not natural, nor is petting as a substitute for intercourse, nor even petting as a preliminary to intercourse.

There are some individuals at lower levels who do see moral issues in sexual behavior, but by and large even they recognize that nature will triumph over morals. . . .

NOTES

1. E.g., F. Bryk, *Voodoo Eros* (New York: privately printed, Falstaff Press, 1933), p. 251.

2. F. A. Beach, "A Review of Physiological and Psychological Studies of Sexual Behavior in Mammals," *Physiological Reviews* 27, 1947: 240–307.

3. Ibid.

4. H. C. Bingham, "Sex Development in Apes," *Comparative Psychology Monographs* 5 (1)

1928: 1–165; R. M. Yerkes and J. H. Elder, "Oestrus, Receptivity, and Mating in Chimpanzee," *Comparative Psychology Monographs* 13 (5) 1936: 1–39; F. A. Beach, op. cit.; V. Nowlis, "Companionship Preference and Dominance in the Social Interaction of Young Chimpanzee," *Comparative Psychology Monographs* 17, 1941: 1–57.

5. B. Malinowski, *The Sexual Life of Savages in North-western Melanesia: An Ethnographic Account of Courtship, Marriage and Family Life among the Natives of the Trobriand Islands, British New Guinea* (New York: Halcyon House, 1929).

6. L. Legrain, *Ur Excavations*, vol. 2: *Archaic Seal-Impressions* (Published by the British Museum and the University of Pennsylvania Museum, 1936).

SEXUAL BEHAVIOR
IN THE HUMAN FEMALE

Alfred C. Kinsey, Wardell B. Pomeroy,
Clyde E. Martin, and Paul H. Gebhard

GENERAL FINDINGS

Married Females: Total Outlet

Among the females in the sample, about 97 per cent had experienced
erotic arousal before marriage. . . . Some 64 per cent had experienced
orgasm at least once before marriage. . . .

Relation to Age.   After marriage the frequencies of total outlet for the
females in the sample had increased considerably over the frequencies
which single females of the same age would have had. This depended, of
course, primarily upon the fact that marital coitus had begun to provide
such a regular and frequent source of sexual activity and outlet as few
females had found in any type of activity before marriage.

"We found that the percentages of married females who were
responding to the point of orgasm in . . . [marital] coitus . . . had
risen more or less steadily in the four decades represented in the
sample."

The number of females reaching orgasm from any source after marriage (the active incidences) had begun at 78 per cent between the ages of

sixteen and twenty. . . . They had then increased steadily to 95 per cent at ages thirty-six to forty, after which they had begun to drop, reaching 89 per cent by age fifty-five and, to judge by our small sample, 82 per cent by age sixty.

The median frequencies of total outlet for the married females who were ever reaching orgasm show marked "aging effects." The active median frequencies between sixteen and twenty had amounted to 2.2 orgasms per week, from which point they had steadily declined, reaching 1.0 per week between the ages of forty-one and forty-five, and 0.5 per week by age sixty. . . .

Relation to Decade of Birth. . . . We found that the percentages of married females who were responding to the point of orgasm in . . . [marital] coitus (the active incidences) had risen more or less steadily in the four decades represented in the sample. . . . For instance, among the females in the sample who were between the ages of twenty-one and twenty-five, some 80 per cent of those born before 1900 had reached orgasm; but of those who were born in the successive decades, 86, 90 and 92 per cent had so responded. . . . Something of the same differences had been maintained in the subsequent age groups. . . .

Relation to Other Factors.   The incidences of total outlet for the married females in the sample had generally been a bit higher for the better educated groups, and lower for the grade school and high school groups. . . . There seem to have been no consistent correlations between the active median frequencies of the total outlet among the married females in the sample and their educational backgrounds, except that the graduate school group had slightly higher frequencies up to the age of thirty-five. . . .

There seem to have been no correlations at all between the occupational classes of the parental homes in which the females in the sample had been raised and the incidences and frequencies of their total outlet. . . .

On the other hand, the religious backgrounds of the females in the sample had definitely and consistently affected their total outlet after marriage. In nearly every age group, and in nearly all the samples that we have from Protestant, Catholic, and Jewish females, smaller percentages of the more devout and larger percentages of the inactive groups had responded to orgasm after marriage. . . . Similarly, the median frequencies of orgasm for those who were responding at all were, in most instances, lower for those who were devout and higher for those who were religiously inactive. In many groups the differences had not been great; but in some instances, as among the Catholic females who were married between the ages of twenty-one and twenty-five, the differences were of some magnitude: an active median frequency of 1.1 orgasms per week for the devoutly Catholic females, and 2.4 for the inactive Catholic females.

Sources of Total Outlet. Coitus in marriage had accounted for something between 84 and 89 per cent of the total outlet of the married females in the sample who were between the ages of sixteen and thirty-five. . . . After the middle thirties, the importance of marital coitus had decreased. In the age group forty-six to fifty, only 73 per cent of the total number of orgasms were coming from that source.

Masturbation was the second most important source of sexual outlet for the married females in the sample, providing something between 7 and 10 per cent of the total number of orgasms for each of the age groups between sixteen and forty. . . . Although 11 per cent of the total outlet had come from this source in the next ten years, the increase in importance of extra-marital coitus had reduced masturbation to a third place in the list.

Extra-marital coitus and orgasms derived in extra-marital petting had accounted, in various age groups, for something between 3 and 13 per cent of the total outlet of the married females in the sample. . . . This had become the second most important source of outlet after age forty, providing 12 to 13 per cent of the total orgasms in that period.

Nocturnal dreams had provided between 1 and 3 per cent of the total outlet of the married females in each of the age groups in the sample. Homosexual contacts had never provided more than a fraction of 1 per cent of the orgasms experienced by the married females in the sample. . . .

Married Females Without Orgasm. There had been an appreciable percentage of the married females who were not reaching orgasm either in their marital coitus or in any other type of sexual activity while they were married. The percentage had been highest in the younger age groups where 22 per cent of the married females between the ages of sixteen and twenty, and 12 per cent of the married females between the ages of twenty-one and twenty-five, had never experienced any orgasm from any source. . . . The number of unresponsive individuals had dropped steadily in the successive age groups, reaching 5 per cent in the late thirties. . . .

". . . there was no factor which showed a higher correlation with the frequency of orgasm in marital coitus than the presence or absence of pre-marital experience in orgasm."

Relation of Pre-marital to Post-marital Activity

Orgasm in Marital Coitus vs. Pre-Marital Orgasm.   In the available sample, there was no factor which showed a higher correlation with the frequency of orgasm in marital coitus than the presence or absence of pre-marital experience in orgasm. Some 36 per cent of the females in the sample had married without having had such previous experience in orgasm. . . . Among those who had had no previous experience, 44 per cent had failed to respond to the point of orgasm in the first year of marriage. . . . But among the females who had had even limited pre-marital experience in orgasm, only 19 per cent had failed to reach orgasm in the first year of marriage; and among those who had experienced orgasm at least twenty-five times before marriage, only 13 per cent had failed to reach orgasm in the first year of marriage.

Among those females who had never experienced pre-marital orgasm from any source prior to marriage, 25 per cent did respond in all or nearly all of their contacts during the first year of marriage; but 45 to 47 per cent of the females who had had pre-marital experience responded to orgasm in all or nearly all of their coitus during the first year of marriage. Similar trends had been evident throughout the later years of marriage, and even for fifteen years in the continuous marriages in the sample. It is doubtful if any type of therapy has ever been as effective as early experience in orgasm, in reducing the incidences of unresponsiveness in marital coitus, and in increasing the frequencies of response to orgasm in that coitus.

These correlations may depend upon selective factors, or upon causal relationships through which the pre-marital experiences contribute to the marital experience. Both types of factors are probably involved. The more responsive females may have been the ones who discovered orgasm in their pre-marital years, either in solitary or socio-sexual activities, and they were the ones who had most often responded in marriage. On the other hand, we have already presented data . . . which show that the female can learn through experience to respond in orgasm, and we have also emphasized . . . the fact that such learning is most effective in the early years, when inhibitions have not yet developed or have not yet become too firmly fixed. Early orgasmic experience may, therefore, contribute directly to the sexual effectiveness of a marriage.

Orgasm in Marital Coitus vs. Pre-marital Coital Experience. The type of pre-marital experience which correlates most specifically with the responses of the female in marital coitus is pre-marital coitus—*provided that that coitus leads to orgasm.* . . . For instance, among the females in the sample who had had pre-marital coitus but who had not reached orgasm in the coitus, 38 to 56 per cent failed to reach orgasm in the first year of marriage. While the percentages had decreased in the later years, there were still 11 to 30 per cent of the pre-maritally unresponsive females who had remained unresponsive in their coitus ten years after marriage. On the other hand, among the females who had had pre-marital coitus in which they had reached orgasm at least twenty-five times, only 3 per cent were totally unresponsive in the first year of marriage, and only 1 per cent in the later years of marriage. For more than half of the females in the sample, coitus without orgasm had been correlated with orgasmic failure in marriage. They had been unresponsive in marriage ten to twenty times as often as the females who had had fairly frequent pre-marital coitus in which they had reached orgasm. . . .

It should be emphasized that pre-marital coital experience which had not led to orgasm had not correlated with successful sexual relations in marriage. . . . On the contrary, it showed a high correlation with failure in the marital coitus. A basic error has been involved in some of the previous studies which have attempted to assay the relation of pre-marital coitus with successful coitus in marriage, because the distinction has not been made between pre-marital coitus that had led to orgasm, and pre-marital coitus that had not led to orgasm.[1]

Whether these correlations are the product of some selection which leads the innately more responsive females to engage in pre-marital coitus in which they reach orgasm, or whether the correlations between the pre-marital and marital records represent causal relationships, are matters which we cannot now determine. In general, it seems probable that selective factors are more often responsible. On the other hand, a girl who becomes involved in pre-marital coitus in which she does not respond may be traumatically affected by such experience, and thus be handicapped in her later adjustments in marriage.

But whether selective factors or causal relationships are responsible for these correlations, it is clear that the possibility that any particular female will respond with regularity in her marital coitus can, other things being equal, be predicted with considerable confidence by examining her orgasm record in pre-marital coitus. For such predictions the pre-marital coitus seems more significant than any other single sexual item, or any social factor in the background of the female.[2]

Orgasm in Marital Coitus vs. Pre-marital Petting to Orgasm.   In the available sample, pre-marital petting which led to orgasm also showed a high correlation with sexual performance after marriage. Among the females who had never done petting to the point of orgasm before marriage, 35 per cent had never reached orgasm in the first year of marriage; but only 10 per cent of those who had reached orgasm in at least some of their pre-marital petting were unresponsive in marriage. . . . The same sorts of differences held for at least fifteen years after marriage. . . .

Again, these correlations may be the product of selective factors or of some causal relationship between pre-marital and marital experience. The most responsive females may be the ones who most often pet to orgasm before marriage, and who similarly respond best in their marital coitus. Or petting to orgasm may have provided the experience which helped the female respond to orgasm after marriage. But whatever the explanation, there are three, five, or more chances to one that a girl who has not done pre-marital petting in which she reaches orgasm will not respond to orgasm after she marries. . . . If she has reached orgasm in her pre-marital petting, there is a much better chance that she will respond in all or nearly all of her marital intercourse during the early years of her marriage and also in the later years of her marriage. . . .

Orgasm in Marital Coitus vs. Pre-marital Experience in Masturbation.
Although the correlations between pre-marital masturbatory expe-

rience that had led to orgasm and the female's subsequent responses in coitus in marriage were not as marked as the correlations with coital or petting experience, the masturbatory experience did show a definite correlation with the marital performance. . . . Among the females who had never masturbated before marriage, or whose masturbation had never led to orgasm, about a third (31 to 37 per cent) had failed to reach orgasm in the first year, and nearly as many had failed in the first five years of their marital coitus. Among those who had previously masturbated to the point of orgasm, only 13 to 16 per cent were totally unresponsive in the first year of marriage. . . .

Once again, the correlations may have depended upon the fact that those who had masturbated were the more responsive females, and therefore the ones who had responded most frequently in marriage. . . . It is probable that the significance of the pre-marital masturbatory experience lay primarily in the fact that it had acquainted the girl with the nature of an orgasmic response. Even after marriage, and even among females who are in their thirties and forties, difficulties in coital responses are sometimes cleared up if they learn how to masturbate to the point of orgasm. The techniques of masturbation and of petting are more specifically calculated to effect orgasm than the techniques of coitus itself, and for that reason it is sometimes possible for a female to learn to masturbate to orgasm even though she has difficulty in effecting the same end in coitus. Having learned what it means to suppress inhibitions, and to abandon herself to the spontaneous physical reactions which represent orgasm in masturbation, she may become more capable of responding in the same way in coitus. There are very few instances, among our several thousand histories, of females who were able to masturbate to orgasm without becoming capable of similar responses in coitus. . . .

DIFFERENCES IN PSYCHOLOGICAL FACTORS IN MALE AND FEMALE AROUSAL

Significance of Conditioning in Females and in Males

In general, males are more often conditioned by their sexual experience, and by a greater variety of associated factors, than females. While there is great individual variation in this respect among both females and males, there is considerable evidence that the sexual responses and behavior of the average male are, on the whole, more often determined by the male's previous experience, by his association with objects that were connected with his previous sexual experience, by his vicarious sharing of another individual's sexual experience, and by his sympathetic reactions to the sexual responses of other individuals. The average female is less often affected by such psychologic factors. It is highly significant to find that there are evidences of such differences between the females and males of infra-human mammalian species, as well as between human females and males.[3]

While we found no basic differences in the anatomy which is involved in the sexual responses of females and of males, and no differences in the physiologic phenomena which are involved when females and males respond sexually, we do find, in these responses to psychologic stimuli, an explanation of some of the differences that we have reported in the incidences and frequencies and the patterns of sexual behavior among females and males. We shall subsequently find . . . that hormonal differences between the human female and male may account for certain other differences between the two sexes.

It cannot be too strongly emphasized that there is tremendous individual variation in the way in which different individuals may be affected by psychologic stimuli. We have already pointed out some of these differences. For instance, . . . there is a considerable proportion of the females who masturbate without associated fantasies, and a considerable proportion of our female sample who had never had specifically sexual dreams while they slept. In this respect, such a female differs considerably from the average male, for nearly all males do fantasy while masturbating, and nearly all of them have nocturnal sex dreams. On the other hand, we have also recorded . . . that there are some females who invariably fantasy while they are masturbating, who have an abundance of sex dreams, and who have daytime fantasies which may so arouse them that they reach orgasm without any physical stimulation of any part of their bodies. It is only one male in a thousand or two who can fantasy to orgasm. In our sample, the range of variation in responses to psychologic stimuli is, therefore, much greater among females than it is among males. While we may emphasize the differences which exist between the average female and the average male, it should constantly be borne in mind that there are many individuals, and particularly many females, who widely depart from these averages.

Observing the Opposite Sex. A third (32 per cent) of the males in the sample reported that they were considerably and regularly aroused by observing certain females (clothed or nude), including their wives, girl friends, and other females of the sort with whom they would like to have sexual relations. Another 40 per cent recorded some response. Only half as many of the females (17 per cent) in the sample reported that they were particularly aroused upon observing males, whether they were their husbands, boy friends, or other males, and another 41 per cent recorded some response. . . .

The responses of these males upon observing females were the physiologic responses characteristic of sexual arousal; they often included genital reactions, and often led the male to approach the female for physical contact. Females who had been aroused with similar intensities did occur in the sample, but most of the females who had been aroused had not responded with such marked physiologic reactions. . . .

Observing Portrayals of Nude Figures. Something more than half (54 per cent) of the males in our sample had been erotically aroused by seeing photographs or drawings or paintings of nude females, just as they were aroused upon observing living females. Most homosexual males are similarly aroused by seeing portrayals of nude males. Fewer (12 per cent) of the females in the sample had ever been aroused by seeing photographs or drawings or paintings of either male or female nudes. . . .

"There were more males . . . who were aroused by observing their own genitalia than there were females . . . who were aroused by observing male genitalia."

Photographs of female nudes and magazines exhibiting nude or near nude females are produced primarily for the consumption of males. There are, however, photographs and magazines portraying nude and near nude males—but these are also produced for the consumption of males. There are almost no male or female nudes which are produced for the consumption of females. The failure of nearly all females to find erotic arousal in such portrayals is so well known to the distributors of nude photographs and nude magazines that they have considered that it would not be financially profitable to produce such material for a primarily female audience. . . .

Observing Genitalia.   Most heterosexual males are aroused by observing female breasts or legs, or some other part of the female body. They are usually aroused when they see female genitalia. A smaller percentage of the females in the sample . . . reported erotic arousal as a product of their observation of male genitalia, and more than half (52 per cent) reported that they had never been aroused by observing male genitalia. . . .

Most human males with homosexual interests are aroused, and in most instances strongly aroused, by seeing male genitalia. Genital exposures and genital exhibitions are frequently employed to interest other males in homosexual contacts. In the course of a homosexual relationship among males, considerable attention may be given to the genital anatomy and genital reactions. Moreover, many males who are not conscious of homosexual reactions are interested in their own genitalia and in the genitalia of other males. But only a small percentage of the homosexual females is ever aroused erotically by seeing the genitalia of other females.

Observing Own Genitalia.   A great many of the males in the sample (56 per cent) had been aroused by observing their own genitalia as they masturbated, or by viewing their genitalia in a mirror. Few (9 per cent) of the females in the sample had found any erotic stimulation in looking at their own genitalia.

There were more males (56 per cent) who were aroused by observing their own genitalia than there were females (48 per cent) who were aroused by observing male genitalia. The male's arousal may have a homosexual element in it, but many of the males who have never consciously recognized any other homosexual interests and have never had homosexual contacts may be aroused at seeing their own genitalia or the genitalia of other males.

Exhibitionism.   Because of their interest in their own genitalia and their arousal upon seeing the genitalia of other persons, males quite generally believe that other persons would be aroused by seeing their genitalia.

This seems to be the prime factor which leads many males to exhibit their genitalia to their wives, to other female partners, and to male partners in homosexual relationships.[4]

It is difficult for most males to comprehend that females are not aroused by seeing male genitalia. Some males never come to comprehend this. Many a male is greatly disappointed when his wife fails to react to such a display, and concludes that she is no longer in love with him. On the contrary, many females feel that their husbands are vulgar, or perverted, or mentally disturbed, because they want to display their genitalia. . . .

The male who exposes himself in a public place similarly secures erotic satisfaction primarily because he believes that the females who observe him are going to be aroused as he would be at seeing a genital exhibition. Sometimes the exhibitionist is aroused by the evident fright or confusion or other emotional reactions of the females who see him and, responding sympathetically, he may be stimulated by such an emotional display. But a considerable portion of the erotic arousal which the exhibitionist finds is a product of his anticipation that the female will be aroused, and this is evidenced by the fact that he is usually in erection before any passerby sees him. His reactions, therefore, may not depend entirely or even primarily upon the responses of the passing female. . . .

There are some females who will show their genitalia to the male partner because they intellectually realize that this may mean something to him. But only an occasional female among those who exhibit receives any erotic arousal from this anticipation of the male's responses. There are no cases in our sample, and practically none in the literature, of females publicly exhibiting their genitalia because they derived erotic satisfaction from such an exhibition.[5]

Interest in Genital Techniques. While the genitalia may be the chief focus of a considerable amount of sexual activity, this does not depend wholly on the fact that these organs are well supplied with end organs of touch. There are many other parts of the body which are similarly supplied with end organs, and the importance attached to the genitalia in a sexual relationship must partly depend upon the fact that most males and some females are psychologically conditioned to consider the genitalia as *the* structures which are primarily associated with sexual response.

This interpretation is favored by the fact that males attach much more importance to the genitalia than females do in a sexual relationship. But there is no reason for believing that the genitalia of the male are more richly supplied with end organs than the genitalia of the female. While genital erection may draw the male's attention to his own genitalia, this does not suffice to interest most females in his genitalia.

Most males, whether heterosexual or homosexual, are inclined to initiate a sexual relationship through some genital exposure or genital manipulation. Most females prefer to be stimulated tactilely in various other parts of the body before the activity is concentrated on the genitalia. It is the constant complaint of married females that their husbands are interested in "nothing but the intercourse," and by that they mean that he is primarily concerned with genital stimulation and an immediate genital union. On the other hand, it is the constant complaint of the married male that his wife "will do nothing to him," which means, in most instances, that she does not tactilely stimulate his genitalia.

". . . one hears homosexual females criticizing homosexual males for exactly the same reasons which lead many wives to criticize their husbands, and . . . one hears homosexual males criticize homosexual females for exactly the things which husbands criticize in their wives. In fact, homosexual males, in their intensified interest in male genitalia and genital activity, often exhibit the most extreme examples of a typically male type of conditioning."

These same differences in the significance of genital activities are to be found in the homosexual activities of females and males. A high proportion of the homosexual contacts among males is initiated through some genital exposure or some sort of genital manipulation (groping). During the actual relationships most homosexual males are likely to prefer more genital than non-genital stimulation. But in female homosexual relationships, the stimulation of all parts of the body may proceed for some period of time before there is any concentration of attention on the genitalia. We have histories of exclusively homosexual females who had had overt relationships for ten or fifteen years before they attempted any sort of genital stimulation.

Homosexual females frequently criticize homosexual males because they are interested in nothing but genitalia; homosexual males, in turn, may criticize homosexual females because "they do nothing" in a homosexual relationship. The idea that homosexuality is a sexual inversion is dispelled when one hears homosexual females criticizing homosexual males for exactly the same reasons which lead many wives to criticize their husbands, and when one hears homosexual males criticize homosexual females for exactly the things which husbands criticize in their wives. In fact, homosexual males, in their intensified interest in male genitalia and genital activity, often exhibit the most extreme examples of a typically male type of conditioning. . . .

Fantasies Concerning the Opposite Sex. The . . . differences between females and males . . . [regarding sexual fantasies and psychic stimuli] provide one explanation of the fact that males are usually aroused and often intensely aroused before the beginning of a sexual relationship and before they have made any physical contact with the female partner. These differences account for the male's desire for frequent sexual contact, his difficulty in getting along without regular sexual contact, and his disturbance when he fails to secure the contact which he has sought. The differences often account for the female's inability to comprehend why her husband finds it difficult to get along with less frequent sexual contacts, or to abandon his plans for coitus when household duties or social activities interfere.

Too many husbands, on the other hand, fail to comprehend that their wives are not aroused as they are in the anticipation of a sexual relationship, and fail to comprehend that their wives may need general physical stimulation before they are sufficiently aroused to want a genital union or completed coitus. Too often the male considers the wife's lesser interest at the beginning of a sexual relationship as evidence that she has lost her affection for him. Sexual adjustments between husbands and wives could be worked out more often if males more often understood that the reactions of their particular wives represent characteristics which are typical of females in general, and if females more often understood that the sexual interests shown by their particular husbands represent qualities which are typical of most males. . . .

Fantasies During Masturbation. Some 89 per cent of the males in our sample had utilized erotic fantasies as one of their sources of stimulation during masturbation. Some 72 per cent had more or less always fantasied while masturbating. Such fantasies usually turn around memories of previous sexual experience, around sexual experience that the male hopes to have in the future, or around sexual experience which he may never allow himself to have but which he anticipates might bring erotic satisfaction if the law and the social custom made it possible for him to engage in such activity. In not a few instances males develop rather elaborate fictional situations which they regularly review as they masturbate. Quite a few males, particularly among the better educated groups, may, at least on occasion, utilize erotic photographs or drawings, or make their own erotic drawings, or read erotic literature, or write their own erotic stories which they use as sources of stimulation during masturbation. Some 56 per cent of the males in the sample indicated that they observed their own genitalia at least on occasion during masturbation, and while this is more likely to be true of males with homosexual histories, it is also true of many others who give no other evidence of homosexual interests. But in any event, these males find the observation of their own genitalia an additional source of erotic stimulation. So dependent are many males on psychologic stimuli in connection with masturbation that it is probable that many of them, especially middle-aged and older males, would have difficulty in reaching orgasm if they did not fantasy while masturbating.

The record shows . . . that only 64 per cent of the females in our sample who had ever masturbated, had fantasied while masturbating.[6] Only 50 per cent of the females who had masturbated, had regularly fantasied for any period of their lives. We have nearly no cases of females utilizing erotic books or pictures as sources of stimulation during masturbation.

Nocturnal Sex Dreams. Nearly all males have nocturnal sex dreams which are erotically stimulating to them. Ultimately some 75 per cent of the females . . . may have such nocturnal dreams.

To judge from our sample, approximately 83 per cent of the males . . . ultimately have sex dreams which are erotically stimulating enough to bring them to orgasm during sleep. The corresponding figure for the females in the sample was 37 per cent. . . .[7]

The frequencies of sex dreams show similar differences between males and females. Among those males in the sample who were having any sex dreams (the active sample), the median frequencies averaged about 10 times per year in the younger age groups, and about 5 times per year in the older age groups. The median female in the sample had had sex dreams which were sufficiently erotic to bring her to orgasm with frequencies of 3 to 4 per year. . . .

Diversion During Coitus. . . . Effective female responses during coitus may depend, in many cases, upon the continuity of physical stimulation. If that stimulation is interrupted, orgasm is delayed, primarily because the female may return to normal physiologic levels in such periods of inactivity. This appears to be due to the fact that she is not sufficiently aroused by psychologic stimuli to maintain her arousal when there is no physical stimulation. We have pointed out that the male, on the contrary, may go through a period in which physical activity is interrupted without losing erection or the other evidences of his erotic arousal, primarily because he continues to be stimulated psychologically during those periods.

Similarly, because the male is more strongly stimulated by psychologic factors during sexual activities, he cannot be distracted from his performance as easily as the female. Many females are easily diverted, and may turn from coitus when a baby cries, when children enter the house, when the doorbell rings, when they recall household duties which they intended to take care of before they retired for the night, and when music, conversation, food, a desire to smoke, or other non-sexual activities present themselves.

Social Factors Affecting Sexual Patterns. For males, we found [8] that social factors were of considerable significance in determining patterns of sexual behavior. In the present volume we have found that social factors are of more minor significance in determining the patterns of sexual behavior among females.

For instance, we found that the educational level which the male ultimately attained showed a marked correlation with his patterns of sexual behavior. . . . Thus, the males who had ultimately gone on into college depended primarily on masturbation and much less frequently on coitus for their pre-marital outlet. On the other hand, the males who had not gone beyond grade school or early high school had drawn only half as much of their pre-marital outlet from masturbation, but they had drawn five times as much of their pre-marital outlet as the upper level males had from coitus. Similarly, kissing habits, breast manipulations, genital manipulations, mouth-genital contacts, positions in coitus, nudity during coitus, the acceptance of nudity or near-nudity during non-sexual activities, and many of the other items in the sexual behavior of a male, are usually in line with the pattern of behavior found among most of the other males in his social group. We have emphasized that such differences do not depend upon anything that is learned in school, for both lower level and upper level males may be together in the same grade school and high school, and the patterns are, for the most part, set soon after the mid-teens and before the average male ever goes on into college. We have emphasized that these differences in patterns of sexual behavior depend upon differences in the sexual attitudes of the different social levels in which the male is raised or into which he may move. This means that he is psychologically conditioned by the attitudes of the social group in which he is raised or toward which his educational attainments will lead him.

In contrast, in connection with most types of sexual activity we have found that patterns of sexual behavior among females show little or no correlation with the educational levels which the females ultimately attain. . . . In her pre-marital petting, pre-marital coitus, and extra-marital coitus, and in her total sexual outlet, there are some differences in the incidences and/or frequencies which appear to be correlated with the educational levels of the females, but the apparent differences prove to depend on the fact that marriage occurs at different ages in the different educational groups; and when the pre-marital activities are compared for the females who marry at about the same age, the average incidences and frequencies of these various types of sexual activity prove to be essentially the same in the several educational levels. . . .

We have also shown that the age at onset of adolescence and the rural or urban backgrounds do not show as marked a correlation with the patterns of behavior among females as they do among males.

For both the females and males in our sample, degrees of religious devotion did correlate with the incidences of the various types of sexual activity, and devoutly religious backgrounds had prevented some of the females and males from ever engaging in certain types of sexual activity. The incidences of nearly all types of sexual activity except marital coitus were, in consequence, lower among the religiously more devout females and males, and higher among the religiously less devout. . . .

The degree of religious devotion, however, had continued to affect those males who finally did become involved in the morally disapproved types of activity, and the median frequencies of such activities were lower among the more devout males and higher among the less devout males . . . ; but among those devout females who had become involved in morally disapproved types of activity, the average rates of activity were, on the whole, the same as those of the less devout females. This was true, for instance, of masturbation, of nocturnal dreams to orgasm, of pre-marital petting, of pre-marital coitus, and of homosexual contacts among females. . . . While religious restraints had prevented many of the females as well as the males from ever engaging in certain types of sexual activity, or had delayed the time at which they became involved, the religious backgrounds had had a minimum effect upon the females after they had once begun such activities. . . .

Summary and Comparisons of Female and Male

. . . The anatomy and physiology of sexual response and orgasm . . . do not show differences between the sexes that might account for the differences in their sexual responses. Females appear to be as capable as males of being aroused by tactile stimuli; they appear as capable as males of responding to the point of orgasm. Their responses are not slower than those of the average male if there is any sufficiently continuous tactile stimulation. We find no reason for believing that the physiologic nature of orgasm in the female or the physical or physiologic or psychologic satisfactions derived from orgasm by the average female are different from those of the average male. But in their capacities to respond to psychosexual stimuli, the average female and the average male do differ.

The possibility of reconciling the different sexual interests and capacities of females and males, the possibility of working out sexual adjustments in marriage, and the possibility of adjusting social concepts to allow for these differences between females and males, will depend upon our willingness to accept the realities which the available data seem to indicate. . . .

NOTES

1. See the following attempts to analyze the possible relationship between pre-marital coital experience and orgasm or happiness in marriage: Davis 1929:59 (of 71 females who had had pre-marital coitus, an undue number was in the unhappily married group).

Hamilton 1929:388 (pre-marital coitus showed no relationship to orgasm in marriage, unless with future spouse, where it was favorable). Terman 1938:383, 387 (a positive relationship between pre-marital experience and orgasm in marriage). Landis et al. 1940:97, 315 (a higher incidence of pre-marital coitus among females with "good general sexual adjustment" in marriage).

2. Example of writers who, on the other hand, have stressed the unfavorable effects which pre-marital coitus might have on later marital adjustments, include: Banning 1937:4–8. Popenoe 1938:15–16. Bowman 1942:232–238. Duvall and Hill 1945:141. Kirkendall 1947:29. Dickerson 1947:68–69. Stokes 1948:19. Landis and Landis 1948:124–31. Foster 1950:69. Christensen 1950:156.

3. In summing up the situation among infra-human mammals, Ford and Beach 1951:241 state: "We are strongly impressed with the evidence for sexual learning and conditioning in the male and the relative absence of such processes in the female."

4. The male chimpanzee frequently solicits the female by coming to erection, spontaneously or by masturbation, and exhibiting the erection to the female, according to: Yerkes and Elder 1936a:9. Nissen, verbal communication. Our observation.

5. That exhibitionism is infrequent among females in comparison to males, has also been recognized by: [Jacolliot] Jacobus X 1900:347. Hirschfeld 1920(3):319; 1948:504. Kronfeld in Marcuse 1923:121. Bilder-Lexikon 1930(1):241. Brown 1940:383. Guyon 1948:319. Allen 1949:108. Exhibitionism is considered non-existent among females by: Walker and Strauss 1939:177–78. Fenichel 1945:346. Rickles 1950:49 (considers it due to the fact that women "have nothing to expose"). In a few pre-literate cultures, women may solicit men by deliberately exposing their own genitalia; see: Ford and Beach 1951:93.

6. Hamilton 1929:429 reports 36 per cent of females, 69 per cent of males record fantasies during masturbation.

7. Hamilton 1929:318–19 reports 66 per cent of females, 42 per cent of males without nocturnal sex dreams.

8. Kinsey, Pomeroy, and Martin 1948:294–96.

BIBLIOGRAPHY

Allen, C. 1949. *The sexual perversions and abnormalities. A study in the psychology of paraphilia.* London, Oxford University Press.
Banning, Margaret C. 1937. "The case for chastity." *Reader's Digest* 31: (Aug.), 1–10.
Bilder-Lexikon (Schidrowitz, L., ed.). 1930. Volume 3. *Sexualwissenschaft.* Wien und Leipzig, Verlag für Sexualforschung.
Bowman, H. A. 1942. *Marriage for moderns.* New York and London, McGraw-Hill Book Co.
Brown, J. F. 1940. *The psychodynamics of abnormal behavior.* New York and London, McGraw-Hill Book Co.
Christensen, H. T. 1950. *Marriage analysis. Foundations for successful family life.* New York, Ronald Press Co.

Davis, Katharine B. 1929. *Factors in the sex life of twenty-two hundred women.* New York and London, Harper and Brothers.

Dickerson, R. E. 1947. *Home study course* [in] *social hygiene guidance.* Lessons I-VI. Portland, Ore., E. C. Brown Trust for Social Hygiene Education.

Duvall, E. M., and Hill, R. 1945. *When you marry.* Boston, D. C. Heath & Co.

Fenichel, O. 1945. Ed. 2 (ed. 1, 1924). *The psychoanalytic theory of neurosis.* New York, W. W. Norton & Company.

Ford, C. S., and Beach. F. A. 1951. *Patterns of sexual behavior.* New York, Harper & Brothers, and Paul B. Hoeber.

Foster, R. G. 1950. (ed. 1, 1944). *Marriage and family relationships.* New York, The Macmillan Co.

Guyon, R. 1948. (Flugel, J. C., and Ingeborg, trans.). *The ethics of sexual acts.* New York, Alfred A. Knopf.

Hamilton, G. V. 1929. *A research in marriage.* New York, Albert & Charles Boni.

Hirschfeld, M. 1916–1921. *Sexualpathologie. Ein Lehrbuch für Arzte und Studierende.* Part 3: Störungen im Sexualstoffwechsel mit besonderer Berücksichtigung der Impotenz. Bonn, A. Marcus & E. Webers Verlag, 3v. in 1. V. 3, 1920.

Hirschfeld, M. 1948, rev. ed. *Sexual anomalies. The origins, nature, and treatment of sexual disorders.* New York, Emerson Books.

Jacolliot, L. (Jacobus X . . . French army surgeon). 1900. *Medico-legal examination of the abuses, aberrations, and dementia of the genital sense.* Paris, Charles Carrington.

Kinsey, A. C., Pomeroy, W. B., and Martin, C. E. 1948. *Sexual behavior in the human male.* Philadelphia and London, W. B. Saunders Co.

Kirkendall, L. A. 1947. *Understanding sex.* Chicago, Science Research Associates.

Kronfeld. A. 1923. "Exhibitionismus." In: Marcuse, M., ed. *Handwörterbuch der Sexualwissenschaft.*

Landis, C., et al. 1940. *Sex in development. A study of the growth and development of the emotional and sexual aspects of personality together with physiological, anatomical, and medical information on a group of 153 normal women and 142 female psychiatric patients.* New York and London, Paul B. Hoeber.

Landis, J. T., and Landis, M. G. 1948. *Building a successful marriage.* New York, Prentice-Hall.

Popenoe, P. 1938. *Preparing for marriage.* Los Angeles, Calif., American Institute of Family Relations.

Rickles, N. K. 1950. *Exhibitionism.* Philadelphia, J. B. Lippincott Co.

Stokes, W. R. 1948. *Modern pattern for marriage. The newer understanding of married love.* New York, Rinehart and Co.

Terman, L. M. 1938. *Psychological factors in marital happiness.* New York and London, McGraw-Hill Book Co.

Walker, K., and Strauss, E. B. 1939. *Sexual disorders in the male.* Baltimore, Williams & Wilkins Co.

Yerkes, R. M., and Elder, J. H. 1936a. Oestrus, receptivity, and mating in chimpanzee. Comparative Psychology Monographs 13, no. 5.

GEBHARD AND ASSOCIATES 4
Continuities in the Typological Approach

After Kinsey's death in 1956, Paul Gebhard became head of the Institute. At that time, the problem facing the Institute was not so much a need to obtain new data as to deal with the mass of data that had already been collected. Thus, a second stage of Institute work began, characterized by the analysis and publication of data on hand.

During this period, Gebhard and his associates continued Kinsey's empirical-taxonomic approach. The two studies they published, which are featured in this chapter, are more specialized than the "Kinsey Reports," yet they are still comprehensive.

Pregnancy, Birth and Abortion, published in 1958, is a fertility study based on interviews with some 7000 white and black women. It examines the number who became pregnant, their marital status at the time of pregnancy, and how their pregnancies ended. Various segments of the population are compared in their experiences of pregnancy, birth, and abortion (both spontaneous and induced).

Sex Offenders: An Analysis of Types was published in 1965. Based on interviews with more than 1500 men imprisoned for various sexual offenses, this book deals with how these prisoners differ from other men, how they differ according to type of sexual offense, and how there are a variety of types within each sexual offense. The offenses dealt with in this excerpt are rape, incest, and peeping.

PREGNANCY, BIRTH AND ABORTION

Paul H. Gebhard, Wardell B. Pomeroy,
Clyde E. Martin, and Cornelia V. Christenson

THE SINGLE [WHITE] WOMAN

There are few sexual problems that receive as much social attention and
individual concern as pregnancy in the unmarried. . . . Our society
makes no real provision for the unmarried parent and has developed
various social sanctions to prevent and punish pregnancy in the unmarried.[1] . . .

The unmarried are caught in a dilemma of our own making: on one
hand there is the strong and basic sexual drive reinforced by the fact that
society encourages the development of heterosexual interests and emotional involvements; on the other hand there is society's insistence that
this must not lead to conception before marriage. . . . To keep one's self
and/or one's suitors at a high pitch of emotional and sexual excitement
for five to ten years, from the beginning of dating to marriage, and
meanwhile to abstain from coitus is, biologically speaking, a most unnatural as well as difficult task.

As is usually the case when social considerations conflict strongly with
biological fundamentals and when society develops partially contradictory goals for its members, a large number of individuals depart from
the social mores in practice although they may uphold them in theory.
As we indicated in our volume, *Sexual Behavior in the Human Female*,
roughly half of the women from the middle and upper socio-economic
levels who married had had coitus prior to marriage. Although our data

regarding females of the lower socio-economic level are inadequate, we know that the younger females of this group have an even greater incidence of pre-marital coitus.

By the age of forty, which for most women is essentially the end of reproductive life, roughly 10 per cent of our total sample had had a pre-marital pregnancy, regardless of their ultimate marital status . . . .[2] This figure was reached gradually: by age twenty, 3 per cent had become pregnant before marriage; by age twenty-five, 8 per cent; and by age thirty, 10 per cent.

. . . It is . . . clear that pre-marital pregnancy is an enormous social phenomenon that has involved not merely a few unfortunates, but millions of women now living.

"There are few sexual problems that receive as much social attention and individual concern as pregnancy in the unmarried."

Immediately one asks what has happened to these women. . . . The answer is: they get married either before or after the end of the pregnancy.

. . . The great majority of these marriages were not, as one might presume, "shotgun marriages," but marriages contracted after the pregnancy had ended. . . .

Since [the research] revealed that the longer a woman delayed marriage the greater the probability of her becoming pregnant, it is not surprising to find that the rate of pregnancy is greater among those who marry later. . . . As one would expect, the older women are more apt than the younger ones to have had more than one pre-marital pregnancy. . . .

Induced abortion is [also] commoner among women who marry later. Of those who conceive before they marry, more of those who marry young carry their pre-marital conceptions into marriage; females who marry at older ages do so much less often.

Education level, our measure of socio-economic status, permits us to extend our findings to a considerable segment of the urban white U.S. population. There is a negative correlation between educational achievement and pre-marital pregnancy: the better educated . . . have fewer pre-marital pregnancies. . . .

. . . The less educated begin pre-marital coitus at an earlier age. . . . They have a higher frequency of pre-marital coitus prior to age twenty-one. . . . There appears to be a difference in the use of and/or the efficiency of contraceptives. For instance, the high school educated, college educated, and postgraduates display roughly the same number of coital years per female, yet differ markedly in conception experience and rates. . . . The inverse relation between educational achievement and pre-marital conception is clear-cut.[3] . . .

. . . The differences disclosed by a study of educational levels are derived in the final analysis from the different attitudes (mores) held by the various socio-economic groups toward pre-marital coitus and pregnancy.

Because more of them became pregnant before marriage, there is a greater incidence of induced abortion among the less educated; but in terms of ratio, a higher proportion of their pregnancies end in live birth or are carried over into marriage than is true of the better educated. . . .

THE MARRIED [WHITE] WOMAN

Our white non-prison married women, taken as a unit, approximate the socio-economic upper 20 per cent of the urban population, but include an overrepresentation of women who have been separated, divorced, or widowed. Ultimately 80 per cent of the ever-married women became pregnant while married, and averaged about three pregnancies each. In any one year an average of between one quarter and one fifth of the wives between ages sixteen and thirty conceived; after age thirty fertility rapidly decreased.

In the course of a lifetime three quarters of the women had a live birth, one quarter experienced spontaneous abortion, and between one quarter and one fifth had an induced abortion. Live birth accounts for three fifths to two thirds of all marital conceptions at any age up to forty; spontaneous abortion ends only about one pregnancy in ten in early life but increases until in late reproductive life about one fifth of all conceptions spontaneously abort. Induced abortion is most prevalent at younger ages when, presumably, the couples do not feel ready to have children: over one quarter of the conceptions of the young wives were deliberately aborted. Later induced abortion becomes less common but shows a tendency to increase in late life when many couples feel their families are sufficiently large. Induced abortion in marriage is commoner among women who later are separated, divorced, or widowed: marital trouble and instability are thought to be causative factors in induced abortion.

Age at marriage is an important factor in reproductive behavior since it determines the number of fecund years within marriage. The later a woman marries the less apt she is to become pregnant; also she will, on the average, have fewer pregnancies than a woman who marries at a younger age. . . .

Analyses indicate that the better educated tend to postpone and limit the number of their conceptions when they are young; hence the less educated surpass them during this period of life in the percentage of wives with conception experience and in the number of conceptions. Later in life, however, the better educated exceed the less educated in conception rate: the former cease their procrastination while the latter have largely completed their families and are now limiting their conceptions. Despite this reversal, in the course of a lifetime fewer of the better educated become pregnant, and they have fewer pregnancies each.

Primarily because fewer of them become pregnant, the percentage of wives who have experienced birth, spontaneous abortion, and induced abortion is smaller among the better educated. The less educated not only have more live births but have them earlier in life. In terms of absolute number, the grade school educated have the most induced abortions and the postgraduate women the least. However, the college educated have a high proportion of the pregnancies they incur during college age aborted; thereafter the induced abortion ratio is roughly the same for the high school educated and the college educated, with the postgraduate women reporting somewhat lower figures. Our fragmentary data on the grade school educated suggest that they probably have a larger proportion of induced abortions, at any age, than do the women of the other educational groups.

Decade of birth presents a more complicated picture. In general one can say that there was a trend toward a decrease in the number of marital conceptions and in the number of women who conceived until the . . . post-World War II "baby boom," when this trend was halted and reversed. The depression of the 1930's lowered the conception rate and it did not return to its predepression level until after World War II.

Live births, like conceptions, tended to decrease among the women of successive birth decades until the "baby boom." Induced abortion showed an increase that was checked by the women born in and after 1910. But during the depression years in the 1930's the proportion of pregnancies that were artificially aborted rose among all wives of reproductive age.

Studying the proportions of marital pregnancies that ended in birth, spontaneous abortion, and induced abortion from roughly 1925 to 1950, we see an over-all slow increase in the proportion of live births and spontaneous abortions, and a corresponding decrease in induced abortions.

Degree of religious devoutness displays a strong and consistent relation to marital reproduction: more of the devout females conceive and they conceive more often than the religiously inactive. Similarly, greater religious devoutness correlates positively with live birth and negatively with induced abortions: relatively few devoutly religious women will have an induced abortion. . . .

THE PREVIOUSLY MARRIED [WHITE] WOMAN

Despite the fact that the proportion of women who have been separated, divorced, or widowed has risen greatly in the twentieth century, virtually nothing has been known of their reproductive behavior during the time following the end of marriage and before remarriage. Much of this lack of knowledge is due to a reluctance to face what many would consider an insolvable moral problem. . . .

"One might say that a male hopes to have coitus with a never-married . . . [woman], but expects to have coitus with a divorcée or widow."

A considerable body of folklore pertaining to sex surrounds women who are separated from their husbands, divorced, or widowed (S.D.W.). The folklore is not without some foundation in fact. . . . In this present study we . . . found that approximately three quarters of the high school educated, college educated, and postgraduate [S.D.W.] women at some time had post-marital coitus (76 per cent, 73 per cent, and 72 per cent, respectively). In brief, the continuation of coitus after the end of marriage is the rule rather than the exception.[4]

. . . Tradition labels her [the previously married woman] as being sexually acceptant, if not actually aggressive, and males react accordingly. One might say that a male hopes to have coitus with a never-married . . . [woman], but expects to have coitus with a divorcée or widow. . . . Unfortunately society makes no special provisions for the divorcée or widow who becomes pregnant. Moreover, she has, compared with the never-married woman, less opportunity and possibly less desire to solve the problem through marriage. In consequence social pressure forces her to the abortionist as inexorably as it forces the single [woman]. . . .

Of our 754 S.D.W. women, 549 (nearly three quarters) had post-marital coitus; of these, 105 became pregnant in the post-marital period. Thus . . . 19 per cent of the sample of those with post-marital coitus conceived. . . . Some of the women attributed their pregnancies to carelessness; it is not uncommon for wives occasionally to "take a chance" when contraceptives are not readily available, and this attitude seems to have carried over into the post-marital lives of some of them.

Examining the percentage of women who conceived as a result of post-marital coitus, we found that educational attainment was no factor. . . .

Of the 157 . . . post-marital conceptions [that had ended at the time of reporting], 4 per cent resulted in live birth, 10 per cent in spontaneous abortion, 79 per cent in induced abortion, and 7 per cent were carried into a subsequent marriage. Comparing these figures with those relating to pre-marital outcome ratios . . . , we see that the proportions of live birth and induced abortion are about the same, but that the S.D.W. women, being generally older, are more prone to abort spontaneously—about twice as often as the single women. . . .

It is of considerable interest to ascertain if and how women who have been separated, divorced, or widowed differ from women who are still married to their first husbands, and to see if anything in pre-marital or marital life foreshadows the subsequent marital dissolution. It should be noted that the majority of our sample of S.D.W. women consists of the separated and divorced: those who were widowed but never separated or divorced comprise 20 per cent of the sample. . . .

In pre-marital life we find that the S.D.W. women, in comparison to the married once, had higher rates of pre-marital conception during their teens and, to a lesser extent, during their twenties.[5] . . . Within marriage also, especially at younger ages, the women who were later separated or divorced . . . had higher marital conception rates than did the married once. . . .

One gains thus far the impression that as a group these S.D.W. women were sexually active and consequently, particularly at younger ages, rather conception prone. This impression, reinforced by our knowledge that a large proportion of them had post-marital coitus and rather high post-marital conception rates, made us suspect that within the S.D.W. sample there existed a group of women who might prove distinctive in their sexual and reproductive behavior. Since we have demonstrated that the women who conceived post-maritally had coitus with greater frequency than those who had coitus but did not conceive, we selected the former for more intensive study.

The 105 women who conceived as a result of post-marital coitus constitute a distinct group in other respects as well. Only three of them were widowed. Their pre-marital sexual life had been different from that of the average woman. Roughly half our total sample of ever-married women had had pre-marital coitus, but for our post-maritally pregnant group the proportion was higher: of the high school educated, 71 per cent; of the college educated, 62 per cent; and of the postgraduates, . . . 82 per cent. Consequently a high per cent (20) had also become pregnant before marriage.

These women also were more experienced in induced abortion. Whereas about 8 per cent of our ever-married women had had an induced abortion before marriage, and roughly one fifth during marriage, 40 per cent of the post-maritally pregnant group of high school education had had an induced abortion in or before marriage, 65 per cent of the college educated, and 46 per cent of the postgraduate.

Occupationally these women were exceptional. We devised an occupational category consisting of professional employment (e.g., physicians, psychologists, college teachers, artists, and so forth) and employment of a managerial or at least highly responsible nature (e.g., store manager, advertisement director, editorial worker, and buyer). Of our sample of post-maritally pregnant women, 34 per cent of the high school educated fell within this occupational category, 65 per cent of the college educated, and 86 per cent of the postgraduates, these percentages being larger than those given by census.[6]

In terms of personality these women were also exceptional. On each of our case histories the interviewer has made brief notes giving his impression of the subject's personality. Examining these notes, we found that between 47 and 58 per cent (varying with educational level) of the post-maritally pregnant women were described as assured, independent, aggressive, or in some way suggesting a high level of energy.

Their dynamism accounts for the fact that many of them went into business and professional occupations where, necessarily, they often faced male competition. Their particular qualities made them, even before marriage, rather independent of social mores. If they felt inclined toward coitus they had it, in or out of marriage. One also senses that these women would not be very tolerant of a husband's defects or play a submissive role, attitudes that may have played a part in the separation or divorce. . . .

While obviously only a portion of the separated or divorced women are similar to those just described, that portion is sufficiently large to justify the apprehension that the average woman feels about the divorcée as a sexual competitor.

THE NEGRO WOMAN

Our sample of Negro non-prison females consists of 572 individuals. Like the white sample, it is predominantly made up of young, urban women of above average education. . . . Of those who married, 63 per cent were subsequently separated, divorced, or widowed by the time they were interviewed.[7] . . .

Negroes in the lower socio-economic level have a distinctive pattern of sexual attitudes and behavior. . . . Insofar as reproductive behavior is concerned, the lower social level Negro pattern may be simply described: coitus is regarded as an inevitable, natural, and desirable activity to be enjoyed both in and out of marriage, contraception is little known and considered at best a nuisance and at worst dangerous or unnatural, and pregnancy is accepted as an inevitable part of life; whether it occurs in or out of wedlock is a secondary issue. The result of this philosophy is a high conception rate, a high live birth rate, a high spontaneous abortion rate (exacerbated by poverty and disease), and a minimal incidence of induced abortion.

The upper socio-economic level Negroes have different attitudes and behavior, similar to those of the middle and upper socio-economic level whites. . . .

. . . In cases of vertical mobility we find the individuals who move upward retain, to varying degrees, the sexual and reproductive patterns of the lower social level; this is true of both Negroes and whites. . . .

The Single Negro Woman

Since in our volume *Sexual Behavior in the Human Female* we presented no Negro data, it is necessary at this point to note the percentages of women with experience in pre-marital coitus and the number of coital years involved. . . . Pre-marital coitus is quite prevalent among Negro women of less than college education, and more prevalent among college educated Negro women than among college educated whites. . . .

Educational level relates to pre-marital conception experience among Negroes much as it does to the experience among whites, the lesser educated showing a higher proportion of women who became pregnant before marriage.[8] . . .

. . . The grade school and high school educated Negro women, for the most part, belong to the lower socio-economic level where social sanctions against pre-marital coitus and illegitimacy are weak. . . .

It is our impression that the conception rates of the Negroes with pre-marital coitus exceed those of the whites primarily because of an absence of, or inadequacy of, contraception. Among Negroes of the lower socio-economic level there is an aversion to all forms of contraception except for the douche, and the douche is not only relatively ineffective but is often too long delayed.[9] . . .

In summary . . . the single Negro women, in comparison with whites of the same education, have a higher percentage of pre-marital coitus and higher rates of pre-marital conception among those having coitus.[10] As far as the outcome of their pregnancies is concerned, the Negro and white single women of college education are similar, but among single women of lesser education the Negroes are far more likely to have live births and less likely to resort to induced abortion.[11] Educational level seems, in general, to correlate with reproductive behavior in Negroes as it does in whites.

The Married Negro Woman

The grade school and high school educated Negro wives of our sample are more fecund than equivalent white wives. However, the college educated Negro wives prove ultimately to have had fewer marital conceptions than their white counterparts. . . .

In view of the [generally] higher marital conception rate it is not surprising to find the Negro live birth rate exceeds that of the whites.[12] . . . Among the college educated, however, there is reason to believe that the whites have more live births than do the Negroes. Despite the small sample, we feel that the finding is probably valid.[13] The college educated Negroes have, unfortunately, considerable difficulty in establishing themselves in positions in society commensurate with their educations, and as a result children are more of an economic handicap to them than to the whites. The decision to have few children so that these few may be given material and educational advantages is probably more of a factor among college educated Negroes than among college educated whites.

One large and inexplicable difference between the Negroes and whites lies in the rates of spontaneous abortion, the Negro rates being roughly double those of the whites by any age.[14] The fact that among the Negro wives the rates decrease with educational level suggests some health factor may be involved, but if so, this is not evident among the white females. However, it is known that syphilis, a factor in spontaneous abortion, is more prevalent among Negroes than among whites,[15] and one would expect its incidence to be greatest among the less educated. It is also feasible to postulate that, owing to economic reasons, the Negroes, as a group, live in less healthful conditions than do whites, and that therefore one might expect a higher spontaneous abortion rate. This supposition receives some indirect support from the fact that our white prison females, who are also an economically depressed group, likewise display high spontaneous abortion rates in marriage.

Induced abortion rates present a different and more complex picture. Among the grade school and high school educated women, the Negro wives have lower rates of induced abortion than do whites, despite the fact that the Negro wives have higher conception rates. Among the college educated the reverse seems true: the Negro rates surpass those of the whites. . . .

One is left with the impression that the Negro wives of less than college education are as a group quite fertile, unusually subject to spontaneous abortion, and rather opposed to induced abortion. The college educated Negroes, on the other hand, appear to have emulated the reproductive behavior of the college educated whites, and matched them in induced abortions. This fact, coupled with the prevalence of spontaneous abortion that also exists among college educated Negroes, resulted in depressing the number and proportion of live births below the level of the white females. . . .

"In cases of vertical mobility we find the individuals who move upward retain, to varying degrees, the sexual and reproductive patterns of the lower social level; this is true of both Negroes and whites."

THE PRISON WOMAN

Between 1941 and 1946 the members of our research organization carried on interviews in three women's correctional institutions. . . .

From the three prisons 1,250 individual case histories were obtained; these represent nearly a 100 per cent coverage of the inmates in the institutions at the times we were working in them. Of the 1,250 women, 900 were white, 309 were Negroes, and the remainder were of other races.[16]
. . .

The White Prison Woman

The characteristics that distinguish females who are convicted by the courts from females who are never tried or convicted are poorly known, and any enumeration of them must be general. One can note that poverty, poor education, mental retardation, alcoholism, and so forth are to be found more commonly among women convicted of offenses. . . .

The importance of this group of white prison women does not lie in their having been convicted and incarcerated, but in the fact that they

give us a better idea of the lowest socio-economic level for which we have otherwise an inadequate sample.

Both before marriage and in marriage the prison women, in comparison with non-prison women, show higher conception rates, more live births and spontaneous abortions, and markedly fewer induced abortions. We believe these are social level differences and have nothing to do with criminality or imprisonment; this belief is strengthened by noting that within the sample of prison women the same educational level differences exist that we saw among non-prison women, the less educated having the greater number of conceptions and live births.

From these prison data, from our grade school educated non-prison females, from our impressions from field work, and from data derived from male case histories, we can arrive at a general idea about fertility among people of urban lower socio-economic level. Two substrata may be differentiated: a lower stratum that furnishes most of our prison sample, and an upper stratum, which furnishes most of our non-prison sample. In the lower stratum, pre-marital coitus is common at younger ages and conception is correspondingly frequent, especially since adequate contraception is seldom employed. The group mores are tolerant regarding pre-marital pregnancy, which is looked upon as a prelude to marriage; effective induced abortion is prohibitively expensive for many; and an element of procrastination and irresponsibility leads others to delay too long. All these factors combine to produce a high pre-marital live birth rate and to minimize induced abortion. With induced abortion low, and in an economically depressed group, it is no surprise to find spontaneous abortion common. . . .

Regardless of which of the several ways of examining outcome ratio is employed, it is clear that the prison women differ dramatically from our sample of non-prison women, having had a vastly larger proportion of live births, a considerably larger proportion of spontaneous abortions, and a much smaller proportion of induced abortions.

. . . In marriage the same picture obtains: high rates of conception, of live birth, and of spontaneous abortion, with induced abortion being rather uncommon. It requires a considerable amount of courage for a wife to seek and to obtain an induced abortion: friends and relatives may know of the pregnancy, she and her husband may have ambivalent feelings, abortion is contrary to religious teachings, abortion is expensive,

abortion is illegal and, of course, a varying amount of physical pain and danger is involved. In many ways it is easier for the pregnant wife to conform to social pressures and bear her unwanted child. In this lower substratum, large families are not looked upon with disapproval and the men and women involved are not especially status-striving.

Turning to the other group, the upper stratum of the grade school educated, one finds more of its members concerned with improving their status socially, economically, and intellectually. It is an unfortunate truth that children interfere with such improvement; children do require expenditure of time, effort, and money. In consequence, as one progresses up the social scale there is an increasing use of contraception and also an increasing resort to induced abortion in cases where contraception fails.

The Negro Prison Woman

The women composing our Negro prison sample came from essentially the same environment as the grade school educated of our Negro non-prison sample; hence the differences in reproductive behavior between these two groups are small in comparison to the differences observed between white prison and white non-prison women.

About the same percentages of prison and grade school educated non-prison women had pre-marital coitus—over three quarters by age twenty. Also, the percentages of women who had pre-marital conceptions, and the frequencies with which they had these conceptions, were similar among the prison and grade school educated non-prison women. However, there are definite differences in how these pre-marital conceptions ended. The prison women had a much higher proportion of live births than did the non-prison women, and fewer of their pregnancies ended in induced abortion.

The prison wives were characterized by low conception rates and by the extraordinarily high proportion of their pregnancies that spontaneously aborted. These two phenomena explain, at least in part, why the Negro prison wives had so few induced abortions. The relative infertility of the married prison women and their proneness to abort spontaneously seem largely the result of the prevalence of syphilis and of prostitution, both being much more frequent among the prison women than among non-prison women of the same socio-economic status.

. . . Prostitutes are surprisingly infertile and not all their infertility can be attributed to venereal disease or contraception; some other and as yet unknown factor may be involved.

NOTES

1. See Kingsley Davis 1939:232 for a thoughtful discussion of social taboos and illegitimacy.

2. There are several other studies reporting experience of pre-marital conception, but it should be kept in mind that the samples vary in important features such as source and method of obtaining data, and the age and marital status, as well as the educational attainment of the women reporting. The figures show a range of from 3.5 to 30 per cent of pre-marital conception experience. . . .

   Hamilton 1929: 125, 133 cited 8 per cent of 100 married women as having experienced a pre-marital conception.

   Dickinson and Beam 1934:33 found 4 per cent with pre-marital conceptions in their total sample of 500 single women.

   Stix 1935:351 reported 35 pre-marital conceptions among 991 married women in a birth control clinic sample. If one assumes that 35 different women were involved, this gives a 3.5 per cent experience figure.

   Raymond Pearl's monumental 1939 study provided fertility data on a sample of over 25,000 white obstetrical patients from 139 co-operating hospitals in the northeastern United States. Calculations made from Table 26, p. 181, fix the pre-marital conception experience of the married sample at 7.3 per cent. If we calculate the present data on the basis of fertile married females in order to make it comparable, we arrive at a 16.8 figure.

   Brunner 1941:163 in a rather selective sample based on gynecology clinic records of 254 single females found 30 per cent had conceived pre-maritally.

   Beebe 1942:61 recorded pre-marital conceptions as reported by 15 per cent of 1,165 married females enlisted for a contraceptive service in Logan County, West Virginia.

   Whelpton in a discussion at the 1942 abortion conference cited 48 definite pre-marital pregnancies and 14 suspected ones among the 1,080 couples in the Indianapolis fertility study. If one uses the total figure and assumes different couples were involved, this would represent a 6.2 per cent pre-marital pregnancy experience. See Taylor 1944:37.

   Lewis-Faning 1949:86 in the British Population Commission report on family limitation found a 17.5 per cent experience of pre-marital conception in a sample of over 3,000 married women.

3. A similar inverse relationship, but based on occupational classification of the husband, was found in Christensen 1953:57. Lowest level of pre-marital pregnancy of wives at time of marriage (5 per cent) was in professional occupations, and highest (16 per cent) among laborers, with farm couples intermediate. An earlier study showed similar results.

   Higher rates of pre-marital pregnancy among lower status groups (manual labor versus nonmanual) were also reflected in the British Family Census, in which live births prior to six and a half months of marriage were tabulated. Here the differences were greater than two to one. See Glass and Grebenik 1954:142–144.

For similar Swedish findings based on the criterion of family income see Sweden, Statistika Centralbryån, Folkräkningen den 31 December 1945, Vol. 7:2, p. 40, Table N.

De Wolff and Meerdink 1957:309 found similar results when comparing the percentages of first births that had been pre-maritally conceived in professional and laboring groups in Amsterdam, 1948–1955.

4. Terman 1938:418–19 found that a high proportion of divorced women who remarried had post-marital coitus: "Roughly four out of five of the divorced wives had premarital intercourse with the present spouse, and about four out of ten with others." Terman's sample, like ours, was predominantly (76 per cent) of females with college or postgraduate education.

5. Christensen and Meissner 1953:643 in a study of pre-marital pregnancy as a factor in divorce state, "Premarital pregnancy has been found to be associated with disproportionately high divorce rates."

6. The 1950 U.S. Census provides data showing that of employed females of college education, 49 per cent may be classed as "professional, technical, and kindred workers" and about 5 per cent as "managers, officials, and proprietors" (excluding farm). This gives a total of 54 per cent for both groups which, when combined, are roughly equivalent to the occupational category we employ here. See U.S. Census, 1950, Special Reports, *Occupational Characteristics*, 1956:108–115, Table 10.

7. From U.S. Census, 1950, Special Reports, *Fertility*, 1955:66–81, Tables 20–21, one can calculate the percentage of ever-married white females who had been separated, divorced, or widowed (S.D.W.), according to educational level. Tables 22–23 provide the same data for Negro females. Considering only urban women of completed fertility (i.e., women aged forty-five to forty-nine at enumeration), one finds that separation, divorce, or widowhood is much more prevalent among Negroes than among whites. For example, of ever-married Negro women with eight grades of schooling, about 61 per cent were S.D.W. as opposed to 31 per cent for the whites; among the college graduates roughly 44 per cent of the Negroes and 24 per cent of the whites had been separated, divorced, or widowed.

8. The same relationship was found in Pearl 1939:182. Of his sample of 5,633 fertile Negro women he reported 37 per cent pre-marital pregnancy experience for those with an elementary school education, 35 per cent for the high school group, and 18 per cent for the college or university educated Negro females.

9. The relative omission of contraception among Negroes, aside from the douche, is cited by Tietze and Lewit 1953:564. Lack of knowledge of contraceptives among a group of unmarried Negro mothers was noted by Hertz and Little 1944:77.

10. Pearl 1939:181 found 36 per cent of his total Negro sample of 5,633 women had pre-maritally conceived, in contrast to 9 per cent in his larger white sample.

Beebe 1942:61–62 also found that pre-marital conception was commoner among Negroes than among whites. The Logan County, W. Va., group he reported on showed 37 per cent experience for Negroes as against 15 for white women.

11. Peckham 1936:112 stated, "In our experience [Johns Hopkins Hospital], it is extremely

rare for a colored woman to induce an abortion upon herself, or to have such a procedure done by midwife or doctor."

Hertz and Little 1944:77–78 noted that their subjects (unmarried Negro mothers) were ignorant of or opposed to induced abortion and added that "a large number of Negroes, predominantly from the lower class, accept illegitimacy more or less as a matter of course." Drake and Cayton 1945:592–595 also discussed the negative attitude toward abortion and the relative acceptance of illegitimate birth.

U.S. Vital Statistics, Special Reports, 1955 (42):256 estimated on the basis of states reporting on illegitimacy, 1938–1953, that 16 to 19 per cent of the registered births of nonwhite women were illegitimate. In the present sample, 66 non-marital births out of a total of 422 provides a percentage of 16.

Young 1954:120–122 warned that while this acceptance of illegitimacy may be true of some Negro groups, the more status-striving Negroes have adopted the upper social level condemnation of illegitimacy.

12. The U.S. Census, 1950, Special Reports, *Fertility*, 1955:66–81, reveals that while more Negro than white wives are childless, those Negro women who bear children do so at a rate sufficiently high to make the Negro birth rate exceed that of the whites. The problem of Negro fertility is discussed by Pearl 1939:113, Beebe 1941:194, Kiser 1942:38–40, Grabill 1955:89–90, and Mayer and Klapprodt 1955:152–154.

13. The 1950 U.S. Census volume on fertility cited previously shows that among urban college educated females, many more Negroes than whites are childless, and that the Negro birth rate in this educational group is less than that of the whites. The decreasing fertility among Negro women with increasing education is also clear in the census tables. This trend was also noted by Kiser 1942:247 and Frazier 1948:330–331.

14. The New York City Department of Health records show that for 1952–1954 spontaneous abortion was about twice as common in nonwhites as in whites. See Erhardt and Jacobziner 1956:831.

15. According to the *Journal of Venereal Disease Information* 1948, Vol. 29, p. 29, U.S. Public Health figures for 1947 show a rate that is 15 times higher for all stages of syphilis among Negro women than among whites.

16. [Editor's note] Gebhard et al. describe these three correctional institutions and the samples they yielded as follows:

Prison A. This institution in a midwestern state was populated chiefly by women convicted of misdemeanors. . . .

The white inmates of Prison A (698 in number) were largely small town or rural in background, and . . . 67 per cent had not gone beyond grammar school. . . . The average age was somewhat high, the median female being 29.8 years old.

Prison B. The institution derived its population chiefly from a large eastern metropolis, accepting misdemeanants, delinquents, and a few first-time felons. It was designed for females ranging in age from the late teens to the late twenties; older females were almost never accepted. The median inmate was aged 19.5 years. . . .

The white inmates were almost wholly urban; only 7 per cent had been primarily rural as adults. Forty-four per cent had grammar school educations and 56 per cent had entered or completed high school. . . .

One aspect of Prison B deserves specific mention: one of the criteria used by the courts in determining whether a . . . [female] was delinquent was whether or not she had had pre-marital coitus. . . .

Prison C. This institution situated in an eastern state served as a training school for Negro girls committed to its custody as delinquents. There were 50 inmates, ranging in age from adolescence to eighteen, and all of them contributed their sexual histories to our research. Twenty-seven girls were aged eleven to fifteen, and 23 were aged sixteen to eighteen. Of the latter, 22 of the 23 had had pre-marital coitus with 14 resultant pregnancies. . . . About half of the girls were in grammar school grades, and half in high school grades.

BIBLIOGRAPHY

Beebe, G. W. 1941. "Differential fertility by color for coal miners in Logan County, West Virginia." *Milbank Quarterly* 19:189–195.
1942. "Contraception and fertility in the southern Appalachians." Medical aspects of human fertility series issued by the National Committee on Maternal Health. Baltimore, Williams & Wilkins.
Brunner, E. K. 1941. "The outcome of 1556 conceptions. A medical and sociological study." *Human Biology* 13:159–176.
Christensen, H. T. 1953. "Studies in child spacing: I—Premarital pregnancy as measured by the spacing of the first birth from marriage." *American Sociological Review* 18:53–59.
Christensen, H. T., and Meissner, H. H. 1953. "Studies in Child spacing: III—Premarital pregnancy as a factor in divorce." *American Sociological Review* 18:641–644.
Davis, K. 1939. "Illegitimacy and the social structure." *American Journal of Sociology* 45:215–233.
Dickinson, R. L., and Beam, L. 1934. *The single woman. A medical study in sex education.* Baltimore, Williams & Wilkins.
Drake, St. C., and Cayton, H. R. 1945. *Black metropolis. A study of Negro life in a northern city.* New York, Harcourt, Brace.
Erhardt, C. L., and Jacobziner, H. 1956. "Ectopic pregnancies and spontaneous abortions in New York City." *American Journal of Public Health* 46:828–835.
Frazier, E. F. 1948 (original, 1939). *The Negro family in the United States.* New York, Citadel.
Glass, D. V., and Grebenik, E. 1954. "The trend and pattern of fertility in Great Britain. A report on the family census of 1946." Papers of the Royal Commission of Population. Vol. 6, Part 1. London, Her Majesty's Stationery Office.
Grabill, W. H. 1955. "Progress report on fertility monograph." In *Milbank Memorial Fund. Current research in human fertility,* pp. 82–92.
Hamilton, G. V. 1929. *A research in marriage.* New York, Boni.
Hertz, H., and Little, S. W. 1944. "Unmarried Negro mothers in a southern urban community." *Social Forces* 23:73–79.
Kiser, C. V. 1942. "Group differences in urban fertility." A study derived from the National Health Survey. Baltimore, Williams & Wilkins.
Lewis-Faning, E. 1949. "Report on an enquiry into family limitation and its influence on

human fertility during the past fifty years." Papers of the Royal Commission on Population. Vol. 1. London, His Majesty's Stationery Office.

Mayer, A., and Klapprodt, C. 1955. "Fertility differentials in Detroit: 1920–1950." *Population Studies* 9:148–158.

Pearl, R. 1939. *The natural history of population*. London, Oxford University Press.

Peckham, C. H. 1936. "Abortion. A statistical analysis of 2287 cases." *Surgery, Gynecology, and Obstetrics* 63:109–115.

Stix, R. K. 1935. "A study of pregnancy wastage." *Milbank Quarterly* 13:347–365.

Taylor, H. C., ed. 1944. "The abortion problem." Proceedings of the conference held under the auspices of the National Committee on Maternal Health, Inc. Baltimore, Williams & Wilkins.

Terman, L. M. 1938. *Psychological factors in marital happiness*. New York, London, McGraw-Hill.

Tietze, C., and Lewit, S. 1953. "Patterns of family limitation in a rural Negro community." *American Sociological Review* 18:563–564.

U. S. Bureau of the Census. 1955. U.S. census of population: 1950. Vol. 4, Special Reports, Part 5, Chapter C, Fertility. Washington, D. C., U. S. Government Printing Office.

1956. U. S. census of population: 1950. Vol. 4, Special Reports, Part 1, Chapter B, Occupation characteristics. Washington, D. C., U. S. Government Printing Office.

U. S. Vital Statistics—Special Reports. National Summaries. 1955. Vol. 42, no. 11, pp. 247–265. Natality: Each state and territory, and specified possessions, 1953. U. S. Department of Health, Education, and Welfare, National Office of Vital Statistics. Washington, D. C., U. S. Government Printing Office.

Wolff, P. de, and Meerdink, J. 1957. (Zajicek, J., and Pressat, R., trans.) La fécondité des mariages à Amsterdam selon l'appartenance sociale et religieuse. *Population* 12:289–318.

Young, L. 1954. *Out of wedlock. A study of the problems of the unmarried mother and her child*. New York, Toronto, London, McGraw-Hill.

SEX OFFENDERS:
AN ANALYSIS OF TYPES

Paul H. Gebhard, John H. Gagnon,
Wardell B. Pomeroy, and Cornelia V. Christenson

HETEROSEXUAL AGGRESSORS . . . [AGAINST] ADULTS

Examination of . . . [heterosexual] aggressors . . . [against] adults leads
us to feel that the majority can be classified into seven varieties, and that
the classification is scientifically and clinically useful.[1]

The commonest variety, accounting for between one quarter and one
third of our sample, we have labeled the assaultive variety. These are
men whose behavior includes unnecessary violence; it seems that sexual
activity alone is insufficient and that in order for it to be maximally gratifying it must be accompanied by physical violence or by serious threat.
In brief, there is a strong sadistic element in these men and they often
feel pronounced hostility to women (and possibly to men also) at a conscious or unconscious level. They generally do not know their victims;
they usually commit the offense alone, without accomplices; preliminary
attempts at seduction are either absent or extremely brief and crude; the
use of weapons is common; the man usually has a past history of violence; he seemingly selects his victim with less than normal regard for
her age, appearance, and deportment. Lastly, there is a tendency for the
offense to be accompanied by bizarre behavior including unnecessary
and trivial theft. Aside from the drunken variety of aggressor, the assaultive type has more cases involving erectile impotence than do the others.

From *Sex Offenders: An Analysis of Types.* Copyright © 1965, Institute for Sex Research, Inc.
Tables omitted. Reprinted by permission of Harper & Row, Publishers, Inc.

In some instances the violence seems to substitute for coitus or at least render the need for it less. In other cases there appears to have been a conflict between sexual desire and hostility resulting in some measure of erectile (less often ejaculatory) impotence.

. . . The assaultive aggressor who seemingly requires violence for his gratification is exemplified by a semiskilled laborer with two marriages and seven prison sentences behind him when he was interviewed in his late forties. While no conscious sadism appeared in his dreams, fantasies, or reactions to stories of brutality, all or nearly all his four rapes or attempted rapes were marked by unnecessary violence. The first rape, committed when he was in his early twenties, was a case of two young men picking up two . . . [women], one of whom fled when the men refused to take them home. While it seems clear that the other . . . [woman] could have been easily subdued and restrained by the two sturdy males, the subject felt it necessary to beat her and, after placing her on the ground, to kick her in the mouth before having coitus. Data are incomplete regarding his second rape when he was in his late twenties, but he entered the bedroom of a sleeping woman and attempted to have coitus with her. His third rape was committed, when he was in his thirties, upon his mother-in-law, who was nearly twenty years his senior. He raped her twice and in the process beat her so severely that she was hospitalized for a month. He evaded prosecution by fleeing the state. His fourth rape, when he was in his late thirties, consisted of forcing a . . . [woman] into his motel cabin and threatening her with a knife. When she tried to escape he struck her with a bottle and beat her up. Before coitus was accomplished, she did manage to run, nearly nude, from the cabin to seek help. The man solaced himself by taking her purse before he fled, but made the error of returning to salvage a bottle of whiskey which he had forgotten to take with him. After serving some years for this offense he was paroled but extradited to another state to stand trial for having raped his former mother-in-law.

The second commonest variety of aggressors . . . [against] adults are the amoral delinquents. . . . These men pay little heed to social controls and operate on a level of disorganized egocentric hedonism, and consequently have numerous brushes with the law. They are not sadistic— they simply want to have coitus and the females' wishes are of no particular consequence. They are not hostile toward females, but look upon them solely as sexual objects whose role in life is to provide sexual pleasure. If a woman is recalcitrant and will not fulfill her role, a man may have to use force, threat, weapons, or anything else at his disposal. The amoral delinquent may or may not have previously known his victim, but this too is a minor point to someone who regards women as mere pleasantly shaped masses of protoplasm for sexual use. It appears that one eighth to one sixth of the aggressors . . . [against] adults may be classed as amoral delinquents.

One case is that of a semiskilled man of twenty-two with a tenth-grade education. The descriptions of him contain terms such as "lazy," "drifter," "reckless," "restless," and "a chronic nuisance in his area." Almost half of his brief army career was spent in the stockade for having been absent without leave. About two years later, by which time he was tattooed and running with local gangs, he and two companions picked up two . . . [women] and, instead of giving them the promised ride to their destination, took them to a rural area where they forced sexual activity by threatening the . . . [women] with a knife. After serving slightly more than a year for this offense, the young man was released on parole. Shortly thereafter he was arrested along with a large group of males and females who were engaged in some sort of street fight. He was also suspected of encouraging a . . . [woman] to write bad checks. In the year he came of age his parole was revoked when he and a friend broke a window and stole several hundred dollars' worth of tools.

An example of an older amoral delinquent is a thirty-seven-year-old in our sample. There was nothing unusual about his life until impending fatherhood forced his marriage at age nineteen. He made his living through semiskilled labor and also got into the entertainment world. His first marriage ended in divorce after three years and his second marriage, when he was in his early twenties, lasted only one year. His wife, complaining of his too frequent sexual demands, made the following highly significant remark, ". . . he treated me as though I were a child," i.e., not as a real person, but as an inferior of use only as a sexual object. Soon after the collapse of this second marriage the man held up a number of stores, in one of which he found a young saleswoman and opportunistically forced her to undress and have coitus. These acts resulted in a long prison term. He was paroled in his early thirties and within about a year was back in prison for petty theft. Paroled again, he supported himself by managing an eating place staffed by waitresses who doubled as prostitutes while he served as the pimp. This remunerative situation came to an end when his attempts to persuade a woman to have coitus resulted in some sort of struggle during which the woman fell, or was pushed, down a flight of stairs, at least partially forced coitus occurred, and the man was injured in his left eye. In any event, he returned to prison on a charge of assault with intent to commit rape.

"The commonest variety [of rapist is] . . . men whose behavior includes unnecessary violence; it seems that sexual activity alone is insufficient and that in order for it to be maximally gratifying it must be accompanied by physical violence or by serious threat. In brief, there is a strong sadistic element in these men and they often feel pronounced hostility to women. . . ."

About as common as the amoral delinquent variety of aggressor is the drunken variety. The student of sex offenders soon comes to realize that drunks are omnipresent, appearing in all offense categories to a greater or lesser degree. The drunk's aggression ranges from uncoordinated grapplings and pawings, which he construes as efforts at seduction, to hostile and truly vicious behavior released by intoxication.

The simplest and least aggressive sort of drunken offense is exemplified by a nineteen-year-old farm laborer of borderline intelligence. The case is summed up in the words of the prison psychologist: "The subject is a dull boy of nineteen. . . . While drunk, he tried to force the young wife of his former employer into a bedroom in an attempt to have sexual intercourse. She resisted and later told her husband. . . ." This resulted in a 90-day sentence for assault and battery. The boy was under the impression that the wife was more amenable than she actually was.

A more bizarre, but still relatively harmless, case is one of a forty-two-year-old, previously married man of average intelligence who was living in a motel and was feeling sexually deprived. He had in the past once forced coitus on a girl friend with whom he had had a mutually voluntary coital relationship and also had once forced coitus on his ex-wife. Both women had resisted, wrestling ensued, and both had finally yielded in order to get it over with and get rid of him. It seems probable that the man looked upon the use of minor force as both effective and safe. He became intoxicated and recalled that a young, unmarried woman lived in a motel cabin nearby. He decided to peep in her window to see if she was with a man, his logic being that if she were with a man this would be evidence that she was sexually loose and, hence, worth cultivating. He peered in and saw her alone asleep in bed and at this moment conceived the idea of having coitus with her then and there. He cut the window screen and then with drunken logic recalled that he was not properly clothed for bed, so he returned to his own cabin and changed into his pajamas. Thus properly dressed, he went back to the . . . [woman's] cabin, removed the cut screen, opened the window, and crawled in. He tiptoed to the bed, turned off the bed lamp which had been left on, and tried to slip unobtrusively into the bed. The . . . [woman] awoke and screamed. The man, frightened, clapped his hand over her mouth and the . . . [woman] became quiet and immobile—possibly fainting. He then crawled on top of her and removed his hand from her mouth in order to kiss her. The . . . [woman] galvanized into action, screaming and scratching. The man was severely scratched before he managed to get out of bed and stumble out of the door into the grasp of a man attracted by the screams.

In contrast to these two examples, which involved no physical harm of any consequence and which were not without some humorous aspects, the cases where intoxication releases a violent pathological response are extremely serious. One of the best illustrations is the case of a young man who up to the time of his offense seemed in no way unusual except for his above-average intelligence, his hatred for his abusive father, and a tendency to want to bite his sexual partners as he reached orgasm. Following graduation from high school he enlisted in military service where he served well and had just re-enlisted before his offense. He had gone on a drunken binge and was frequenting bars in order to pick up . . . [women]. He finally found one; they drank and left together. They went into an alley and began petting. According to the man, while they were deep-kissing she suddenly bit his tongue severely, and subsequent medical examination disclosed a deep cut nearly halfway through his tongue. This intense pain coming on top of erotic arousal and extreme intoxication precipitated a sadistic assault in which he not only beat the woman but repeatedly bit her face, breasts, and genitals. Portions of flesh were actually bitten off. He claimed only vague memory of this and had no memory of taking the woman's wristwatch and dental plate when he left her. The psychologists and psychiatrists who examined him reported deep underlying hostile impulses which were released during intoxication. . . .

The next commonest variety of aggressor, constituting perhaps 10 to 15 per cent of the aggressors . . . [against] adults, might be termed the explosive variety. These are men whose prior lives offer no surface indications of what is to come. Sometimes they are average, law-abiding citizens, sometimes they are criminals, but their aggression appears suddenly and, at the time, inexplicably. As one would expect in situations where individuals snap under hidden emotional stresses, there are often psychotic elements in their behavior. The stereotype of this variety of aggressor is the mild, straight-A high school student who suddenly rapes and kills. For total unexpectedness, one of our cases is equally dramatic. A small, physically delicate, devoutly religious eighteen-year-old had been reared by his mother, who seems to have dominated him. While heterosexually oriented, he never developed sociosexually with girls of his own age; instead, on rare occasions he engaged female children in what would be called childhood sex play had he been preadolescent rather than fifteen or older. He was never able to achieve coitus, but usually ejaculated when the children struggled or when his penis touched their genital area. This behavior resulted in his being sent to a juvenile institution for about a year. On his return home and only a few days after his eighteenth birthday, during his mother's absence he asked a neighbor woman to come into the kitchen and light the oven for him. When she entered he struck her on the head with a hammer, hoping to knock her unconscious so that he could have coitus. She was not rendered unconscious by the blow and succeeded in escaping.

While the above case is unusual in that the subject was so sociosexually underdeveloped, in the following case the man's sexual history was normal. He was a hard-working, semiskilled laborer described by the prison psychologist as having "many fine traits, . . . deep respect for authority, family pride, sense of personal responsibility, a knowledge of right and wrong and a willingness to abide by the same, . . . etc." His dossier contained numerous and various letters attesting to his good character and respectability. The only negative note was his wife's statement that he tended to worry excessively and became emotionally upset easily. This statement is biased by the fact that the behavior of the wife and her relatives directly led to the sex offense. This conservative and respectable man had made the error of marrying a . . .[woman] from a very low socioeconomic stratum who brought with her to marriage not only an unborn child, but a number of shiftless, drunken, parasitic relatives. The resultant bitter arguments essentially destroyed the marriage, and the man decided to make the best of a bad situation by having extramarital coitus with some of his promiscuous female in-laws. He chose his mother-in-law, having interpreted her behavior toward him as provocative; the psychologists say that this choice also was unconsciously motivated by a desire for revenge against his wife and all her relatives. In any case, coitus occurred and the woman was at least partly forced.

The next variety of aggressor . . . [against] adults, and one accounting for perhaps as much as 10 per cent of the group, is the double-standard variety. The males so classified divide females into good females whom one treats with some respect and bad females who are not entitled to consideration if they become obstinate. While one would not ordinarily think of maltreating a good girl, any girl one can pick up easily has in essence agreed to coitus and can legitimately be forced to keep her promise. These double-standard aggressors are somewhat like the amoral delinquents in attitude, but differ from them in being less criminal, in resorting to force only after persuasion fails, and in not being so generally asocial. In brief, the double-standard variety may be described as rather average males of lower socioeconomic background who feel that with provocation the use of moderate threat or force is justifiable when applied to females judged to be sexually lax or promiscuous. . . . These double-standard males share with the amoral delinquents a penchant for group activity, the logical result when several males cruise about looking for female pickups. This trend may include a sort of man-to-man generosity, the female being shared much as men would share food or liquor, and with about the same emotional affect. Indeed, we have one case in which the man left a pickup . . . [woman] and his friend in his car to go to a nearby parked car containing three other men and suggested sharing the . . . [woman] in exchange for a gallon of wine. Yet this man strongly desired to marry a virgin and had refrained from coitus with his fiancée.

Another man of limited intellect and education who had a clear record, save for juvenile car theft (not uncommon behavior in his social milieu), helped a woman get her stalled auto started, mistook her appreciation and offer of a lift for an indication of sexual willingness and then threatened and struck her when she refused coitus. The prison report is illuminating: "[The subject has] habitually a naive expression . . . anxious to have everyone understand that he was neither brutal nor violent with his victim . . . admits that when he could not persuade her in friendly fashion he uttered threats. . . . Frank to admit he sees nothing wrong with what he did for the victim was not harmed in any way and it was nothing more than what he has done on many occasions in the past to other girls. . . ."

The rationalization of a double-standard aggressor might often be in the following vein, to quote one of them: "Man, these dumb broads don't know what they want. They get you worked up and then they try to chicken out. You let 'em get away with stuff like that and the next thing you know they'll be walking all over you."

After subtracting the above [five] varieties, nearly one third of the aggressors . . . [against] adults remain. A few of them may be recognized as clear cases of mental defectives and a few others as unquestionable psychotics, but the others strike one as being mixtures of the varieties described. . . .

INCEST OFFENDERS . . . [AGAINST] ADULTS

Incest offenders . . . [against] adults are adult males who have had sexual contact with their daughters or stepdaughters who were aged sixteen or older at the time. As in the other incest groups, the use of force will not be a separate category. When a female is sixteen or older, the presence or absence of threat or force is more easily determined than when she is younger; both parental authority and the disparity in physical strength are less and, to be effective, physical force or threat must ordinarily be so extreme as to be easily identified.

All the elements that served as real or fancied mitigating factors in the case of incest offenders . . . [against] minors are intensified in the incest offenders . . . [against] adults. The females were all physically mature and would be considered appropriate sexual partners by most men. The "child molesting" element of the other incest offenders no longer exists. Bluntly speaking, society tells the father or stepfather of a female aged sixteen or over, "You must live on rather intimate terms with a female who is old enough for sex and who is sexually attractive, but you must not allow yourself to take advantage of this situation." To the average person this dictate seems a reasonable law and one easy to obey. However, in certain circumstances even the most conservative person must admit that obedience to the law requires an iron will. For example, there are cases where a man marries a woman who has a full-grown daughter perhaps far more attractive than her mother; here the man may find himself sharing a home with a female with whom he could have a socially acceptable sexual relationship were it not for the fact that he married her mother. To view this female, whom he can scarcely look upon as a true daughter, in provocative dishabille without any thought of sex entering his mind is a virtual impossibility. The daughter, looking upon him not as a father but merely as her mother's husband, may make the situation more acute by applying to him the semisexual behaviorisms that have proved useful in obtaining her way with other males.

Many a father who would rather commit suicide than have sexual contact with his daughter has guiltily repressed incestuous thoughts that come unbidden to his mind. It is hard to recognize sexual attractiveness without being sexually attracted.

At the other extreme one sometimes finds cases that bring to mind the primate families or European peasant families of the past, where the wife and nubile daughters were regarded as the personal property of the male to do with as he pleased. Even today in some nations incest is looked upon as a family problem rather than a matter calling for legal action by society. In these cases the male's basic attitude is a simple and not illogical one: "I've reared them, fed them, and protected them for years; by rights I should have sexual access to them in recompense." Vestiges of this old pattern remain in some of our culturally "backward" communities and urban slums. These vestiges are not only recognized but expected by the persons involved—"Pop's drinking again tonight, Sis; you'd better go over and stay with Aunt Jennie." Such a situation, accepted as one of life's hazards by the participants, is enough to send the college-educated social worker running for the nearest policeman. . . .

The over-all impression is of a group of impoverished uneducated farmers or ranchers of less than average intelligence. This impression is substantiated by the facts: 14 of the 25 grew to adulthood in rural surroundings, another three were rural for a large proportion of their formative years, 11 were well below average in intelligence, and only five above. Four families could rival the Jukes and Kallikaks.

". . . the commonest incest offender . . . was a member of a Tobacco Road type milieu wherein incest was regarded as unfortunate but not unexpected."

As one would judge from all this, the commonest incest offender . . . [against] adults was of the subculture variety. Such an offender was a member of a Tobacco Road type milieu wherein incest was regarded as unfortunate but not unexpected. A few were of the amoral delinquent variety. An amoral delinquent in a subculture situation can be recognized chiefly by his greater tendency toward serious crime, marital instability, and aggressiveness, but differentiation is admittedly difficult in some instances.

One example of a subculture offender is a male, aged about forty at conviction, who had been born and reared in rural Oklahoma until he was eighteen, and thereafter lived a nomadic life in the Western states doing unskilled and semiskilled labor. He did not go beyond the eighth grade and was rated as "dull-normal" in intelligence. At fifteen he had his first coitus with a divorcee over twice his age; four years later he married a . . . [woman] of his own age who was pregnant by her uncle. The marriage broke up after five years and they did not see one another for about 15 years, when they met by accident at a carnival where the woman (still legally married to the subject) and her common-law husband were employed. Through their conversation at this chance meeting the wife learned enough to find him later, and she and the nineteen-year-old daughter, who was already a mother and divorcee, appeared and took up residence with him. He was not particularly interested in a reconciliation, and his wife was in the terminal stages of a pregnancy by her common-law husband. His daughter (actually his stepdaughter), on the other hand, was sexually attractive, and since he had not seen her since her early childhood it "seemed just like being with a strange woman." Flirtation developed into petting and finally coitus. The wife caught them and in the ensuing quarrel the man told her to leave the house, which she did. The incestuous arrangement continued (and resulted in pregnancy) until the father and daughter had a fight, the police were called, and the daughter, in a fury, told about the incest. The officials recognized this as a subculture case, the probation officer stating, "The girl of nineteen appears to be mentally and morally below average—no force or threats were probably necessary." The district attorney stated, "In view of the low intellectual and moral conditions surrounding all the members of this family it is the recommendation of this office that the defendant be given a short sentence"; and the prison psychologist remarked that the man's actions were "mostly explained by the social and cultural patterns of a primitively organized family group and his behavior is not uncommon in his native locale."

Aside from the subculture and amoral delinquent varieties, the remaining offenders who could be classified were a motley group: two senile deteriorates, two situational cases, and several other varieties represented by only one or two men each.[2]

One important aspect of the incest offenders . . . [against] adults was obvious during the reading of each case history in our search for varieties of offenders. This is their ability to be religious, moralistic, intolerant, and sexually inhibited, and at the same time to live a life of disorganization, drunkenness, violence, and sexual activity opposed to their religious tenets. This incongruence usually occasions no psychological stress, or at least none that cannot be relieved by periodic open repentance. The incest offenders . . . [against] adults were the "most religious" of any offenders, nearly half being classed as devout. Nearly all of these devout men were members of Pentecostal sects or were "hardshell" Baptists and Methodists.

A second and more important aspect of the incest offenders . . . [against] adults is that most were behaviorally but not legally offenders . . . [against] minors: of the 21 cases with sufficient data for determining the age of the daughter when the incestuous behavior began, in 13 the initial contact took place when the daughter was aged twelve to fifteen. In three cases she was under twelve and in only five cases was she sixteen or more. The general rule seems to be that in the eyes of these offenders puberty renders a female eligible for sexual exploitation. One might very well regard the incest offenders . . . [against] adults as chiefly incest offenders . . . [against] minors who were not found out until later. Why were they belatedly apprehended? Probably because their familial and social milieu (their subculture) was such that the incest came to the attention of the authorities only through unlikely chance.

This likeness between the incest offenders . . . [against] adults and the incest offenders . . . [against] minors explains why the two groups are so frequently similar in various measurements.

The five men who began their incest after their daughters were sixteen were all rural in their formative years, all had moderate to restrained sexual histories (none had extramarital coitus except with a daughter, and only three had premarital coitus), at least four of the five did not rate better than dull-normal in intelligence, and only one of the five was devoutly religious. None had more than a grammar school education. Aside from their lack of devoutness, these five men look much like the other incest offenders . . . [against] adults. . . .

PEEPERS

Peepers are ádult males who, for their own sexual gratification, looked into some private domicile or into some area or room reserved exclusively for females with the hope of seeing females nude or partially nude, the observation being without the consent of the females concerned. The term peeper, as thus defined, is not quite synonymous with the term voyeur, which is broader. A voyeur is a person who, according to the dictionary, ". . . attains sexual gratification by looking at sexual objects or situations." Thus, a lounger on the street watching passing . . . [women], or a person watching a strip-tease act could qualify as a voyeur, or so could the peruser of "cheesecake" magazines. One might say the peeper is a voyeur who has no legal right to be at the location from whence he observes, but even this definition is imperfect since a man has a right to be on a public street at night, but is liable to arrest if he stands on the sidewalk looking into the window of the adjacent apartmenthouse.

We prefer to limit our classification to the stereotype of the "Peeping Tom," the man who looks at females through some opening in a building. Such limitation excludes only a very few cases and, frankly, these cases should be excluded. Whereas the basic motivation may be the same, there is great psychologic and personality difference between the ordinary surreptitious peeper and the man who, let us say, persuades or hires a female to undress before him. The peeper in our sense of the word seldom desires any prearrangement with the person or persons observed; he wants to see them behaving in presumed privacy; he prefers the authentic to the contrived.[3] True, on rare occasions the peeper may believe (sometimes rightly) that the female has become aware of his presence and is "putting on a show," and this he finds contributes more to his sexual excitement. However, in these rare circumstances we are no longer dealing with pure peeping; an unsolicited element of deliberate feminine seductiveness, an erotic stimulus under any circumstances, has been added. A few peepers deliberately draw attention to themselves by, for example, tapping on the window or slipping a note under a door, but here again this represents an extraneous element: a desire to frighten or embarrass, or a desire to elicit a reciprocal interest—motivations usually associated with exhibitionists. The vast majority of peepers try to avoid detection.

One of the complications in studying peeping is the fact that virtually all males have voyeuristic and peeping tendencies. No one is apt to quarrel with this generalization even though we do not have statistical data to substantiate it.[4] The differentiation between the average man and the peeper is not one of seeking visual stimuli, but of willingness to assume risks in obtaining the stimuli. To cite a simple example, the average man may slow his step as he passes a window with the shade up, but he is unwilling to cross the lawn and press his nose against the pane. Unfortunately, for our analyses, the hypothetical average man may yield to temptation a few times in his life (especially when younger) and thereby become a part of our category of convicted peepers. Thus this category is a mixture of "real" peepers who have a long-standing and rather compulsive pattern of peeping, and individuals who have simply yielded to impulse once or twice and had the misfortune to be caught.

Still another, though minor, complication is constituted by the prowler, the opportunistic amateur burglar. Such a person roves about, usually by night, on the lookout for anything of value. If in the course of his prowling he has the opportunity to see nudity or sexual activity, he avails himself of it as an unexpected bit of luck. If he is arrested as a peeper, he is not apt to state that he was in actuality looking for something to steal; in fact, if he has a prior record of larceny, he may be happy to plead guilty to a peeping charge.

Like all men, the peepers have preferences and standards of sexual attractiveness; the simple act of peeping is not sufficient gratification—the person observed must be aesthetically acceptable. Virtually all peepers are looking for adult females with at least a modicum of physical attractiveness. The ideal, of course, is to see an attractive female engaged in some sort of sexual activity. As a group, peepers are persevering optimists. In this way they remind one of ardent fishermen, undaunted by failure and always hoping that the next time their luck will be better. Just as the fisherman will wait patiently for hours, so will the peeper wait patiently for a female to finish some interminable minor chores before going to bed—and then, like as not, she may turn off the light before undressing. Again like the fisherman who keeps a list of areas where fishing is especially good, the peeper not infrequently has in mind a number of particularly likely places to which he returns.

"The commonest variety of peepers . . . have much less heterosexual experience than is customary for their age and socioeconomic status, they are shy with females, and have strong feelings of inferiority."

In childhood and youth peeping is commonly a joint venture involving two or more persons, but in adult life it is always a solitary activity. There seem to be two major reasons for this. First of all, it is difficult to find another adult male willing to admit that he is a peeper and willing to share the risks of peeping expeditions. One can scarcely take a census of one's friends and acquaintances in a search for possible peeping partners without disclosing one's own proclivities and incurring censure. Secondly, the presence of a witness almost necessarily inhibits one's sexual response. A substantial number of peepers masturbate while watching, and in our culture to be seen masturbating, as an adult, is an extreme embarrassment. The masturbating peeper would be doubly vulnerable to ribald remarks and derogatory jests.

One characteristic of the peeper is that he almost never watches females whom he knows well. This is not a precaution against being recognized; he simply does not find in known females the satisfaction he seeks.

Acquaintanceship does not necessarily disqualify a woman, but it is extremely rare to find adults peeping at a "girl friend," relative, or spouse. All the peepers who were questioned on this point expressed a definite preference for females who were strangers. The human, and especially masculine, interest in novelty and diversity is doubtless an important factor here. . . .

The commonest variety of peepers are the sociosexually underdeveloped: nearly one third of the peepers fit this description. They have much less heterosexual experience than is customary for their age and socioeconomic status, they are shy with females, and have strong feelings of inferiority. Intelligence does not seem a significant variable; these men range from dull to superior. As we have said, marriage does not remove a man from this category—it is no cure for peeping.

Among the sociosexually underdeveloped, peeping often becomes a repetitive and important part of sexual life, frequently substituting for masturbation fantasy. The linkage between masturbation and peeping is mutually reinforcing, and for some men peeping-plus-masturbation becomes a truly compulsive activity carried on over lengthy periods of time.

A classic example is a man who was in his midtwenties when we interviewed him. He had begun petting at fourteen and had petted with a modest number of females, but had gone beyond above-the-waist stimulation with only two girls. When he was seventeen he had coitus three times with one girl and none thereafter. Timidity and an overwhelming fear of being rejected kept him from seeking more heterosexual activity which he strongly desired. His fear of rejection began, insofar as he knows, with a traumatic event shortly after he reached puberty and was experiencing the usual quick and intense sexual arousal at that period of life. Circumstances forced him to share a bed with his married sister and he became extremely aroused and desirous of coitus. Unable to express his wish, he simply showed her his erect penis. She rejected him violently and harangued him at length on how vile he was. Ever since then he had felt extremely awkward and hesitant about approaching females sexually, and every rebuff was excruciating.

He began peeping regularly, first at his sister through a keyhole, and later at other women through windows, usually masturbating while doing so and reaching orgasm. The peeping became a compulsion which he was unable to resist despite repeated arrests. Heterosexual petting—in which he engaged to a mild degree—did not satisfy his sexual or emotional needs, and his sensitivity about being rejected was so great that he ceased trying for coitus after four rebuffs. He found the idea of coitus with a prostitute unappealing and, moreover, he was strongly afraid of catching a venereal disease.

Of the five peepers who exhibited fetishistic behavior (in every case female lingerie was the fetish), three belonged to the sociosexually underdeveloped variety.

Another variety, constituting perhaps one peeper in ten, is the drunk. In essence, these are men who would not, and did not, peep while sober, but when their control was weakened by alcohol they either deliberately set out to peep or else took advantage of an unexpected opportunity to do so. Of the six men whom we classed as of the drunken variety, three were chronic vagrants and one was a professional criminal. . . .

About one fifth of the peepers may be regarded as of the situational variety—men who availed themselves, while sober or reasonably sober, of the opportunity to peep. This variety runs a wide gamut. At one end of the range is a virgin college freshman who had never seen a nude woman and who stopped to peep into a room where a woman was undressing. At the other end of the range is a married man with a grammar school education, in his thirties, who had spent nearly half of his life in juvenile homes, jails, and prisons, who evidently combined pleasure (peeping) with business (burglary) when the opportunity presented itself.

Perhaps one eighth of the peepers owed their trouble with the law to their mental deficiency. These men could not control their impulses adequately nor could they peep discreetly enough to avoid being caught. Many of these mental defectives tend to blend with the situational and drunken varieties of peepers, but the root of their trouble was their low intelligence rather than circumstances or alcohol.

After subtracting these four varieties, we are still left with about one quarter of the peepers unclassified. These men were neither drunken nor mentally deficient, their sociosexual behavior was generally within normal limits, and their peeping was not an opportunistic offense. Upon closer examination it was found that ten of these 14 men had been convicted of rape and three of exhibition. In the case of five rapists the peeping antedated the rape: these are the men who generate the popular notion that peepers become, in time, rapists. While it is true that an occasional peeper of one of our four varieties may rape, the use of force is generally uncommon—it happened in only three cases (all of the socio-sexually underdeveloped variety) . . . .

We cannot determine from our data what behaviorisms differentiate the harmless peeper from the peeper who will subsequently rape, but we do have the impression that peepers who enter homes or other buildings in order to peep, and peepers who deliberately attract the female's attention (tapping on windows, leaving notes, etc.) are more likely to become rapists than are the others.

NOTES

1. A classification of types of rapists and their variant personalities can be found in Manfred S. Guttmacher and Henry Weihofen, *Psychiatry and the Law* (New York: Norton, 1952), pp. 116–117; Paul Plaut, *Der Sexualverbrecher und seine Persönlichkeit* (Stuttgart: Ferdinand Enke, 1960), pp. 75–81.

2. Various types of incest offenders, some similar to those found here . . . were identified in these studies: Olof Kinberg, Gunnar Inghe, and Svend Riemer, *Incestproblemet i Sverige* (Stockholm: Natur och Kultur, 1943), p. 309 (the "despotic father" accounted for about half the cases with data); Denis Szabo, "L'Incest en Milieu Urbain," *L'Année Sociologique*, Troisième Série (1957–58), 1958, pp. 79–80; [S. Kirson] Weinberg, *Incest Behavior* [(New York: Citadel, 1955)], pp. 98–105.

3. The factors of stealth and of a stranger as an object in peeping were stressed by Irvin E. Yalom, "Aggression and Forbiddenness in Voyeurism," *Archives of General Psychiatry*, 3 (September 1960), p. 317.

4. G. V. Hamilton supplied some verification of this, He found that out of 100 married males, 73 per cent remembered youthful pleasure from "stealing peeps" of others' sex organs, 81 per cent admitted the tendency remained in adulthood, and 63 per cent had indulged such desires after growing up. *A Research in Marriage* (New York: Albert & Charles Boni, 1929), pp. 455–456.

THE TRANSITION PERIOD 5
Think-Pieces and New Research

In the 1960's, there was a major turnover in the Institute's research staff. In 1960 and 1963, two of Kinsey's original research team left the Institute. Clyde Martin resigned to pursue an advanced degree in sociology, and Wardell Pomeroy left to begin private practice as a psychotherapist.

John Gagnon and William Simon, both sociologists, joined the Institute in 1959 and 1965, respectively. In addition, a number of graduate students became affiliated with the Institute and contributed a great deal to the work of this period. By 1968, though, except for a few graduate students, these people had all left the Institute. It was Paul Gebhard, director of the Institute throughout this decade of turnover, who provided the core around which the Institute, and a sense of continuity, were sustained.

The work during this third stage continued the Institute's sociological tradition. The period was, however, distinctively characterized by the publication of a number of think-pieces. With an accumulation of extant knowledge about sexuality, such pieces, in which to "collect one's thoughts," were timely. Publications during this period had less scope but greater depth than earlier Institute works. Journal articles became a fitting vehicle of publication.

In addition to these think-pieces, a number of research projects to gather new data were initiated. These studies included a pilot study for future research on homosexuality and a survey of college students with regard to their sexual experiences.

The selections in this chapter represent the various kinds of work that were being done during this period.[1] The first selection is by David Sonenschein. While he was a graduate student in anthropology, Sonenschein worked for the Institute and did much of the ethnography for the homosexual research that the Institute was undertaking. In this selection, Sonenschein describes six types of sociosexual relationships that he found to be common among homosexual males.

The second selection is a think-piece by Paul Gebhard. In this selection, Gebhard discusses fetishism and sadomasochism, and he provides some provocative theorizing on these topics.

---

[1] Gagnon and Simon have recently integrated into book form the various think-pieces they collaborated on during this period and have requested that these articles not be reprinted here.

The final selection is by Donald Carns, who, as a graduate student in sociology, worked on the 1967 Institute study of college students. In this study, interviews were conducted with a national random sample of 1177 undergraduates representing secular colleges and universities with enrollments over 1000. In this selection, Carns discusses the project's data on first coitus and integrates some of the ideas that were contained in the think-pieces of this period.

14. Institute staff, 1961. Back row, left to right: Gebhard, Dellenback, Mary Winther, Elizabeth Egan, Henry Remak, Bettie Silverstein, Hedwig Leser, Richard Scammon, Blaine Johnson; front row, seated left to right: Pomeroy, Mary Louise Carter, Gagnon, Christenson. *Dellenback*

15. Christenson, Gebhard, Gagnon, and Simon. 1969. *Dellenback*

16. Pomeroy supervising coders. Circa 1963 *Dellenback*

MALE HOMOSEXUAL RELATIONSHIPS

David Sonenschein

This work has largely come about because of a dissatisfaction with previous psychological approaches and some of the recent sociological research on male homosexuality. It has been pointed out (Sonenschein, 1966) that psychology has furnished us with most of our data and methodological viewpoints of homosexuality; most of this research and rhetoric has dealt excessively with the definition, origin and operation of etiologic behaviors. Simon and Gagnon (1967) have more explicitly pointed out, however, that this approach has resulted in an extremely "simplistic and homogeneous" conception of homosexual individuals and groups; their lives are characterized in much of the literature by bizarre case histories of personal, social and sexual pathology. On the other hand, such people as Evelyn Hooker (1956, 1962), Maurice Leznoff and W. A. Westley (1956) and Albert Reiss (1961) have formed the basis of what is essentially an ethnographic tradition in the description and functional analysis of the homosexual community. Others such as Nancy Achilles (1967) have done more specifically anthropological work in the analysis of what is called in this paper the "cultural system" of the homosexual world. This paper hopes to contribute to this area of objective description, and also to the newly developing sociological approach, in that certain variables are suggested which if adequately measured, may reveal a much more systematic picture of the varieties of homosexual relationships.

From "The Ethnography of Male Homosexual Relationships." *The Journal of Sex Research*, Vol. 4, No. 2 (May 1968), 69–83. Copyright © 1968, The Society for the Scientific Study of Sex. Reprinted by permission.

In other words, what the newer social approaches to homosexuality mean to do is: firstly, anthropologically describe and analyze the synchronic particular social and sexual subculture that a given homosexual both finds himself in and structures for himself, and, secondly, to sociologically describe and analyze various modes of relation and interaction of homosexuals with society as a whole (cf. Simon and Gagnon 1967). Basically, the kinds of answers one seeks then now center around the question: "Given a homosexual individual, what does he do about it, what does he do with it, and what happens to him as a result?" This writer feels that this is a much more immediately important and crucial approach—to the homosexual and heterosexual alike—rather than what seems to be at this time, the unanswerable question of etiology.

The data used in this paper come from observations and interviews of informants of a homosexual community in the Southwestern United States; as a check on these initial data, subsequent brief observations were made in five other cities around the country. The subject community was roughly divided into (1) an "upper status" homosexual group composed of individuals in the higher socioeconomic brackets of the city; (2) a "lower status" homosexual group composed of the city's middle and lower class members, students and military men; and (3) an unstructured body of "marginals" composed of such individuals as transients, homosexuals who did not identify with either of the two main groups and "hustlers" or male prostitutes. Most of the observations were made of the lower status group. While it was impossible to estimate the total homosexual population in the city, observed groups ranged in size from three individuals to approximately 100. The age range of the subjects was from 16 to 57, the modal age falling roughly in the middle 20's.

The introduction into this community was a result of personal friendship and professional affiliation rather than being based on any research design.[1] Actual observations did not begin until about six months after the initial introduction in 1961. The period of association with the subject community as a heterosexual friend then lasted for about 1½ years until 1963; at no time did the members of the community know observations were being made. The directions that the ethnographic work followed included considerations of (1) the position of the homosexual community in relation to the city, (2) the social and cultural structure of the homosexual community itself, (3) the special language of homosexuality in relation to the group, and (4) the nature and structure of the interac-

TABLE I

Typology of Male Homosexual Relationships in the Subject Community

	Duration	
Sexuality	Permanent	Non-permanent
Social	First order friendships (I)	Second order friendships (II)
Sexual	Extended encounters (III)	Brief encounters (IV)
Sociosexual	Mateships (V)	Circumstantial encounters (VI)

tion of individuals within their groups. This paper is a partial report on the latter set of observations and analysis of interpersonal relations.

Table I, then, is an attempt at a systematization of the dyadic relationships as were seen in the subject community. The organizing variables are those that were the most important in the relationships, those of sexuality and duration; the cells of the table are thus a function of the relative saliency of these variables to the participants.

I. PERMANENT SOCIAL RELATIONSHIPS

These are what may be called first order friendships and included individuals that the subjects described as their "best and closest friends." The individuals who described each other in this manner were usually found within the same clique structure and were in constant face-to-face interaction. These cliques held members who were much alike in interests, intellects, occupations, general social and sexual status-roles and attitudes.[2] Members felt strongly committed to each other in three main areas: social psychologically (in terms of constant association, confidence in intimate matters and behavioral reinforcement), economically (such as loans of money, job placements, etc.) and materially (loans or gifts of clothes, personal items, etc.). Based then on these kinds of bonds, these friendships were mutually maintained over time and distance. Most subjects claimed that they had anywhere from two to five "really close friends" with whom they always kept in contact regardless of how far apart they were.

II. NON-PERMANENT SOCIAL RELATIONSHIPS

What are here called second order friendships describe those individuals that were spoken of as "good friends" but were usually found outside of an individual's clique. The sociometric choice or labeling of friendships in this case need not be reciprocal or equal; that is, A may call B his "good friend" while B may not think of A as such (cf. Lundberg and Lawsing 1937). A lesser degree of congruence of attitudes and expectations was called for in second order friendships than in those of the first order. Second order friendships did not call for continued contact over distance; a moving away of one member of the dyad usually meant an end to the relationship until such time as face-to-face contact was reestablished. Even still, communication was maintained as long as the individuals were in the same community.

It is to be noticed that first and second order friendships were seen to be entirely social and non-sexual in nature. Members were fairly explicit in their statements regarding the possible sexual desirability of good or close friends. Most cited reasons were: "knowing them too well to have sex" and/or that sexual needs were amply satisfied from other sources. However, whether or not such statements come before or after the fact is not clear at this point. In other words, whether the category of "friends" is really a residual category of individuals who did not work out as sexual partners or whether there are differential expectations through which individuals are initially screened to become either "friends" or "partners" is a matter now set for future research. Leznoff and Westley (1956) discuss the question of friendships briefly in functional terms indicating that there are a few individuals that are selected specifically to form the basis of some kind of "primary group cohesiveness" which is pitted against a category of "all others," i.e., sexual partners. The observational data from the subject community suggest that in reality both processes may operate due to the fact that many homosexuals had friends with whom they had never attempted to have sex as well as friends who were once sexual partners but had since moved into a non-sexual friendship category. There were, in addition, a few individuals who were both sexual and social partners, depending on the social situation and needs of the individuals. They will be discussed below in more detail as third order friendships under cell VI of the typology, but it is important to note at this point that this very category seems to indicate a process of "trial and selection" whereby certain individuals who may not succeed as sexual partners may still be retained as a certain class of "friends."

Where both friends and sexual partners must be drawn from the same sex, the processes involved seem to particularly depend upon sociocultural factors as well as the psychological ones. For example, while genital relations between first and second order friends were extremely rare, sex play was very common. There seemed to be a rather definite joking relationship among these individuals that allowed on the one hand for affectionate behavior and on the other, more hostile verbal behavior of teasing and chiding. A. J. M. Sykes (1966) has noted a similar relationship in heterosexual groups, where it helps to define and differentiate between sexual and non-sexual partners. The operation of this kind of relationship may prove significant not only with regard to processes of selection but even with regard to the management of friends and sexual partners in interpersonal interaction. It was interesting to note that in the subject community as members became socialized into their proper status group and clique, they shared with the others a kind of group cohesiveness which presented a relatively homogeneous social and sexual front to other groups. On the other hand, members within each group became more competitive with each other for social and sexual partners. This many times resulted in a good deal of tension in the confrontations in the context of the homosexual institutions. The strains on the relationships seemed to be both manifested and managed in such ways as (1) gossip, an extremely constant and common activity, (2) humor, containing unusually high amounts of self-mockery and the projection of homosexuality onto heterosexuals, and (3) "campy" or effeminate behavior, the sporadic nature of which will be discussed below.

As an initial step to analysis, Table II, while being minimally descriptive of the subject community, suggests an approach to more quantitatively define the three classes of friendship as indicated by the observational data. It is suggested that the variable "degree of interaction," when broken into several indices, will yield the "strength of relationships" in clusters which correspond to the three categories of friendship as held by the subjects.

Before leaving cell II of the typology, there is one further important example of a non-permanent social relationship which is here simply called the roommate relation. It has been previously assumed that if two homosexuals were living together, they were sexual partners and may

TABLE II
Discrimination of Friendship Relations

	Strength of relationship		
Degree of interaction	Best friends	Good friends	Acquaintances
Maintains face-to-face contact in social situations	yes	yes	yes
Seeks contact within the community	yes	yes	no
Maintains relationship over time within the community	yes	may or may not	no
Maintains relationship over distances	yes	no	no

even be included in that vague class of "homosexual marrieds." Upon a closer examination, however, it can be seen that there are several types of living arrangements, each with its special form and content. The roommate relation is a case where friends live together for varying lengths of time, usually for reasons of economics (not being able to afford a place alone) or for social psychological reasons (loneliness, wanting to be at the centers of social and sexual action, and other reasons as mentioned above). The emotional involvement between roommates was as between first and second order friends: most of the roommates in the subject community were members of the same clique.

Although Hauser's *The Homosexual Society* (1962) is the only study to discuss the non-sexual living arrangement, he makes a series of statements that are entirely unsupported by the present data. First of all, he sees the roommate relationship solely as a degenerated form of a love or sex relationship. This paper proposes the contrary: that the category of non-sexually involved housemates is an extension and function of a greater realm of asexual friendship relations. Secondly, Hauser suggests that this kind of arrangement can exist only between what he calls "two similarly sex-oriented" individuals, that is, two homosexuals equally masculine or equally feminine. Too many exceptions to this were observed in the subject community and others for this statement to hold true. Implicit in this is the assumption that Hauser and others make which says that instances of effeminate behavior are valid indicators of a consistent role and self-conception that is essentially feminine. While there are indeed some individuals who consistently occupy very masculine or very feminine sociosexual roles both in and out of the homosexual community, there is a good deal of evidence that most of the obvious effeminate behavior is situation-specific; that is, sporadic, circumstantial and usually satirical. In other words, much of this behavior is a function of sociocultural structure: the intersection of time and place within the homosexual community and a homosexual's idea of what he has to do to fit into the group. In short, there is doubt at this point as to whether or not a given instance of behavior does in fact indicate any sort of consistent and/or conceptualized role within the community.

Returning to the subject community and the roommates within it, it was noted that for the most part, the division of labor in terms of household duties was a matter of personal choice rather than any function of so-called masculine or feminine roles. The breaking of the roommate relation was due sometimes, as Hauser insists (1962), to some form of jealousy, but in the subject community, it was due more often to matters of more mundane affairs such as financial irresponsibility, conflict over the maintenance of the house, moving away and the usual assortment of "personality clashes." It is this often less interesting realm of activities and events of managing a day-to-day life that previous accounts have neglected but when they are taken into account, they prove significant in the recharacterization of the homosexual and his life.

III. PERMANENT SEXUAL RELATIONSHIPS

This form included what was called "being kept." Because the basis of this relationship was materialistic and sexual, the explanation of it, as a relationship, varied as to an individual's attitude toward and involvement in the dyad. The homosexual who is being "kept" is in the role of a mistress; the "kept boy" was a younger individual whose interest in the relationship was primarily materialistic and monetary and whose emotional involvement with his partner was superficial and exploitative. He did not usually enter into such a relationship unless there was a high probability of a stable income of goods and money; his role was to produce a stable output of sexual services. This individual then conceived of the relationship as "permanent" in the sense of "as long as the money holds out."

This younger individual was "kept" by an older, more well-to-do homosexual whose physical appearance and/or aging had tended to move him out of the system of competition for partners in the homosexual community. The older homosexual had greater expectations of "permanence" involving a hope or fantasy of actual emotional involvement, but he would not have committed himself to this kind of relationship unless he could have kept up a constant output of money and goods; this he realized he must do in order to "keep" (in both senses) his partner.

Group participation by these individuals was low due on the one hand to the fear on the part of the older man that his "boy" would be stolen from him, and on the other hand, to the fact that the other members of the group held a rather low opinion of such a relationship and the individuals involved in it. The "kept boy," however, apparently served a social function to his "keeper" in that the older homosexual liked to occasionally "show off" his partner and the manner in which he could "keep" him to the rest of the community. Despite the expectations of permanence in this relationship, it was very unstable, the biggest factor of breakup being the infidelity of the "kept boy."

IV. NON-PERMANENT SEXUAL RELATIONSHIPS

This cell in the Table contains two main examples: the "one night stand" and the "affair." The two tend to separate out by considering the relative duration of the interactions and the content of the relationships.

The "one night stand" is perhaps the homosexual's most frequent sexual relationship yet surprisingly little is known of its forms and even less of its dynamics and content. There were two rather distinct types of relationships under this rubric, differentiated from each other again by using the criteria of the duration of the brief encounter and the relative degree of social interaction with the partner. Both types were extremely depersonalized, the sole basis of the relationship being the purpose of sexual activity and orgasm. The briefest and most superficial of the two was known as the "quicky" and may be consummated in anywhere from a few hours of activity to the few minutes it takes to reach orgasm. This form involved the highest degree of anonymity; it seemed to be the most popular form of sex for those homosexuals with a good deal of social rank and for those who were tremendously committed to sexuality. In this activity, the partners usually had never seen one another before and usually never saw each other again.

The other type of the "one night stand" was a more prolonged relationship such as for a whole night or a weekend. Here participants were more likely to learn at least each other's name and a few mutual interests. Much like the above, however, the relationship was entered into and departed from in an entirely non-committal manner.

". . . male homosexuals in the subject community tend to separate and keep separated those individuals who served their social needs from those who served their sexual needs."

The variety called an "affair" was defined by the subject group as a primarily sexual relationship lasting over an indefinite period of time; it may or may not involve what the participants called "love," even though the participants were seen as "lovers" by the rest of the group. Duration varied in terms of weeks or months. It would be distorting to impose an arbitrary time criterion here for definition as does Schofield (1960) when he suggests an affair last over a year. What is important is the conception of the relationship by the participants themselves; it was seen in the subject community that relationships lasting a year or more were spoken about and conceived of in entirely different terms. Participants rarely lived together in affairs. They acknowledged a relative instability in the relationship and an uncertainty of the depth of the emotional involvement. Thus for some, an affair was a trial relationship, a prelude to a more committal one and a testing of mutual emotional and sexual adjustments in terms of the individuals' relations to each other and their relation to the community as a couple.

For others, however, it was a kind of "going steady," referred to as a kind of young puppy love that was frequently indulged in many times during one's life and may or may not be intended as a "test" of a future mate at all. In this case, a couple may spend a varying amount of time in intense association with the implicit knowledge that the affair will end when the novelty wears off or in some cases when the risk of discovery becomes too great. Finally, for still others, the affair was merely an intensely physical relationship with another, ending when both partners were sexually satiated.

The "fear of discovery" leads to another aspect of the affair that characterized it in the subject community. Pressures of exposure were both external (the police, one's employer) and internal (other group members) to the community. To the participants, however, the latter was the more important. The affair was often spoken of with illicit overtones indicating either that a homosexual was involved in a clandestine relationship with a respected and/or heterosexually married man in the city, or, more usually, that one was involved with another homosexual who was the partner of a third party. In this latter sense, "extra-marital" affairs were common in the subject group.

It is this modal category of the depersonalized sexual relationship, and more particularly the "one night stand," that has attracted the most attention from the psychological field but opinion here has largely overlooked its sociocultural context. It has been implied and stated in the psychiatric literature that all homosexual sexual encounters were of the "one night stand" variety and due in reality to a searching for the ultimate and permanent partner, or, alternately, that it was due simply to "the neurotic basis of homosexuality" (Harper 1963; cf. Hauser 1962, Schofield 1960). In the subject community however it was clearly evident that there were differential expectations operating in the formation of the various sexual relationships discussed here. Very simply, the partner desired for a "one night stand" was usually not the one a homosexual saw as a good bet for a more permanent partner. One acted very differently with a purely sexual partner than with a sociosexual partner.

It is in this connection then that one is stimulated to look to the sociocultural contexts of the behaviors involved in the relationships. It was seen that there were two major systems in the homosexual community that directly influenced interpersonal behavior: the "cultural system" and the "social system." [3] The major part of the cultural system in the subject community was a series of institutions that served the needs of its members. Places such as bars (cf. Achilles 1967), steam baths, parties and even the streets provided backdrops that were more conducive to one kind of expected relationship than another. For example, one would walk the streets or "cruise" (look for partners) the public restrooms as well as go to the bars if one wanted a purely sexual partner. On the other hand, one may have looked more in some bars, gone to parties or depended upon personal introductions by friends if one wanted a partner for a more lasting relationship, social or sexual. Even within the system of bars, there were differences; some may be more of a social rather than a sexual "market place" to paraphrase Hooker (1965). Just then as there was a difference of role behaviors as a function of the sociocultural situation, so too was there a difference in the relationships that took place in and grew out of the institutions of the homosexual subculture.

In addition to this, there was the social system of the subject community which directly involved the structure and behavior of groups and the individuals in them. One aspect of this was the status differentiation found in the community. This was very similar to what Leznoff and Westley (1956) found but although severe social distance was maintained, the separation of sexual interaction was not as great. Members of the subject community preferred and sought sexual partners from opposing groups and cliques. Based on the intention of action, the graph in Figure 1 is a representation of the tendency in the subject community for social choice to vary inversely with sexual choice. In other words, male homosexuals in the subject community tend to separate and keep separated those individuals who served their social needs from those who served their sexual needs. Also in Figure 1, the relationships from the typology are shown in the directions that they tended to distribute themselves.

It must be mentioned again however that many times these relationships are a function of the sociocultural structure of the community;

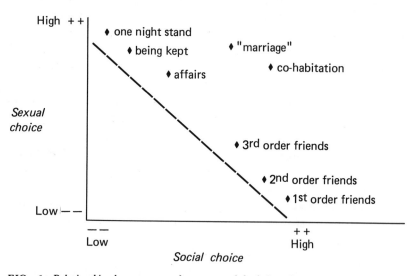

FIG. 1. *Relationship between sexual versus social choice of partners in the subject community and clustering of relationships.*

the variables may tend to merge as the range is narrowed by the opportunity structure of any given community. For example, in a community small in numbers of members, there would be more repetitive sexual relationships with given individuals. The direction of alternatives in this case would either be to limit the numbers of members in the social and sexual categories or to tend to combine them into a more unified category.

V. PERMANENT SOCIOSEXUAL RELATIONSHIPS

To find a permanent partner was certainly a common goal of many homosexuals in the subject group but it was not as universal, as constant or as compulsive as the psychological literature would have us believe. Most of the younger individuals were more intent upon the satisfactions of the moment or having partners in extended encounters rather than questing after a permanent mate. It was usually only after "aging" set in (about age 30) that finding a steadier mate became a significant concern.[4]

The psychological conception of the so-called homosexual marriage has been simplistic and misleading. It has assumed that all homosexuals living together were to be construed as being "married" in some rather homogeneous way and has defined both the form and content of this category as pathological. Thus previous conceptions of the relationship have been too inclusive [5] and have not distinguished the forms of paired relationships we have even thus far covered in this paper.

Yet there is a category of homosexual relationships that is indeed in many aspects much like a heterosexual marriage. But within this concept, there appeared in the subject community two rather separable patterns of behavior that so-called "married" couples exhibited.

The first form, for which the term "marriage" (in quotes) will be reserved, was characterized by the following complex of traits: (1) some sort of ritual, usually in imitation of the heterosexual marriage ceremony; (2) a material demarcation of the union as in the exchange and wearing of wedding rings; (3) a value system of the participants, based on a romantic conception of ideally unending love; and (4) a tendency to dichotomize social roles. It is this form that is the most obvious and most closely approaches the psychological characterization.

It has been commonly thought that role dichotomization was a "natural" and automatic event in homosexual marriages: one man stays home in an essentially feminine and domestic role and is called the "wife" and the other partner assumes the occupational responsibilities and the more masculine domestic chores and is called the "husband" (Hauser 1962; Bergler 1956). This also was supposed to correspond to the gender role identification and sexual behavior of the partners: one is effeminate, conceives of himself as a "woman trapped in a man's body" and is "passive" in sex; the other is more masculine in appearance and behavior, sees himself as a man and is "active" in sex. In actuality, however, it was seen in the subject community and in other homosexual communities that these kinds of gender and role distinctions were typical only of a minority and special type of paired homosexual partners.

The second kind of mateship was less formalized, often the only event being a personal exchange of rings and/or the setting up of a household. It too was based on a conception of love but the relationship was less predominately sexual as was the previous variety; there was a more conscious attempt by the individuals involved to aim at a congruence of values and interests. This kind of stable pairing may be called simply "cohabitation" to differentiate it from the actual homosexual "marriage."

"It was continually observed in the subject community that as soon as any two individuals entered into a sexual or sociosexual relationship that was hoped to last for any period of time, these individuals rapidly withdrew from the activity of the community and decreased their participation in group affairs, regardless of how active or popular they had been before. . . ."

The first variety of the permanent relationship was less stable than the second variety. It seemed that in fact, the ritual, rather than being an attempt to cement the relationship, was more of an excuse for the ever-present and ever-needed party. It seemed in a sense to reintegrate the group in terms of its own values, particularly those that mock the heterosexual world. The pairing off into permanent mateships became, through the mock marriage, a group event in contrast to the private event of pairing for the co-habitants.

The relative publicness or privateness of interpersonal relations in the homosexual community profoundly affected their stability and duration.

It was continually observed in the subject community that as soon as any two individuals entered into a sexual or sociosexual relationship that was hoped to last for any period of time, these individuals rapidly withdrew from the activity of the community and decreased their participation in group affairs, regardless of how active or popular they had been before; the institutions that were more conducive to sexual interaction, and hence more competitive, were particularly avoided. This applies not only to permanent mateships but also to the relationship of "being kept" as above.

VI. NON-PERMANENT SOCIOSEXUAL RELATIONSHIPS

In this final cell are included situational face-to-face contacts. They were between individuals who considered themselves "friends" but also potential sexual partners. These may be called third order friendships and comprise individuals whom ego might call an "acquaintance" or speak of as "just a friend." Social encounters seemed to occur before sexual activity with these individuals in contrast to those in cell IV, where sexual interaction usually preceded social acquaintance.

It seemed in the subject community that although there were people who might fall into this category, they were relatively rare. Individuals were pointed out as to whether they were sexual partners or social partners; only rarely could they be both. As mentioned earlier, given the hypothesis of the separation of sexual from social partners, this category might then represent a category of selection rather than a static unit. It might be here that a homosexual makes the decision as to whether an individual becomes a friend of a higher order or a sexual partner.

NOTES

1. Pomeroy (1963) and Hooker (1963) discuss the problems of sex research and research on homosexuality respectively. Honigmann (1954) provides some anthropological perspectives on the Kinsey reports and sex research in general.

2. This is similar to Lazarsfeld's concept of "homophily" (1954).

3. This distinction is somewhat forced as both systems are aspects of a unified phenome-

non. The "cultural system" focuses not only on the tangibles such as artifacts and dress but also on such intangibles as overriding value orientations, language and communication and so on (Parsons and Shils 1951). The "social system" focuses upon the structuring and relationships of groups. Communication mediates this relation of values and behaviors (Parsons 1961). Institutions become then in this sense situations or environments in time and space in which a number of fairly specific and sanctioned behaviors occur (Sheldon 1951). These are exemplified in the text of this paper.

4. Observations outside the subject community indicate that this concern may be in part a variant of the social structure in which a homosexual has to operate in the sense that it is a function of the kind of opportunity structure in his society that allows for the presentation of potential partners plus the community's system of values that may define him as a potential partner.

5. Robbins (1943) defines a homosexual marriage as "an essentially monogamous, relatively durable intimacy existing between members of the same sex"; it is also defined as inherently pathological. Other definitions are by Leznoff and Westley (1956): "a stable social and sexual relationship between two homosexuals . . ." and by Hauser (1962): "only the homosexuals who have a lasting affair and are faithful to one another will be considered 'married.' "

BIBLIOGRAPHY

Achilles, N. B. The Development of the Homosexual Bar as an Institution. In *Sexual Deviance* (ed. Gagnon, J. H. and Simon, W.) New York: Harper and Row, 223–244, 1967.

Bergler, E. *Homosexuality: Disease or Way of Life?* New York: Hill and Wang, 1956.

Harper, R. A. Psychological Aspects of Homosexuality. In *Advances in Sex Research* (ed. Beigel, H. G.) New York: Hoeber-Harper, 187–197, 1963.

Hauser, R. *The Homosexual Society.* London: Bodley Head, 1962.

Honigmann, J. J. An Anthropological Approach to Sex. *Social Problems 2:* 7–16, 1954.

Hooker, E. A. Preliminary Analysis of the Group Behavior of Homosexuals. *Journal of Psychology 42:* 217–225, 1956.

Hooker, E. The Homosexual Community. In *Proceedings of the XIV International Congress of Applied Psychology.* Copenhagen: Nielson, 40–59 (Vol. II), 1962.

Hooker, E. Male Homosexuality. In *Taboo Topics* (ed. Farberow, N.) New York: Atherton, 44–55, 1963.

Hooker, E. Male Homosexuals and Their "Worlds." In *Sexual Inversion* (ed. Marmor, J.) New York: Basic Books, 83–107, 1965.

Lazarsfeld, P. F. and Merton, R. K. Friendship as a Social Process: a Substantive and Methodological Analysis. In *Freedom and Control in Modern Society* (ed. Berger, M., Abel, T., and Page, C. H.) New York: Nostrand, 18–66, 1954.

Leznoff, M. and Westley, W. A. The Homosexual Community. *Social Problems 3:* 257–263, 1956.

Lundberg, G. A. and Lawsing, M. The Sociology of Some Community Relations. *American Sociological Review 2:* 318–335, 1937.

Parsons, T. Introduction. In *Theories of Society* (ed. Parsons, T., *et al.*) Glencoe, Ill.: Free Press, 963–993 (Vol. II), 1961.

Parsons, T. and Shils, E. A. (Eds.) *Toward a General Theory of Action*. New York: Harper Torchbooks, 1951.

Pomeroy, W. Human Sexual Behavior. In *Taboo Topics* (ed. Farberow, N.) New York: Atherton, 22–32, 1963.

Reiss, A. J., Jr. The Social Integration of Peers and Queers. *Social Problems 9:* 102–120, 1961.

Robbins, B. S. Psychological Implications of the Male Homosexual "Marriage." *Psychoanalytic Review 30:* 428–437, 1943.

Schofield, M. G. (pseud. Westwood, G.) *A Minority*. London: Longmans, 1960.

Sheldon, R. C. Some observations on theory in the social sciences. In *Parsons and Shils* 1951, 30–44.

Simon, W. and Gagnon, J. H. Homosexuality: the Development of a Sociological Perspective. *Journal of Health and Social Behavior 8:* 177–185, 1967.

Sonenschein, D. Homosexuality as a Subject of Anthropological Inquiry. *Anthropological Quarterly 39:* 73–82, 1966.

Sykes, A. J. M. Joking Relationships in an Industrial Setting. *American Anthropologist 68:* 188–193, 1966.

FETISHISM AND SADOMASOCHISM

Paul H. Gebhard

It is appropriate to consider these two phenomena together since they frequently intermingle. Sadomasochism very often incorporates fetishistic elements, and one may with justification regard much of the sadomasochistic paraphernalia as fetish objects since the sight or touch of these devices can engender sexual arousal. On the other hand, fetishism is less dependent on sadomasochism: one type of fetishism is almost devoid of it. However, the two phenomena share certain relationships. In mild and often unconscious form they are both moderately common in the general population; they occur in both heterosexuality and homosexuality; and in more extreme form they are true paraphilias with neurotic compulsive elements.

While there exists a substantial literature on both fetishism and sadomasochism, virtually all of it is based on the more extreme forms which have come to clinical or legal attention. The milder forms have largely escaped attention except for speculative essays or for passing observations appended to a study of some other phenomenon such as violence. Those fetishists and sadomasochists who have not run afoul of the law or who have not encountered clinical scrutiny remain an unknown majority.

In their milder forms—such as the opinion that high heels add to feminine allure or the impulse to pinch a well-rounded buttock—these phenomena involve millions of U.S. males. Even the more extreme manifes-

From *Science and Psychoanalysis*, Vol. XV (1969), 71–80. Copyright © 1969, Grune & Stratton, Inc. Reprinted by permission of publisher and author.

tations may be found in thousands rather than hundreds of individuals. These quantitative aspects fully justify fetishism and sadomasochism receiving more attention, especially in a social era marked by increasing concern about mental health and violence. Even beyond this, studies of these phenomena can elucidate much of the etiology and function of normal sexuality, just as study of a malfunctioning or atypical organ of the body can show us something about the function of the normal organ.

In our present state of knowledge the Institute for Sex Research cannot offer any reasoned theories buttressed by factual data. We can, however, present some findings and ideas which should prove useful and suggest future lines of investigation.

FETISHISM

The initial stumbling block in sexual studies is generally a lack of reasonably precise definition, and my first task is to describe what I consider fetishism. Freud and most psychiatrists and analysts use substitution as the basic criterion: the fetish functions much as a substitute for the "normal sexual object." [1] This criterion at once gives rise to vexing questions. Must the substitution be total or partial? What if the putative fetish is not a substitute, but a highly desirable adjunct to sexual activity? Or, to push the matter to the boundary of absurdity, is a sex-starved shepherd a victim of ewe fetishism? Obviously supplementary criteria are required. Phyllis Greenacre attempted to fulfill this need with a more rigorous definition: "We may define fetishism as the obligatory use of some non-genital object as a part of the sexual act without which gratification cannot be obtained. The object may be some other body part or some article of clothing and less frequently some more impersonal object." [2] Even this definition has deficiencies. The word "obligatory" rules out too many cases, and the "non-genital object" which may be a "body part" implies that use of the mouth or hand could constitute fetishism.

Rather than become involved in a definition of Talmudic intricacy I wish to present an operational definition which has proved satisfactory in dealing with fetishism in overt form or at a conscious level. I envision the whole matter of fetishism as a gradated phenomenon. At one end of the range is slight preference; next is strong preference; next is the point where the fetish item is a necessity to sexual activity; and at the terminal end of the range the fetish item substitutes for a living sexual partner. Nearly all humans have preferences as to the physical or sartorial attributes of their sexual partners. Hence I feel that statistical normality ends and fetishism begins somewhere at the level of strong preference. This is nicely exemplified by one man who had his first recognition of his own fetishism when he realized he had ignored a beautiful girl to court a plain girl with a particular hair style. The next stage, that of necessity, would be the case of a man who is impotent unless his partner wears a certain type of shoe. The ultimate stage is the man who habitually dispenses with the female and achieves orgasm with only the shoe.

". . . the fetishist falls victim to what Whitehead called 'the fallacy of misplaced concreteness': the symbol is given all the power and reality of the actual thing and the person responds to the symbol just as he would to the thing."

As more speculation than information I suggest that there seems to be escalation of degree of fetishism only when the individual suffers from some other sexual maladjustment. A youth who has not yet established a satisfactory sociosexual life may experience an upsurge of fetishism (often female lingerie) which declines when he later develops hetero- or homosexual liaisons. An old man may also experience an escalation of fetishism as problems of impotence appear—here the fetish is employed as a crutch upon which he may increasingly depend. If age or poor health radically diminishes the sexual drive the fetishism tends to die out before the basic sexuality is extinguished. This same gerontological denouement is seen equally often in cases of sadomasochism. Some fairly substantial amount of sexual drive seems necessary to maintain a paraphilia. Several middle aged men have told me that obtaining sexual partners is difficult enough without the additional burden of finding one with, or tolerant of, the paraphilia. An aging person cannot afford to be particular lest he doom himself to involuntary celibacy. In some respects the decline of paraphilia reminds one of the "burning out" seen in aging narcotic addicts.

One can divide fetishism into two major classes: In one the fetish in its purer—or at least more distinctive—form is an inanimate object; in the other the fetish is some physical attribute of the sexual partner, aptly labelled "partialism."[3] The latter blends with normality so inextricably that it can be differentiated only in certain extreme forms. Thus we would not call a man a breast fetishist because he insisted his female partners had at least vestigial mammae, but we would label as a hair fetishist a man who could have coitus only with red heads. Because of this difficulty of differentiating and because in partialism the stage of substitution cannot be attained (except for hair fetishists) short of necrophilic amputation, I shall confine the remainder of this discussion of fetishism to the class of inanimate objects.

We have divided inanimate fetishism into two types: media and form. Fetish items are often a combination of both, but in such instances one type is considered more important by the individual than the other. Also a person may have several fetishes, some of one type and some of the other, but generally one is dominant. A media fetish is one wherein the substance rather than the form of the object is the important aspect. Leather fetishism is an excellent example: the person responds to leather and whether it be a coat, glove, or shoe is less consequential. A form fetish is one wherein the form of the object is more important than the material of which it is constituted. Shoe fetishism is a good example of this.

Media fetishism can be usefully subdivided into two subtypes. Without intending any humor I have labelled these "hard" and "soft." Hard fetish objects are generally smooth, slick, and with a hard metallic sheen. Leather, rubber, and lately plastics, exemplify this. Hard fetish items are often tight constricting garments or shoes, usually black. Note that in our culture a tight black shiny dress is regarded as the trademark of the *femme fatale*. Hard media fetishism very frequently is associated with sadomasochism. In other cases the hard media fetishist in his or her tight garb feels secure and armored against the world, much like a matron who feels soft and vulnerable without her corset, or the military officer who feels ineffectual out of uniform.

Soft media fetish objects are fluffy, frilly, or soft in texture. Fur and lingerie are common examples. There is no emphasis on constriction or tightness. Color is generally less important, although black is a favorite. Soft media fetishism, despite Sacher-Masoch, is not usually associated with sadomasochism. Effective combinations of hard and soft media fetishism are commonly exploited in burlesque and floor shows.

Form fetishism is potentially limitless, but the commonest items are clothing and foot gear. Shoe fetishism nearly always involves high heels which in our society symbolize adulthood and sexuality. High heels often are associated with sadomasochism: to be stepped upon by a female with long sharp heels on her shoes is a classic masochistic theme. Conversely, extremely high heels functionally cripple a female and turn her into a sexual object incapable of flight and hence appeal to the bondage enthusiast or sadist. Boot fetishism is almost totally affiliated with sadomasochism. Until the recent fashion for them, high boots were the trademark of prostitutes specializing in sadomasochism.

Lingerie fetishism is the extreme form of an interest common to many males. Every Christmas the stores sell large quantites of black or red lingerie and the purchasers are predominately males buying these sexually enhancing garments for their wives or girl friends. Clothesline thefts of lingerie are a common police problem.

Garter fetishism has undergone a metamorphosis. The garter has been associated with sex for centuries. Note, for example, its role in Jewish weddings and the inevitable garter on chorus girls from can-can dancer days to recent times. However, in the past fifteen years the garter as a fetish item has been largely replaced by the garter belt, which has become almost a standard fixture in pornographic photographs and films.

Stockings, especially black mesh hose, have a strong fetishistic value, but at the preference level. True stocking fetishists are quite rare. The same is true of glove fetishism, but the glove seems to be suffering a decline since it plays a lesser part in current feminine dress. Black opera length gloves nevertheless remain a part of sadomasochistic costume.

Corset fetishism was once prevalent and certain corsetry shops sold space at peepholes whereby men could glimpse customers trying on corsets. As the corset declined in popularity and became a symbol of stout matrons rather than of beauties such as Lillian Russell it rapidly declined as a fetish item. Corset fetishism now survives chiefly as an adjunct to bondage and sadomasochism.

Other form fetishes are numerically less important. Interestingly enough, some items of dress seem unsuited for fetishism. Hats are one example. One might reasonably expect that brassieres would be almost as popular as underpants, but inexplicably they are seldom fetish items despite our cultural emphasis on breasts as sexual centers of interest.

At this juncture it must be noted that transvestism is related to fetishism, but not synonymous with it. Many transvestites report no conscious sexual arousal from wearing clothing of the opposite sex and do not fixate on any special piece of clothing. In a questionnaire distributed by Virginia Prince to 390 transvestites only 13 per cent reported any fetishistic feelings. Two-thirds of the males said they felt they had a feminine component which was seeking expression through transvestism. The remaining 11 per cent were transsexuals who felt they were women trapped in male bodies.[4]

The various theories as to the etiology of fetishism all suffer from fatal flaws. Freud's hypothesis that the fetish substitutes for the male genitals and hence protests against castration fear seems corroborated by the rarity of fetishism among females, but it does not stand up under scientific scrutiny. Michael Balint suggests the fetishist's entire body is phallic and hence the fetishist inserts it into hollow objects such as shoes, gloves, and clothing—all being symbols of female genitalia.[5] Phyllis Greenacre thinks fetishism arises from a disturbance of body image in early life.[6] Caprio regards it as symbolic masturbation.[7] Allen says it is an attempt to return to mother.[8] Frankly, I find all these and other theories grossly inadequate. Actually the only important elements of fetishism now known are these: (1) It is confined to well-developed civilizations, especially European-American cultures. It is essentially non-existent in preliterate cultures. (2) It is far rarer in females than in males. (3) It is usually associated with the body, clothing, or body by-products. (4) It seems almost wholly a sexual phenomenon. Aside from the fixation of some children on their blankets or particular toys, and an occasional adult's dependence on some lucky piece, it is difficult to think of non-sexual analogies. (5) It generally manifests itself in puberty or adolescence, but can be induced even in adult life by some trauma or powerful experience.

I agree with psychoanalysts that fetishism is basically a matter of symbolism. Physical attributes or objects assume a sexual symbolic value through association. The process stops here with the average person, but the fetishist falls victim to what Whitehead called "the fallacy of misplaced concreteness": the symbol is given all the power and reality of the actual thing and the person responds to the symbol just as he would to the thing. Due to the greater sexual responsiveness of the male he is more liable to such sexual association than the average female, and he is especially vulnerable in puberty and adolescence when sexuality becomes powerful and when he has been exposed to the symbols of sex before experiencing the actuality of sociosexual gratification. Perhaps the seeming absence of fetishism in preliterate cultures is due to the frequent tolerance of childhood sex play and early knowledge of coitus. If this be true, a study of a prudish preliterate society should unearth cases of fetishism. On the other hand perhaps fetishism can develop only in a literate civilization wherein there is from infancy on a great use of and dependence on a multiplicity of verbal, written, and other symbols. This seemingly feeble idea is reinforced by the fact that fetishism seems largely confined to literate people taught to be imaginative and to make extensive use of symbolism in verbal and written communication and hence in their thought processes.

"Sadomasochism is extremely complex. Some achieve orgasm during the pain; in other cases the sadomasochism only constitutes the foreplay and the session culminates in conventional sexual behavior. Some masochists dislike the pain while it is being inflicted, but obtain gratification by anticipation of the pain or by thinking about it after it has ceased. Lastly, there are the bondage people who do not enjoy pain but are stimulated by constraint, mild discomfort, and a sense of helplessness."

This theory does not explain why some people become fetishists and others in the same culture do not, but it at least is in agreement with what little we know about fetishism.

SADOMASOCHISM

Sadomasochism may be operationally defined as obtaining sexual arousal through receiving or giving physical or mental pain. Unlike fetishism, analogues are common among other mammalian species wherein coitus is preceded by behavior which under other circumstances would be interpreted as combatative. Temporary phases of actual fighting may be interspread in such pre-coital activity. In some species, such as mink, sexual activity not infrequently results in considerable wounds. This pre-coital activity has definite neurophysiological value in establishing, or reinforcing, many of the physiological concomitants of sexual arousal such as increased pulse and blood pressure, hyperventilation, and muscular tension. Indeed one may elicit sexual behavior in some animals by exciting them with non-sexual stimuli. This may explain why sadomasochism is used as a crutch by aging men in our society who require some extra impetus to achieve arousal. From a phylogenetic viewpoint it is no surprise to find sadomasochism in human beings.

Sadomasochism is embedded in our culture since our culture operates on the basis of dominance-submission relationships, and aggression is socially valued. Even our gender relationships have been formulated in a framework conducive to sadomasochism: the male is supposed to be dominant and aggressive sexually and the female reluctant or submissive. Violence and sex are commingled to make a profitable package to sell through the mass media. This is no innovation—for centuries the masochistic damsel in distress has been victimized by the evil sadist who is finally defeated by the hero through violent means.

Relatively few sadomasochists are exclusively sadists or exclusively masochists; there is generally a mixture with one aspect predominant. This mixing is sometimes necessitated by circumstances: sexual partners are extremely difficult to find and consequently, for example, if two masochists meet they are obliged to take turns at the sadist role. This role trading is made easier by ability to project. The masochist playing the sadist may fantasy himself receiving the pain he is inflicting.

Sadists are far rarer than masochists, and female sadists are so highly prized that masochists will travel hundreds of miles to meet them. I postulate that this imbalance between sadists and masochists is a product of our culture wherein physical violence, particularly to someone of the opposite gender, is taboo and productive of intense guilt. To strike is sin; to be struck is guiltless or even virtuous in a martyrdom sense. Even more psychodynamically important is masochism as an expiation for the sin of sexuality. During childhood, puberty, and part of adolescence sexual behavior is punished and it is easy to form an association between sexual pleasure and punishment. The masochist has a nice guilt relieving system—he gets his punishment simultaneously with his sexual pleasure or else is entitled to his pleasure by first enduring the punishment.

It is important to realize that pain *per se* is not attractive to the masochist, and generally not to the sadist, unless it occurs in an arranged situation. Accidental pain is not perceived as pleasurable or sexual. The average sadomasochistic session is usually scripted: the masochist must allegedly have done something meriting punishment, there must be threats and suspense before the punishment is meted out, etc. Often the phenomenon reminds one of a planned ritual or theatrical production. Indeed, sadomasochistic prostitutes often report their clients give them specialized instructions to follow. Genet's *Balcony* is true to life. When one appreciates this one realizes that often in the relationship the sadist is not truly in charge—the sadist is merely servicing the masochist. The sadist must develop an extraordinary perceptiveness to know when to continue, despite cries and protests, and when to cease. A sadist who goes too far or stops prematurely may find his ineptitude has cost him a sexual partner. Not infrequently sadomasochistic activity is interspersed with loving and tenderness. This alternation makes the process far more powerful. Police and brainwashers use the same technique of alternate brutality and sympathy to break their subjects.

Sadomasochism is extremely complex. Some achieve orgasm during the pain; in other cases the sadomasochism only constitutes the foreplay and the session culminates in conventional sexual behavior. Some masochists dislike the pain while it is being inflicted, but obtain gratification by anticipation of the pain or by thinking about it after it has ceased. Lastly, there are the bondage people who do not enjoy pain but are stimulated by constraint, mild discomfort, and a sense of helplessness. Bondage has both sadistic and masochistic aspects. The sadist has the pleasure of rendering his partner helpless and at his mercy—a favorite sexual theme in mythology, literature, and fantasy. The masochist bondage enthusiast enjoys not only the restraint itself but the guilt relieving knowledge that if anything sexual occurs it is not his or her fault. Also as Dr. Douglas Alcorn points out, some persons derive a sense of comfort and security from physical constraint.[9] Lastly, the hood, often used in bondage, offers the advantage of depersonalization and heightens the helplessness through interfering with sight, hearing, and vocalization.

Both sadomasochism and bondage are often replete with fetish items including specialized clothing and restraint or torture devices. All this offers the devotee substantial additional gratification. The average heterosexual or homosexual has relatively little paraphernalia for supplementary pleasure and it offers scant opportunity for ingenuity or creativity.

The prevalence of unconscious sadomasochism is impossible to ascertain, but it must be large if one can make inferences from book and magazine sales and from box office reports. We do know that consciously recognized sexual arousal from sadomasochistic stimuli are not rare. The Institute for Sex Research found that about one in eight females and one in five males were aroused by sadomasochistic stories, and roughly half of both sexes were aroused by being bitten.

The etiology of sadomasochism, while the subject of much writing especially in the form of interminable German books, is not well understood. In individual cases the genesis may be clear as psychoanalysis and psychiatry amply demonstrates, but these individualistic explanations do not suffice for the phenomenon as a whole. After all, the supply of English headmasters and Austrian girl friends is limited. We must turn to broad hypotheses, and I will offer a rather simplistic one.

"It may be that a society must be extremely complex and heavily reliant upon symbolism before the inescapable repressions and frustrations of life in such a society can be expressed symbolically by sadomasochism."

First, we may assume on the basis of mammalian studies and history that we humans have built-in aggressive tendencies. Second, it is equally clear that males are on the whole more aggressive than females. Experiments indicate this is in large part an endocrine matter: androgens elicit or enhance aggression. Thirdly, animal and human social organization is generally based on a dominance-submissiveness relationship, a peck-order. Fourthly, when one couples the difficulties of sexual gratification with the problems involved in living in a peck-order society, one has an endless source of frustration which lends itself to expression in pathological combinations of sex and violence. Note that in our own culture when we wish to say that someone was badly victimized we use sexual terms such as, "he got screwed." From a rational viewpoint we should apply the words "he got screwed" to someone who had had a pleasurable experience, but we have unfortunately mixed sex with dominance-submissiveness behavior.

This using sex as a symbol brings up the puzzle as to why explicitly sexual sadomasochism, like fetishism, seems the monopoly of well-developed civilizations. One never hears of an aged Polynesian having to be flogged to obtain an erection, and for all their torture and bloodshed there seem to have been no de Sades amongst the Plains Indians or Aztecs. While it is true that in various preliterate societies sexual activity often involves moderate scratching and biting, well-developed sadomasochism as a life style is conspicuous by its absence. It may be that a society must be extremely complex and heavily reliant upon symbolism before the inescapable repressions and frustrations of life in such a society can be expressed symbolically in sadomasochism. Sadomasochism is beautifully suited to symbolism: what better proof of power and status is there than inflicting humiliation or pain upon someone who does not retaliate? And what better proof of love is there than enduring or even seeking such treatment?

NOTES

1. Freud, Sigmund: Collected Papers. Vol. 5, London, Hogarth Press, 1950, pp. 198–204.

2. Greenacre, Phyllis: Certain relationships between fetishism and faulty development of the body image. *In:* Psychoanalytic Study of the Child, Vol. 8, 1953, pp. 79–98.

3. Caprio, Frank: Variations in Sexual Behavior. New York, Citadel Press, 1955, p. 268.

4. Prince, Virginia: A Survey of 390 Cases of Transvestism, Los Angeles, 1965, privately printed.

5. Balint, Michael: A contribution of fetishism. Int. J. Psychoanal., Vol. 16, 1935, pp. 481–483.

6. Greenacre, Phyllis: Op. cit.

7. Caprio, Frank: Fetishism. *In:* Ellis, A., and Abarbanel, A., eds., Encyclopedia of Sexual Behavior, Vol. 1, 1961, pp. 435.

8. Allen, Clifford: The Sexual Perversions and Abnormalities (second edition). London, Oxford University Press, 1949, pp. 175–180.

9. Alcorn, Douglas: Personal communication.

FIRST COITUS
AND THE DOUBLE STANDARD

Donald E. Carns[1]

If we rid much of what has been written on sexual socialization of its polemical bent, and look at certain underlying themes, a fairly coherent and plausible view of male versus female sexual learning is emerging. Especially from the sociological, social-psychological, and neo-psychiatric viewpoints, the importance of puberty as a pivotal event having different meanings in two sexual socialization subcultures . . . has supplanted earlier theories which took their leads from childhood experiences, primal family dynamics, and subconscious states.

In particular, this revisionism has tended to reinforce, on a scientific and therapeutic level, something which has borne a cultural label for many years, the so-called "double sexual standard." [2] For by reemphasizing sexual learning in the home, institutions, peer groups, and society as a whole, one is ineluctably led to a position which stresses the very different patterns of sexual initiation, scripting, legitimation, and context which exist for men as opposed to women, especially in Western societies. . . .

One pair of essayists, reacting to Freudian concentration on preadolescent dynamics in adult sexual behavior, offered a synthesis of social learning views of sexuality that resulted in a sharply different view of modal male and female sexual consciousness (Simon and Gagnon, 1969).

From "Talking About Sex: Notes on First Coitus and the Double Sexual Standard." *Journal of Marriage and the Family*, Vol. 35, No. 4 (November 1973), 677–88. Copyright © 1973, National Council on Family Relations. Tables omitted. Reprinted by permission of publisher and author.

To summarize and paraphrase part of their argument, young males, at or soon after puberty, initiate masturbatory activity and, especially in the case of middle-class children, continue masturbation until well into marriage (Kinsey, 1948:505–508). But more importantly, for the male, masturbation at this age is accompanied by the development of rich and varied erotic fantasies, direct analogs of fiction and graphics which are designed to "appeal to prurient interests." . . .

. . . The female does not typically initiate masturbatory activity until much later in the age cycle, and most especially not until after some significant amount of socio-sexual experience as, for example, genital petting or even coitus.[3] Such a disparity, which is suggested in Kinsey (1953:173) as well as the data upon which this paper was prepared, implies two additional differences between adolescent boys and girls. First, unlike males, girls, perhaps because they do not develop such early and heavy commitments to auto-erotic self-manipulation, do not typically form the same rich and uncontextualized set of erotic fantasies that the male does (Kinsey, 1953:687–689; 174).[4] This term "uncontextualized" is used here in the sense that the adolescent male's sexual fantasies are not typically grounded in real life relationships which he is experiencing with one or more girls, but rather tend to take their content from source materials such as pornography, from the media (including films and film stars), even from his relatives (if Freud is at all correct on this point).[5] Secondly, female fantasies at this age, to the extent they have even the remotest sexual content at all, typically center on contexts which emphasize feeling states—"romantic love"—in which the female is the center of male attention but in which there is minimal or nonexistent sexual activity. . . .[6]

We may add a third generalization to this set, that of the homosocial bond during adolescence. To the extent sexual behavior before marriage is prescribed for the male, it is likely that he receives his status feedback from the same sex, same age peers. This suggests that he must socialize his sexual experiences to those who count, for it is in this way that his identity is validated. Since we presume that sexuality is an integral part of adolescent male identity, he most certainly will report his experiences, embellishing and editing them as it fits his style, purpose, and the reactions of his audience. And, we may go so far as to suggest that, in the absence of real experience, he will draw on his pornotopic fantasies and create a fictive sexual identity using imaginary exploits. His skill at doing this will determine, in many important ways, his acceptance into the group and the degree of identity validation that takes place. One could even take a long-term view of this process, that the creation of fictive experience and the embellishment (and reportage) of real experience is, in form, anticipatory socialization into later adolescent and young adult sexual roles. He creates his identity and then, in a sense, must live up to it.

"In later adolescence, when the female modally begins to experiment in a socio-sexual sense, she is not only considerably behind her male counterpart, statistically speaking, but she finds the major sources of legitimation for her acts from her definition of the emotional relationship she shares with the male."

The female's proscriptive sexual situation (culturally speaking) has its roots in, among other things, the Judaeo-Christian tradition (Kinsey, 1948:483 ff.), the Victorian and post-Victorian periods (Marcuse, 1955), and the problem of unwanted pregnancy (Winch, 1971:525–527). In later adolescence, when the female modally begins to experiment in a socio-sexual sense, she is not only considerably behind her male counterpart, statistically speaking,[7] but she finds the major sources of legitimation for her acts from her definition of the emotional relationship she shares with the male. If the relationship is "serious," or even better, has a high probability of ending in family formation in the relatively near future, she can, to a limited degree, socialize her sexual experiences with same age, same gender peers and receive something other than negative feedback. Indeed, on college campuses in such situations, a girl who did not become sexually involved with a male in whom she had placed fairly high levels of emotion would probably be considered slightly odd, and certainly stuffy and not "with it."

Thus males and females in the postadolescent period (roughly the college years) each have sexual audiences and sexual identities, but they are based on quite different scripts. If this reasoning is correct, the double sexual standard should show up quite dramatically in the varied ways males and females manage the fact of first coitus, and in particular the immediacy of· reportage, the pervasiveness of their audience and its nature in relation to them, the audience's reactions, and the like. For in this way, we should be approaching the double standard through the back door, so to speak; an oblique interpretation, but one which surely goes to the heart of the matter: *i.e.*, sexual identity and its public presentation and management.

One additional introductory note. Premarital sexual intercourse is used in this paper as a pivotal behavior, one which creates either problems or prospects. Its pivotal nature, in turn, stems from our culture's conception of first coitus—it is decidedly an irreversible event. One possesses one sexual status before the act—"virgin"—and another afterwards. It is the management of the post-coital status which shall be our concern in this paper. . . .

As suggested . . . , the concept of a double sexual standard sensitizes us to expect quite different patterns in the management of personal sexual experience depending upon whether the actor is male or female. . . .

In line with our reasoning that males seek approval for their sexual exploits from other males, one could reasonably assume that sharing such knowledge with greater numbers of friends would bear a higher pay-off. . . . It is the category "5 or more" friends which contains over half of the experienced males in this sample. We have no way of knowing if the identity of the female coital partner is part of this knowledge-sharing process, although a strong case could be made in the affirmative. If so, it suggests that a woman's decision to enter coitus also implies that she is creating for herself a sexual status which will have a relatively pervasive distribution. If she has sexual relations with two males, or more, her new sexual status increases arithmetically in terms of the size of the knowledgeable audience, and assuming they talk to others, is spreading at an alarming, perhaps logarithmic, rate. Further, through interaction of knowledgeable others, a qualitative change will also occur, *i.e.*, she will be evaluated downwardly. Such is the nature of the male bond.

On the other hand, about 56 per cent of the experienced females in the sample have told only two or fewer friends about their entry into coitus, and indeed nearly 27 per cent have told no one. This contrasts sharply with the male pattern discussed in the paragraph above. Clearly then, to the extent publicizing sexual experience is an indicator of sexual selves and sexual identity management, these data reveal . . . quite different patterns for males and females. . . .

As one would expect, women have a much greater investment in a virginal status than men in relation to their parents. . . . [The data] reveal that well over half of the females in the sample are certain their parents do not know they have had coitus before marriage, while about a third of the males could report this with certainty. This is not at all surprising, for the double standard should be most pervasive and imperative in the context of intergenerational information management as, indeed, other kinds of information remain privy to a specific generation.

Notwithstanding our reasoning to this point, the motives which impel a person to discuss a first coital experience are, of course, complex and varied. Generally, though, the nature of masculinity and its maintenance in this culture, coupled with the double standard which, we have suggested, has relevance to one's sexual status, would suggest that males should talk about their experiences more quickly than women. We have elsewhere (Carns, 1973) characterized much of male sexuality in this society as "ego-sex," [8] thus suggesting that, for example, vocalizing sexual exploits should be gratifying, especially (although not exclusively) when associated with the occurrence of actual genital sexual experience. That is, one of the primary rewards for experience would be to share the knowledge of it with one's . . . peers, if one is a male. And the more the better. Using nothing more than a criterion of one month as relatively rapid reportage of the act . . . note that over 60 per cent of experienced males in this sample talked to someone within that period of time. Conversely, only about 40 per cent of the coeds fall in that category. . . .

. . . It is also noteworthy that about equal proportions of each gender never talked about their first coital encounters (24 per cent of females, 20 per cent of males). If our reasoning is correct, . . . then the female pattern of sexual de-privitization is motivated by elements other than ego enhancement, except in a curiously reverse sense. That is, one would suspect that the sharing of sexual knowledge (and especially coital acts) by a female is brought about by . . . intimacy (best friend, roommate) and/or status management. The sharing of secret knowledge is, at once, a way of dispelling pluralistic ignorance, the latter functioning to foster guilt and a sense of special status, and is a technique for building intimacy between small numbers of intimate friends. . . .

. . . When a respondent talked to someone about his or her first coital experience, it was generally to a friend of the same gender. . . . Males receive positive feedback for their reported actions far more than women do. In both cases—males and females—few are totally disapproved of, with more disapproval for women than men. But mixed (ambivalent) reactions abound for women.

Certainly this bears strongly on one of our central theses: that sexual scripts for male and female undergraduates (and more generally, most premarital actors in the United States) are quite different as a reflection of the cultural pattern of the double sexual standard, that when a script is violated the audience expresses sanctions in the form of disapproval, or in the case of males, adherence to the script produces applause. Many females are then faced with a dual, interrelated problem: the private management of guilt (which may or may not be religiously based) (Carns, 1970a; 1970b) or the socialization of guilt in order to neutralize its meaning through sharing it and receiving positive feedback for the sexual act. For about two women out of three (in this sample) this procedure would seem to work, but for a third it either does not work or meets with ambivalence, and this in turn must be neutralized in some other fashion. As noted earlier, the male is probably not socializing guilt when he talks to others of his experiences. He is either reaffirming the male bond and his sense of masculinity and belongingness, or he is sharing with his friends a confidence about his relationship with his girl. Both meet with approval: the first because he is acting out a cultural prescription of his gender, the second because he has received affirmation for his sexual rights with a female defined as his.

Age and relational elements in first coitus are not unrelated. It is probable that the earlier the entry into premarital coitus the less likely the act occurs in the context of emotional bonding, . . . Naturally other factors enter to specify this generalization, in particular socioeconomic status, since adolescents who do not attend college tend to marry younger and thus at a younger age enter relationships which have a high probability of resulting in legal mating. In this section we shall explore this dimension by cross-classifying age of first coitus and the respondent's definition of the relationship by our reportage variables. Our overall guiding assumption is still in force: the double standard should still manifest itself. But by controlling age and relational status, we may be able to specify this basic relationship to a considerable degree.

For this analysis, only two of the "talking about sex" variables shall be used—immediacy of talking and the reaction of the person talked to. . . .

. . . Over half the experienced males in the sample first had coitus before college. This contrasts sharply with the female pattern which is fully rectilineal over the four . . . age periods with . . . only about 27 per cent of the coeds reporting pre-college coital onset. . . . [Keeping in mind] that males have had a considerably longer time (on the average) in which to report the event to someone . . . it is nonetheless interesting that there is a steady increase in the proportions of males who never talk as . . . age increases. . . .

. . . [Also,] if we look at [those who talked about their first coital experience "immediately,"] there is a monotonic decrease of [such talk with advancing age]. . . . The motive underlying entry into premarital coitus apparently shifts dramatically for males as a function of age, and the composition of . . . those to whom he reports the event . . . also shifts as he (and they) grow older. . . . While advancing age does not materially affect the probability of a woman immediately reporting the event, it does have a considerable impact on the male probability.[9]

These patterns emerge more clearly when the reactions of those told are related to the . . . age of coital entry. . . . Only about three per cent of the young male coital initiators are disapproved of when they share their knowledge with others, and this drops to zero for sophomores through seniors. Clearly disapproval of coital entry is a rare event for these males just as it must be more generally a rare event in male culture. Indeed, if premarital sex is prescribed for males, then not only would disapproval be absent (as it is), but we should expect to find disapproving reactions if, for example, our actor reported that he had failed to have coitus, that he had suffered a loss of nerve or the pangs of conscience.[10]

On the other hand, the female . . . [data] again substantiate our thesis—that premarital coitus can be legitimated most effectively for women if (1) there is an understood emotional relationship . . . and (2) the reality principle of approaching graduation makes it probable that such a relationship will result in mating. . . . Thus, . . . the proportion of clear disapproving reactions is highest in the freshman year, but drops somewhat in the upperclass period.[11] Even more significant, though, is the considerable drop in proportions expressing a "mixed" or ambivalent reaction to the news: 30.5 per cent for pre-college coital initiation; 8.4 per cent for the last two years of college. This suggests, by inference, that with increasing . . . age, approaching social maturity (legal mating, remunerative work role, etc.), the consequent socially-shared bonding behavior ("love," "going steady," engagement, and the like), the sexual self of the coed becomes more coherent and less ambivalent, as the pattern of feedback tends to converge on this set of social meanings. In her junior and senior years of college, for perhaps the first time in her life, she can engage in sexual intercourse and (to a limited and specific degree) talk of it and not . . . be stigmatized. Her self-labeling, to the extent it is almost certainly a product of others' labeling of her and her actions, is positive,[12] and she is fully *au courant* with her age-graded station in a pattern of American love-sex-marriage values. But it did not come about until age 20 or 21.[13]

Data are available on the respondents' assessments of the nature of the relationship with the first coital partner. . . .

Most of the 101 males who report "pick-up/prostitute" as the context of their first coital relationship actually fall into the "pick-up" (nonprofessional) category. Thus, it is particularly interesting that 61.4 per cent of this group talked immediately upon completion of their first coital act. The proportions in the "immediate" column decline monotonically to the most involved relational status—"to marry." As before, this finding strongly underscores our position on male sexuality: to the extent coitus first occurs in non-involved situations, one of the primary rewards accrues from sharing it with one's fellows. In this way a socio-sexual status is created which is, as noted, fully in line with prescriptive elements in the premarital male role. . . .

"For males, the more involved the relationship of first coitus, the lower the proportions of approving reactions. . . ."

Some aspects of the female . . . [data] parallel those of the men, especially the general decrease in "immediate" talkers with increasing emotional commitment. To be sure, the . . . [data] suggest that first coital involvement for males is related most strongly to less intense relationships [e.g., casual date or pick-up]; for females to more intense ones [e.g., in love with, planning to marry]. This finding parallels the variant patterns in the relationship between . . . age and coital onset between men and women. If our reasoning to this point has been correct, the tendency by women to socialize their new status immediately as an inverse function of the closeness of the relationship would reflect guilt-management efforts rather than (as for men) the socializing of prescriptive success in the male role. For this reason, if the pick-up and casual dates categories are ignored, males and females are remarkably alike in the proportions who talk immediately—*i.e.*, in the "emotion," "love," and "to marry" categories of relationships.

But convergence between men and women in relation to the reactions of others does not hold up so neatly. . . . For males, the more involved the relationship of first coitus, the lower the proportions of approving reactions for the first person told. From the point of view of male sexual socialization and the male bond discussed earlier, this makes sense, but only in the sense that non-involved relationships would be applauded. Why males who enter coitus in "love" or "to marry" relationships should get relatively less positive feedback is an open question. One possible explanation may take the form of "hurting someone." Alternatively, and more likely, overwhelming positive feedback for sexual performance (say in the 90 per cent and above range) simply cannot result from anything but the male culture and its peculiar standards for male sexual performance. Any other reason for coital entry, no matter how much it may fit our general cultural standards for relationships and family formation, simply cannot rate such a high approval response. (In line with these speculations, note that the "mixed" or ambivalent column . . . increases monotonically for males with the strength of the first coital relationship.) . . . [As a result,] males and females alike receive about the same proportions of positive feedback for love-sex relationships.

SUMMARY

We have posited the existence of a double sexual standard for men and women in American society and have explicated that concept to center on the public and private management of the sexual status. For these reasons, men were expected to respond to a prescriptive sexual norm, and this assumption was reflected in the male's sharing of knowledge of first coital experiences with other males. Substantial evidence emerged which suggested that this sexual script changes with advancing age, thus increasing the tendency to create emotional bonds around coital entry.

Women, on the other hand, have historically responded to a proscriptive sexual script and, in order to legitimate the act of first coitus, have relied on the rhetoric of romantic love and the probability that the relationship had some durability. For these reasons, males and females can be viewed as converging, in later adolescence or postadolescence, into a very similar normative system with regard to premarital sexuality: that which centers on relatively stable relationships and romantic love. Such a convergence has been suggested by others (Winch, 1971; Simon and Gagnon, 1969) and, in a sense, reflects Freud's notion that the triumph of civilization produced, especially in men, the tendency to deflect (sublimate) polymorphous perverse and later aggressive (and male bonded) sexual impulses into stable, institutionalized relationships (Freud, 1962).

As we noted earlier, most of the treatments of the sexual revolution pay undue attention to genital behavior—*i.e.*, number of episodes, age of entry, orgasmic experiences [14]—reflecting, in all probability, our cultural dialogue (and dialectic) with the now-past Puritan era. But what we must pay attention to is the meaning of the act to the participant and most especially how that meaning shifts subtly as the person matures. If we had found that women first experienced coitus with substantially the same set of meanings as men have traditionally done, we could speak of a revolution, albeit one with a questionable future. No such finding emerged from this analysis. Correspondingly, if the evidence had suggested that men at younger and younger ages were employing at least the rhetoric of love and relationship and seeking less feedback from their same sex peers, we could also speak of a revolution of sorts. Ironically, it is probable that both these trends are occurring, each at its own pace. The net result, obviously, would be gender convergence, not of the number of genital acts, but of the meaning of the acts to the participants. This would constitute a kind of revolution on top of two revolutions if it came about; premarital sex would then not be "repressively de-sublimated" to use Marcuse's phrase (1964) but rather would be "non-repressively sublimated." Puritanism and Victorianism would have died along with the male bond and its manifold implications for the adolescent boy.

Obviously, if such a second-level "revolution" came to pass, it would resemble the synthesis stage in the historical dialectic (at least since Victorianism) between the male bond and the Romantic, home-oriented female. One would hope that, if indeed these trends are occurring, the genders do not pass each other in the night, women on their part seeking the genital expression so long denied them by a sexually repressive culture, men looking for situations of affection and tenderness unalloyed by the performance principle forced upon them by the restrictions of hyper-masculinity.

NOTES

1. This paper is based upon data gathered under the auspices of PHS Grant HD 02257.

2. The idea of a double standard with reference to premarital sexuality has been with us for a long time. There is strong evidence that such a double standard existed (at the normative level) in certain ancient codes of law—The Code of Hammurabi, The Law of Eshunna, The Middle Assyrian Laws (Pritchard, 1950). The Old Testament itself reflects, at times, the view of women as property, not to be sullied by coitus before marriage (as for example, Exodus 22:16–17). Cross-cultural evidence suggests that the pattern is relatively pervasive around the world (Blumberg, Carns, and Winch, 1970), although Murdock (1949:264–265) disagrees. Research conducted in industrially developed, particularly Western societies, strongly underscores the existence of a double behavioral standard, especially at the level of norms.

3. Nor are female-male differences (of the sort we are characterizing) based upon physiologic deficiencies in the female. Kinsey attempted to lay that notion to rest (1953:688). Masters and Johnson (1966) administered the *coup de grace*.

4. For example, fantasy "almost always" accompanied masturbation among 72 per cent of experienced males but only 50 per cent of experienced females in the Kinsey samples (1953:174).

5. The reference, of course, is to Freud's essay, "The Transformations of Puberty" (1962), in which he states: "Certain of the sexual fantasies of puberty stand out distinguished as quite universal in occurrence and to a very great degree independent of the experience of the individual. Thus the fantasies of spying upon parental coitus; of early seduction through beloved persons; of the threat of castration; fantasies of the mother's womb . . ." (p. 83).

6. Without unduly leaning on Freud, it is instructive to note one of his views of some women: among some people, mostly girls, he says, ". . . the apparently nonsexual love for the parents and the sexual love are nourished from the same source, that is, that the first merely corresponds to an infantile fixation of the libido" (1962:84). It is much more plausible to suggest that women in Freud's day were responding to the severe cultural separation of sex and romantic love which saw its fullest flowering in the Victorian era. "Mature libidinal cathexis" (Eros) is quite difficult to achieve under such circumstances; it is perhaps as difficult today for both men and women (Marcuse, 1955; 1956:79; 1964: esp. 73).

7. This has become a controversial point, the debate revolving around the existence or nonexistence of a "real" revolution in sexuality, and especially with relation to premarital coitus among women. Some trend studies using fairly comparable but narrowly restrictive samples show a considerably higher incidence of premarital coitus among college attending women (Bell and Chaskes, 1970; Christensen and Gregg, 1970). Ehr-

mann (1959) flatly asserted the existence of such a revolution, at least in terms of real increase of coital incidence for women. Carns (forthcoming, 1973) agrees with certain of the reported patterns but offers interpretations at odds with a "sexual revolution," a state of affairs which should ideally include a revolution in female sexual consciousness. No data on the latter have been forthcoming except those reported in this paper, or those which may be derived by implication from the very interesting work of Reiss (1967) and the recent body of literature stemming from the women's movement.

8. The relationship between "ego sex" and the "sexual revolution" deserves mention. The extent to which women, in liberating themselves sexually, follow the stereotypical male model of sexual expression—genital, ego-gratifying, and expressive of maleness and the male bond—then women will not have become liberated at all (on this point, Marcuse, 1964, is quite instructive). And when the middle-class male matures, he has available a well-developed sexual script comparable to that of his adolescence—the "Playboy Philosophy" of Hugh Hefner (1962). Again, in any truly erotic (Eros) sense, the Playboy Philosophy is anti-sexual (Cox, 1968:40) and women are little more than another accouterment in an endless array of status-confirming objects for the successful young executive.

9. And, of course, the "immediate" response would not be spuriously affected by age as the "never" column could.

10. We should bear in mind that different sexual subcultures exist for men and women. Religiosity is especially significant in predicting not only premarital sexual behavior and norms but also appropriate sexual selves and verbal scripts (Carns, 1970a; 1970b).

11. These data (in the "disapproving" column) are more suggestive than conclusive for they do not stand the test of chance replication. Note also that pre-college coital entry is less disapproved than freshman entry. Whether or not this reflects the reality principle of future mating (least for freshman, higher for high school seniors) is unknown.

12. With the caution noted before, that religious subcultures specify this generalization to a certain degree as do other sexually restrictive statuses, notably rural origin or the type of college milieu.

13. To be sure, those coeds who started college and then formed strong emotional and sexual bonds early on (say, the freshmen or sophomore years) probably would not stay in this sample; that is, they would have dropped out to get married. Thus, one could presume that the same process of sexual legitimation would occur for this earlier "bloomer" and, prior to dropping out and legally mating, she would have experienced a certain amount of positive feedback for her sexual involvement. . . .

14. Not unlike the (unfair) accusation frequently made of Kinsey, that he was an "orgasm counter," or of Masters and Johnson (1966) and other scientists who deal with sexuality in a non-normative way.

BIBLIOGRAPHY

Bell, Robert R.
1966   Premarital Sex in a Changing Society. Englewood Cliffs, N.J.:Prentice-Hall.

Bell, Robert R. and Jay B. Chaskes
1970 "Premarital sexual experience among coeds, 1958 and 1968." Journal of Marriage and the Family 32:81–84.
Blumberg, Rae, Donald E. Carns, and Robert F. Winch
1970 "High gods, virgin brides and societal complexity." Paper read before the annual meetings of the American Sociological Association.
Cannon, Kenneth L. and Richard Long
1971 "Premarital sexual behavior in the sixties." Journal of Marriage and the Family 33:36–49.
Carns, Donald E.
1970a "Religiosity, premarital sexuality and the American college student." Unpublished thesis, Indiana University, Bloomington.
1970b "Religiosity and the double sexual standard." Paper read before the annual meetings of the Midwest Sociological Society.
1973 "Identity, deviance and change in conventional settings: the case of 'sexual revolution.' " In James McIntosh (ed.), The Deviant Paradigm. Boston:Allyn-Bacon.
Christensen, Harold T. and Christina F. Gregg
1970 "Changing sex norms in America and Scandinavia." Journal of Marriage and the Family 32:616–627.
Cox, Harvey
1968 In J. D. Brown (ed.), Sex in the 60's. New York:Time-Life.
Ehrmann, Winston
1959 Premarital Dating Behavior. New York:Holt, Rinehart and Winston.
Freud, Sigmund
1962 Three Contributions to the Theory of Sex. New York:E. P. Dutton. (Originally published in 1905 in Germany by Deuticke.)
Hefner, Hugh M.
1962 "The Playboy Philosophy." (3 pamphlets) Chicago:HMH Publishing.
Kinsey, Alfred et al.
1948 Sexual Behavior in the Human Male. Phildelphia:Saunders.
1953 Sexual Behavior in the Human Female. Philadelphia:Saunders.
Marcuse, Herbert
1955 Eros and Civilization. Boston:Beacon.
1956 "A reply to Erich Fromm." Dissent (Winter):79.
1964 One Dimensional Man. Boston:Beacon.
Masters, William H. and Virginia E. Johnson
1966 Human Sexual Response. Boston: Little, Brown
Murdock, George P.
1949 Social Structure. New York:Macmillan.
Pritchard, J. B. (ed.)
1950 Eastern Texts Relating to the Old Testament. Princeton, N.J.:Princeton University Press.
Reiss, Ira
1967 The Social Context of Premarital Sexual Permissiveness. New York:Holt, Rinehart and Winston.
Robinson, Ira E., Karl King, Charles Dudley, and Francis J. Clune
1968 "Change in sexual behavior and attitudes of college students." The Family Coordinator 17:119–123.

Simon, William and John H. Gagnon
1969 "On psychosexual development." Pp. 733–752 in David A. Goslin (ed.), Handbook of Socialization Theory and Research. Chicago: Rand McNally.
Simon, William, John H. Gagnon, and Donald E. Carns
1968 "Sexual behavior of college students." Paper read before the American Academy of Psychoanalysis.
Winch, Robert F.
1971 The Modern Family. 3rd Ed. New York:Holt, Rinehart and Winston.

BELL
Sexual Development and Diversity

Alan Bell joined the Institute near the end of the transition stage and, as a developmental and counseling psychologist, brought an added dimension to the Institute. His first book, *The Personality of a Child Molester: An Analysis of Dreams*, published in 1971, is excerpted here. (Bell coauthored this book with Calvin Hall, a well-known authority on dream analysis.) Like the work of the '60's, *The Personality of a Child Molester* has narrower scope but greater depth than the early Institute works. Bell's theoretical emphasis (which is psychoanalytic) is also apparent.

The second selection from Bell's writing reflects another change in the Institute's work—namely, an increasing interest in acquainting professionals in a variety of fields with the practical implications of our findings.[1] This selection, published as a chapter in a textbook on human sexuality, provides health personnel with guidelines for counseling their homosexual patients.

This selection draws on preliminary data from a large-scale study of homosexuality, on which Bell and I are collaborating. This research involves in-depth interviews with 1500 people—males and females, blacks and whites, homosexuals and heterosexuals. We are planning to publish this research soon, in two volumes tentatively titled *The Development and Management of Homosexuality*.

From our review of the literature for this project, Bell and I published *Homosexuality: An Annotated Bibliography*.[2] The bibliography describes all the scholarly books and articles on homosexuality published in English between 1940 and 1968, including physiological, psychological, and sociological works.

Bell's chief interest at present is developing a typology of homosexuals and delineating the developmental processes that produce each type.

---

[1] This interest is also highlighted in the last chapter of another Institute work, Martin S. Weinberg and Colin J. Williams, *Male Homosexuals: Their Problems and Adaptations* (New York: Oxford University press, 1974).

[2] Martin S. Weinberg and Alan P. Bell, *Homosexuality: An Annotated Bibliography* (New York: Harper & Row, 1972).

THE PERSONALITY
OF A CHILD MOLESTER

Alan P. Bell and Calvin S. Hall

The present study was undertaken with two aims in mind. The first aim was to determine the relationship between what a person dreams while he is asleep and recalls in the morning and his behavior and personality in waking life. The second aim was to identify and to describe the specific variables that constitute the character of [Norman,] a pedophile (child molester) and to attempt to discover the origin of his sexual preoccupations and outlets.

NORMAN'S BACKGROUND

Norman was born in 1928 in a large Midwestern city where he grew up and attended school until the age of 15. After working at a series of jobs in order to augment the family's relatively meager income, Norman entered the United States Army in 1946 at the age of 18 and was given an honorable medical discharge 15 months later. Norman was first institutionalized in the spring of 1949 at the age of 20 and, until the age of 37, spent approximately seven years in five different mental institutions. Despite his difficulties Norman received a high school diploma through a correspondence course at the age of 23 and, when he was not in an institution, continued to live at home with his mother and sister and to work in a series of jobs in the printing field. When first seen by the senior author, Norman was 37 years old and was about to be discharged from a mental institution. He has not been institutionalized since that summer of 1966 and is presently attending college full-time. . . .

Norman was born . . . at home about a year after his parents' marriage. His mother had a cold and fever at the time and, in a generally weakened condition, gave birth three weeks prematurely. Although his father had not wanted a child, on this occasion he cooperated to the extent that he procured the services of a midwife who prophesied that the boy would be strong, a prophecy based on the strength of his urinations. She also observed "as how I looked like the infant Jesus." They were living in a cold water flat not far from where his father worked in a shoe factory. He earned very little, and even the rent of ten dollars a month was not always available. Whenever they were evicted for failing to pay the rent—which was every six months—Norman's father would retaliate by damaging some portion of the landlord's property. . . . When Norman was eight years old his parents were separated briefly, but it was not long before his father begged to be taken back. His wife assented, for reasons perhaps unknown even to her.

Before the 1929 depression, Norman's father would become involved in fights with his fellow workers and lose whatever job he had at the time. He was no more successful working for the W.P.A. during the depression. Ultimately, he found that door-to-door selling was more suitable to his temperament. But by this time his relationship with his wife had deteriorated completely. There had been the usual arguments, the threats of separation, and finally his expulsion from the household when his wife learned that he had contracted venereal disease. Norman was twelve years old at the time and, according to his mother, he was relieved by the enforced absence of his father. As Norman now recalls, "He was more like a boarder anyway." Nine years later, when Norman was informed of his father's death, he reacted with little or no apparent emotion.

After Norman's father had been removed from the home, his mother became increasingly preoccupied with her son. Her controlling behaviors were particularly evident in Norman's relationship with his sister who had been born three years after him. He recalls, "She was always careful that my sister and I not see each other without our clothes on." . . . Whatever concerns she had became more exaggerated when Norman displayed a persistent interest in looking at his sister's genitals. . . .

The reaction of Norman's mother to his interest was severe. She became increasingly restrictive with regard to their relationship, and did all that she could to reinforce the incest taboo with reference to her own relationship with her son as well as to her children's relationship. . . . Instead of extinguishing Norman's voyeurism, his mother's reaction seems to have served only to heighten his preoccupation. It did not help matters when, according to Norman, a stranger entered the house where they were living and attempted to molest his sister who was eight years old at the time:

"Whenever they were evicted for failing to pay the rent—which was every six months—Norman's father would retaliate by damaging some portion of the landlord's property."

"I heard her screaming. Some man came down the stairs. He looked at me, and then he left."

Norman claims that this incident piqued his curiosity about girls— "how they were constructed"—despite his mother's and sister's obvious irritation:

"As far as they were concerned, sex was nasty. My sister would never let me see her. In fact it wasn't until the Army that I had any idea that there was such a thing as a clitoris."

This enforced ignorance is perhaps reflected in Norman's incestuous wishes that went beyond the voyeuristic interests he had initially with respect to his sister. . . .

During his elementary school years Norman did fairly well academically. Outside of school he spent most of his leisure hours by himself at home where he would practice the violin and work with chalk at his blackboard. He had few friends, and in fact over the years became more and more an object of ridicule among his peers. The high school years, in an all-male parochial school, were passed a little more easily. He spent a good deal of time bicycling with his only friend or playing the tuba in the school band or at home reading dog stories. . . .

Norman describes those years as marked with indecision over what to do vocationally, loneliness, and various internal conflicts having to do chiefly with "an attraction to sex and at the same time a fear of it."

At the age of 15, at his mother's insistence, Norman quit school and went to work. He was employed first as an elevator operator in a hospital for tubercular diseases and then for approximately one year in a printing firm where he learned how to feed the presses. Then he worked several months in a linotype shop where a buzz saw cut through one of his fingers. He left, to work on and off in four different printing establishments before he was drafted and entered the Army in 1946. He was discharged a little more than a year later on medical grounds—there were hypochondriacal complaints about his stomach—and returned home. Norman continued to work, without enthusiasm, in numerous printing firms, until his first conviction and incarceration.

Norman was twenty-one years old the first time he was committed to a state hospital. He was there six months, but the first three he does not remember:

"I actually thought I was in hell. Once when my mother came to visit me I asked, 'What are you doing *down* here?' I thought the colored attendants were devils, and I would wrestle with them. Things didn't look real. The walls didn't look natural; it was as though they had no beginning and no end. There was one doctor I remember who put the hose in my mouth during shock treatment. He had a hard look like my father. His gaze was like my father's. There were twenty-one treatments in all, and I think as a result I can't concentrate as well as I used to." . . .

Two years later he was sent to another state hospital:

"My state of mind was different then. I had been picked up for molesting a child and sent there for observation. I remember a lot of homosexuals being there, the masculine kind. They were very aggressive and kept referring to me as 'a good lay.'. . . I ran away with another patient, but the police picked us up. I felt frustrated being there, at the idea of not being free. Besides, it wasn't doing me any good. I think I saw a psychologist exactly once. The day I passed staff, the doctor told me I'd better not come back or it would be hell. But a voice told me I'd already been in hell and it was the doctor's fault."

Nine years later, when Norman was 31 years old, he was charged with impairing the morals of a minor and admitted to a state mental institution from which he was transferred to a veterans' hospital and, several months later, to a state hospital for the criminally insane:

"There I felt undignified. I would have felt more dignified if they'd put me in prison. A mental patient is like a senile person; it's as though he's not a part of society. The officers always treated the persons coming there from prison much better than those who came from hospitals. They kept referring to us as 'nuts.' I would prefer to have been called bad rather than sick. "

"Norman describes those years as marked with indecision over what to do vocationally, loneliness, and various internal conflicts having to do chiefly with 'an attraction to sex and at the same time a fear of it.' "

Norman's lawyer had requested that he be sent there for observation. He could have been sent to prison for life for his felonious sex offense, but that offense was reduced to simple assault. . . .

DREAM AND WAKING BEHAVIOR ANALYSES

Dreams

The contents of Norman's dreams, either in themselves or when compared with the dreams of . . . [a] norm group, provide a great deal of information pertaining to his personality and waking behaviors. They also suggest some of the reasons that Norman has become the person he is. *What follows is based entirely on the dream analysis.* It must be remembered that other than the age and gender of the dreamer, no other information was provided [to Calvin Hall, the coauthor who does the dream analysis].

The most outstanding feature of Norman's personality is his extraordinary emotional immaturity. On every level of his existence, he remains a child. His infantile status is reflected in a polymorphously perverse disposition which fails to distinguish between one sexual object and another or one sexual act and another. . . .

A child was standing on a table. I ran my hand on his buttocks. A woman came and wanted to be intimate with me and I did so.

I was walking with a slim gray haired woman. She smiled mischievously at me and grabbed me in the crotch.

A young boy and I became friendly and I played the passive role in an act of fellatio. . . .

I was actively and passively intimate with another man.

A woman had breasts but she had a male organ. I let her perform pederasty with me. We were flying in an airplane. . . .

. . . Although Norman's sexual interests include a wide range of objects—male and female, child and adult—most of his sexual feelings are not acted out. In fact he is less active sexually than most males his age. Norman is probably a chronic masturbator, but even in this regard he tries to control himself to an unusual degree. Breasts, hips, legs, and hair excite him sexually; but it is the buttocks of both males and females which have the greatest erotic potential for Norman. He tends to be ambivalent towards female genitals. Another reflection of Norman's childlike personality is his unusual dependence upon his mother and sister for his emotional security. This dependency is of long-standing. . . .

I was in a house with my mother and sister. My mother left on a trip. The woman who lived downstairs tried to persuade me to let her use our rooms, but I would not yield. . . .

I was running for a subway with my sister. She caught it but I did not. I decided to run to the next station. After going several blocks, I discovered that I had turned left when I should have turned right. I was on a deserted street, and I felt very lonely. . . .

. . . During his childhood, possibly because his mother encouraged it or because his family did not stay in one place for any length of time, Norman had few friendships. Then, as now, Norman invested little of himself in others with whom he remained only superficially friendly. Another reason that Norman was and remains a "loner" is that his associations with other children were very painful. In fact it is reasonable to suppose that Norman's sexual activities with children represent, in part, the effort to make up for his original experience of loneliness in childhood. At that time Norman was forced to retreat to the nuclear family where he enjoyed a particularly close relationship with his sister (who was his father's favorite) whom he tended to protect in much the same way as his mother did with him. One aspect of their "union against the world" possibly included an explicitly sexual relationship which may have served as a model for his subsequent child "molestations." The fact that Norman was raised in an exclusively female environment and that his mother was probably hostile toward males in general probably accounts for the considerable confusion which Norman displays with regard to his own gender identity. He tends to reject any firm gender allegiance—he is no more male than female—and the fact that he is noncommittal in this regard can be considered further evidence of Norman's infantile fixation. His ambiguous gender identification, expressed in certain fantasies about being a woman and in occasional instances of cross-sex dressing, may also be the result of a paternal relationship which made it impossible for Norman to identify with a male role model. . . .

> I was with a boy. Later, I was in a room. I dressed in a woman's dress, and I went into the next room to view myself in the mirror. The skirt had pleats in it. When I came to the mirror, I danced lightly and let the skirt twirl around my legs. I felt a thrill. . . .

> I was in a place with other men. A man near me began telling me that I had feminine charms. I became angry and I told him that I have a man's body and he should leave me alone. . . .

. . . His father, now dead, and possibly the result of suicide, was probably absent during much of Norman's childhood, or else there was something about his relationship with Norman that was so traumatic that Norman has entirely repressed it. It is possible that Norman's father used him sexually, and that this is the reason he was banished from the family and from the family's memory. Perhaps this is why Norman perceives the father as powerful, dangerous, and impulsive. On the other hand, there is evidence that Norman has identified with an ineffectual, "castrated" father. . . .

> I was the son of a knight. Suddenly, about ten ornamental balls topped with birds fell from the balcony I was on. A woman came and said that because of that accident my father would lose his knighthood. I was angry. I said, "Woman, I will see that you don't take away his knighthood. I have something to say about that."

. . . In either case, it would appear that Norman's distorted relationship with his father was the crucial determinant of Norman's renunciation of adulthood. The latter is most evident in Norman's inability to postpone certain gratifications, most notably those associated with his eliminative functions. In his childhood, and perhaps even at the present time, Norman was a chronic bedwetter. This lack of control over urination, and defecation as well, indicative of a strong expulsive mode in his psychological make-up, probably means that Norman is not able to save money, to keep a job, or to lead an orderly life. . . .

I was on a muddy slope. Water was running down, and the ground was eroding.

A fire hydrant near the house was leaking and a faucet in a neighbor's garage was leaking. The plumbing in our house was shut off, so I urinated by the plug. A neighbor saw me and I was embarrassed. When I went back upstairs, my mother asked me if the rag was still in the plug in the sink, and I said, "No.". . .

. . . This lack of control is accompanied by an externalized superego. When Norman's defenses (primarily intellectualization) fail—which they usually do, accounting for his frequent incarcerations—he experiences little guilt or shame. He is either embarrassed by his misdeeds or else annoyed by the inconvenience of hospitalization. He is not apt to see much wrong with having his penis sucked or held by little children or with seating children on his lap and fondling various parts of their bodies. Although he tries to control his pedophilic interests and behaviors, in this as in other matters, his attempts at self-control are unsuccessful. He has sought children out, not in aggressive or sadistic ways, but with an affection which may be reminiscent of the relationship he had with a highly nurturant but seductive mother. . . .

The phallic imagery in Norman's dreams demonstrates a fundamental and recurring conflict: the need to overcome an insufferable sense of impotence and inferiority by an assertiveness which is equally threatening. Fears of castration by others or even by himself are followed by equal fears about the consequences of a potency which has not been defused:

A man who owned a fish market was showing a movie at his store about how he traveled the country to get his fish. I showed him a transparent fish. He said he would return shortly to examine it. Before he returned, the fish shriveled up.

I came to a motor powered paper cutter. Someone said it was for killing fish. The fish would trip a switch, releasing the blade which then came down upon the fish. It needed some glycerin. I went to get some.

I was carrying a gun in my pocket. I tried to adjust it so it would not bulge from my pocket.

I was told that I would be released on parole. But the meat from a small bone on the table had to be scraped off first.

Whether or not sexuality and aggression are the most problematic features of civilized man's existence, they are certainly the chief issues in the life of our dreamer. In Norman they are hardly separate issues; the one is no more or less eschewed than the other. If one gives in to one *or* the other, one's lifesaving control is forfeited. "Death" comes as quickly and easily in orgasm as in anger.

"On every level of his existence, he remains a child."

Although . . .[there is a] low incidence of weapons and . . . [a] high proportion of non-aggressive encounters with others in Norman's dreams . . . explicit fears relating to aggression are also expressed in the dream material:

> I was in a state of anxiety throughout the dream. I saw a man lying on the floor, shot.

> I had a jack knife. It fell out of my hand onto the porch below. I heard someone gasp down there, and I was afraid the knife had hurt someone.

> I was a patient in a hospital. I was going to be released. I accidentally hit a young patient in the face. I was excused. Later, I accidentally poked another patient in the face. He thought that I had done it purposely. I was afraid that I would not be released because of the incident. I asked to see the doctor so I could explain that it was an accident.

Norman seems to equate sexuality with aggression and both with a loss of control which endangers himself as well as others. There are aggressive as well as erotic elements to Norman's anal rebellion. By withholding his feces and defecating in inappropriate settings, Norman simultaneously thwarted his mother's will, secretly delighted in his anal eroticism, and deposited a contempt for his unrewarding immediate environs. And presumably others' punishing responses to his untimely acts reinforced the sado-masochistic features of Norman's interchange with the world. In most of his interpersonal transactions—whether they occur in his dreams or his waking life—Norman is the passive victim, and any occasion which suggests the assumption of a different role is avoided by an immobilization produced by equal measures of repulsion and attraction. The female genitals are a stimulus which elicits aggressive feelings in him ("The first time I saw female genitalia I felt like a tiger that had caught its prey.") and for that reason are avoided by a voyeurism which reflects his immobilized state or by a seduction for which he claims no responsibility or by the sexual activities of a pedophile which he can believe are more platonic than erotic. . . .

Of considerable interest is the correspondence of Norman's apparent lack of aggressiveness, his masochism, and his experience of castration, to what others might suppose is the female's experience of self and others. If the . . . data had not indicated otherwise, it might have been concluded that the chief issues in Norman's life pertained to his confusion over his gender identity. That this is not the case suggests that more attention must be given to the possibility that human behavior can be understood as more a function of fears concerning new experiences of the self and of others than concerns about gender or conflicts between the self and the ideal self. While Freud and other theorists offer constructs which pertain to the human disinclination to "grow up," none really focuses upon the extent to which this is possible, upon the trauma of new inputs, upon the human insistence that an original experience of the world be maintained. Perhaps one of the chief contributions of the present study is that it suggests a human being's behavior can be explained in large part as the result of fixation at an exceedingly primitive level, in which other issues such as gender identity or the claims of conscience are quite beside the point.

Another important contribution is an understanding of the way in which dreams reveal what is being defended against in waking behavior. Waking life may consist largely of defensive behavior—as Roheim spoke of culture as a massive defensive operation. Dreams tell us what the tasks are that waking behavior tries to solve, usually through displacements, symbolizations, reaction formations, projections, sublimations, negations, inhibitions, and repressions. It is only when defenses break down that the raw wish is revealed. . . .

Waking Behavior

The data provided by personal conversations and correspondence with Norman, by psychological tests administered over a seven-year period, and by records from the six different hospitals to which Norman had been committed, present the following picture.

Norman has failed to grow up in any real sense. He has been extremely dependent upon his mother throughout the course of his life, and he has come to rely upon her concern for him in very fundamental ways. In that as in other relationships he is more childlike than adult, and Norman's style of life indicates that he has sought to preserve an almost womblike existence. In keeping with his infantile status, there is some confusion with regard to his gender identification. He seems to have renounced masculine traits in himself, but at the same time he has not made a true feminine identification either. This gender ambivalence is probably the result of many factors. It was his mother who assumed the male functions in the household. He could not identify with his father whose extraordinary sexual relationship with his son further enhanced Norman's gender confusion. . . .

When Norman was four years old, his father forced him to suck his penis:

"I felt bewildered. The size of his erection frightened me. I had never been approached like that before by my father. In fact, I can't recall ever having had sexual thoughts prior to that time. All I can remember is my father's hypnotic, angry stare as I tried to push his penis away from my face. It depicted vengeance, retribution, destruction. The memory of that stare is vivid and was reinforced by subsequent ones. I feared for my life. I felt drawn by my father's almost hypnotic force." . . .

According to one of the hospital reports, this incestuous activity— Norman's sucking of his father's penis—continued until his father left the family. The report also suggests that although Norman was traumatized by the initial experience, he came to enjoy this unusual attention from his father. Norman's latest report, made at the time of this present investigation, indicates his strong ambivalence:

"During the early years, I tried desperately to decide what to do about my father's actions with me. I decided to do nothing, and I never did decide whether I was doing the right thing by doing nothing or whether I was sinning. I often had spells in which the feeling that I was being exploited was mingled with a feeling that I wanted to be exploited, and in the midst of these feelings came the feeling of erotic ecstasy, mingled with a feeling that I was taking something that I did not deserve to have. I then would pound my pillow in anguish at being involved in this human situation, and rage against the human condition that was manifested by my inability to cope with it and grasp the meaning of my father's behavior." . . .

. . . A principal result of these incestuous encounters was that Norman suffered an identity crisis from which he has never recovered.

Other reasons for Norman's lack of a strong masculine identification include his having been raised in a female-dominated environment and his isolation from same-sex peers.

Another chief impression of Norman which is gained from these particular data is that of his attempts to control his bodily impulses. He is less active sexually than other males his age, and all that is unusual about his sexual interests and sexual expression is their infantile quality: in the past, at least, most of his sexual arousal has occurred in the company of children and in connection with primarily voyeuristic behaviors. These activities can best be understood as the expression of an inadequate, infantile personality. At the time that they took place Norman was not experiencing a psychotic episode, and, on the other hand, his molestations were accompanied by feelings not usually found in the sociopath. They were probably more a continuation of his childhood preoccupations and conducted from a child's point of view. On one occasion in which Norman's behaviors amounted to more than this, he was so appalled that he sought an extraordinary self-control which would guarantee that such a thing would not happen again. It is this determination, reflected in Norman's intellectualization and obsessive-compulsive defenses, which is most clearly evident in the data derived from his waking behaviors.

NORMAN'S PRESENT AND FUTURE

Norman was released from the veterans' hospital in late spring, 1966. He has not been hospitalized since. After he returned home, Norman made arrangements to pursue his education at a local community college where he has obtained an Associate in Arts degree. He is continuing his education at a local university where he hopes to receive a bachelor's degree which will enable him to go on to graduate study. Thus he remains a "perpetual student," spending much of his leisure time in the school library or in his own bedroom, studying at home doing the two things—reading and writing—which he really enjoys. It is interesting to note, and perhaps indicative of an improved psychological adjustment, that Norman is beginning to enjoy biographies. Most of his life he had not appreciated stories about people because people had seemed "unnatural" and "artificial."

At home Norman has little contact with either his mother, who spends most of her time tending the lawn or looking over the bills, or with his sister, who works on the assembly line of a local industry and spends her leisure time watching television. Although they take their meals together, do the shopping together, and go to church as a family, one gets the impression that in fact each has gone his separate way, bound together by a lethargy or a mutual dependency which makes any alternative arrangement unthinkable. They will probably continue to live together in this way until Norman's mother dies. After that, it is difficult to say what will happen or who will assume her role and function in her children's lives. Neither Norman nor his sister has been prepared for life without their mother, and it is difficult to predict what adjustments will be made when the time comes that she is no longer with them.

Of the two children, it is Norman who has made more of an attempt to enter into relationships with people outside the home. At school Norman has begun to make satisfying social contacts, particularly with older, married females. He has lunch with his fellow students in the school cafeteria and has come to enjoy discussing academic matters with them. Norman has received average grades in his courses, and there is every reason to believe that he will complete his course work satisfactorily.

With regard to his current psychological adjustment, Norman reports that he is rarely depressed or very unhappy, bored, or restless. However, he often feels very lonely or remote from other people. He has no psychosomatic complaints and rates his health at the present time as good. He does not appear to worry a great deal, but when he does it is usually about his future plans as well as his loneliness. There are other concerns as well. He writes, "I have experienced emotional distresses, periods of feelings of aimlessness and uselessness, stemming mainly from the difficulty I am having in distinguishing which of my experiences of the unusual type are in the long run going to be harmful to me and which are going to be beneficial. I feel great forces within my organism, and I do not want any of them to serve any immature desires that lead to self-destruction rather than the self-actualization that I seek." Another letter indicates that residues of his past torments remain: "I am attending _____ University now. I still have the same sexual 'hang-ups' that I had at _____ College. The mini skirts and the small panties under them still remind me that I am caught in the web of 'civilization.' I still have a longing to break from this web, the same longing that I had in those high school days when I used to read those dog stories like Jack London's *Call of the Wild*. I want to go where I can communicate telepathically with the animals, and know the freedom to be wild." Norman's recent correspondence reflects a continuing consternation over sexual interests which he can neither accept nor understand. Describing the central character in a novel which he had finished reading, he writes: "The hero is part brute as he peeps into a woman's room and watches her undress, and at times the hero is human as he sees two lovers and senses their pathos, their tenderness and their uncertainty; and he loathes the animal in himself. When he sees the swaying dresses of the women, it is not sexual intercourse that he wants, but 'some indefinable freedom of which the women, with their veiled and hidden nakedness, are a symbol.' This hero is so much like myself that when I read it, a surge of emotion came upon me." He refers, in another letter, to an article he had read on male voyeurism: "Sexuality exhibits the characteristic of tension caused by inadequate information and causes curiosity and conflict. The female with her internal genitalia poses an enigma for the male. Her upright posture and pubic hair prevent him from seeing her genitalia—further stimulating his curiosity." Clearly, Norman's present life includes issues and questions which have not been resolved either intellectually or emotionally.

Norman keeps up with politics in magazines, newspapers, and television. Although he sometimes votes in local elections, he is not politically active. On most issues of the day he would call himself a liberal. He is an independent voter, belonging to neither party. Norman goes to church with his mother and sister every week, even though he gives Zoroastrianism and Hinduism as his present religious preference. This illustrates his disinclination to refuse the requests his mother makes of him even now that he has reached middle age. His independence remains unexpressed. One of their most serious and open confrontations involved his determination to attend school fulltime. Although she considered this a waste of time and strenuously objected to these educational pursuits, Norman remained adamant.

More recently a disagreement arose between Norman and his mother with regard to the publication of the present book. Norman had known from the very beginning that such a book would be written and to this end had given his complete cooperation, meeting with Bell from time to time whenever additional information was needed. Often Norman would take the initiative himself, writing to Bell whenever he felt that certain matters pertaining to his past needed further clarification. It was in the spirit of what had become, over the years, a collaborative undertaking that Bell invited Norman to review the manuscript. However, Norman's mother, in characteristic fashion, opened the letter addressed to her son, read its contents, and then insisted that Norman join with her in an effort to have absolute control over every aspect of the report. Despite his own feelings on the matter, Norman enclosed a letter with his mother's list of demands which indicated that he agreed with his mother's statements. At the same time, in other private communications with Bell, Norman wrote: "My mother is upset about the book. She thinks that you are taking advantage of me. And she wants to read the book, because if anything is in it about her, she wants to have it omitted if she would rather not have it published or if, in her opinion, it is false. She says that I have no head for business, and always let people swindle me. She says it's been like that ever since I let my father bully me into not telling her what he did that day when I was four years old. . . . No use trying to convince mother that I am competent enough to handle my affairs. All letters sent to me must be read by mother. I wrote that letter to appease mother, not because I agree with her." In subsequent letters Norman made it clear that he supported the publication of the manuscript. They also provide evidence of Norman's increasing dissatisfaction with his present home situation and of Norman's increasing attempts to establish viable relationships with others outside the home. For example, he writes to Bell: "Dear Alan: I hope you don't mind my addressing you by your first name. Since the encounter with my mother (over the publication of the manuscript), I feel more close to you." In a more recent letter, he makes the following disclosures: "Here is something that may surprise you: Last February, I wrote to a woman in reply to an ad in the personal column of a newspaper. Her ad said she was lonely, and wanted an acquaintance with a man interested in astrology or E.S.P. She is nine years older than I am . . . I received her reply about a week after the Easter mail strike . . . I replied to two of her letters and received a third one. I sent her a polaroid snapshot and she has sent me one of her. She has confided with me that she is in a state of sadness, confusion, and indecision. She had written something about this in an earlier letter. This is one reason for my pensive mood. I am afraid that as we correspond further, she may be disappointed in me or I may find things about her which are disappointing. I would welcome your advice regarding this relationship. . . . Another thing depresses me. There is a meeting on E.S.P. that I would like to attend. If only I lived alone, I would certainly go there, since my final exams have been cancelled due to the strike. But my mother would never hear of it."

Norman is probably more independent of his mother than at any other time in his life. How much more independent Norman will become remains to be seen. Needless to say, it will not be an easy accomplishment.

". . . Norman's style of life indicates that he has sought to preserve an almost womblike existence."

When a record of dreams is kept by a person over a period of years, it is customarily found that what he dreams about does not change substantially in any systematic way from year to year. The usual consistency in a person's dreams over time has also been found in Norman's dream production.

There are, however, a few systematic changes which do occur over the three and one-half years that Norman recorded his dreams and which deserve attention.

With regard to characters, the proportion of females in Norman's dreams decreases, and the proportion of males increases over the five year period. Norman is becoming more like other males in having a higher proportion of male characters than female characters in his dreams. Part of the decrease in the number of females is due to the decreasing appearances of his mother. Both of these changes might be thought of as constituting an improvement in Norman's condition to the extent that they reflect a greater adult male identification and a diminution of Norman's dependency needs.

On the other hand, the proportion of familiar characters steadily decreases and the proportion of unfamiliar characters steadily increases over the five year period. A large number of strangers appearing in dreams is usually interpreted as representing a dreamer's alienation or isolation from people. If this interpretation is valid, then Norman's dream record indicates that he may be jumping from the "frying pan" of dependency into the "fire" of alienation. Alienation may increase the strain upon his infantile character to such an extent that even worse problems are precipitated. Unless his ego and superego are strengthened, he may find that living in a world of strangers, unprotected by family and friends, is intolerable. There is a systematic increase in the proportion of dreams in which Norman suffers a misfortune. If this indicates increasing self-punishment by an internalized superego, it could be a good sign, and one could consider this a transition phase from which Norman will emerge with a stronger and more effective personality. There is, however, no strong indication of this in his dreams at the present time. And the fact that the proportion of minors in Norman's dreams does not change over the five year period provides no grounds for optimism. In addition, sexual encounters with males and with minors actually *increase* while those with females *decrease*. Although there are those who would scarcely interpret this as progress, it may be that a homosexual orientation is evolving which represents a kind of maturity that is lacking in his pedophilic history.

Although the references in Norman's dreams to his mother decrease, the number of aggressive interactions with her increases, and the number of friendly interactions with her decreases. Friendly interactions with his sister also decrease. This could be interpreted as a good sign if it were balanced by fewer aggressions and more friendliness with other characters. But it is not. To lose affectional and dependency ties with the nuclear family can only be beneficial if positive cathexes are established with other adults. There is no indication in Norman's dreams of this taking place.

There is only one systematic change in the objects categories. The proportion of references to communication objects steadily rises from 1963 to 1967. This could represent an increasing need to communicate with others or else a diversion (sublimation) of libido into reading and writing activities. This is evident in his present style of correspondence and in his determination to pursue his higher education. If such a sublimation could be effected, it would probably offer the best chance Norman has for bringing about a real improvement in his condition. There is evidence from his most recent correspondence that Norman is attempting to move in this direction. He writes, "I am considering preparing some article or book that perhaps I could get published. I don't expect to complete anything of more than about ten pages, but it would be a start.

. . . Next Fall, I'm determined to join the Sensitivity Group at _____ University. This semester I kept putting it off until when I did get enough courage to act about it, it was after Easter and too late to join. The emotional intimacy kind of frightens me away, but I'm sure it would be rewarding." Norman will probably remain an infantile character, but this does not necessarily present a handicap for a writer, particularly if he addresses himself to themes which express his wishes and concerns. Were Norman younger it might be possible for a therapist to transform him into a reasonably well socialized, independent, heterosexual adult. This does not appear to be a present possibility for Norman.

With regard to Norman's sexual proclivities, . . . [it has been] found that the peak of pedophilic activity occurs from the mid to late thirties. Norman is now past this age, and this should be an opportune time for him to divert his interests into substitute channels while his impulses are in a relatively quiescent state. [It has also been found that] another peak of pedophilic activities [occurs] in late adulthood and at the onset of old age. Such behaviors, however, are conducted by males with predominately heterosexual histories and who are motivated by concerns to which Norman is well-nigh a stranger. But even if there were an onslaught of impulses which occurs when Norman reaches that age, it is possible that defenses developed between now and then will effectively contain them.

Finally, another reason to believe that the future will not present new crises for Norman is the fact that he is not predominantly an oral character. He is not prone to use alcohol in order to allay his anxiety or to bolster a diminished masculinity. If Norman were an oral and not predominately an anal character, there would be little reason to hope for more than the chaos and confusion which he has known in the past. But because the anal mode is productive and potentially creative, at the present time there is reason to believe that Norman may be able to manage his future circumstances more adequately than he did in the past.

THE HOMOSEXUAL AS PATIENT

Alan P. Bell

There is no such thing as homosexuality. By this I mean that the homosexual experience is so diverse, the variety of its psychological, social, and sexual correlates so enormous, its originating factors so numerous, that to use the word "homosexuality" or "homosexual" as if it meant more than simply the nature of a person's sexual object choice is misleading and imprecise. When a male or female patient announces his or her homosexuality to the physician, the doctor must conclude nothing more than that the patient becomes erotically aroused by persons of the same sex and/or engages in sexual behaviors with persons of the same sex. As we consider the diversity of homosexual experience, we shall see the crucial mistake in inferring anything more. To put it another way, there are as many different kinds of homosexuals as heterosexuals, and thus it is impossible to predict the nature of any patient's personality, social adjustment, or sexual functioning on the basis of his or her sexual orientation. . . .

THE DEGREE OF HOMOSEXUALITY

One of the first things that must be determined is the extent to which a person's erotic arousal and behavior are homosexual. The matter can be pursued in several ways. . . . [Persons may be asked] to rate themselves

From "The Homosexual as Patient," in *Human Sexuality: A Health Practitioner's Text*, edited by Richard Green. Copyright © 1975, Williams & Wilkins Co. Reprinted by permission.

on the so-called Kinsey Scale, first with regard to their behaviors and then with regard to their feelings. The scale goes from zero (exclusively heterosexual) to six (exclusively homosexual). It has been estimated that approximately 4 to 5% of American males—and half that percentage of females—are exclusively homosexual (or sixes on the Kinsey Scale) in their behaviors throughout their lives. Additionally, much larger numbers at any given time are exclusively homosexual in their behaviors, and even larger numbers engage in both homosexual and heterosexual acts from time to time. For a given individual, ratings on this homosexual-heterosexual continuum may go up or down depending upon the person's age, life circumstances, and the culture in which he or she lives. It is sometimes helpful to have an individual review his or her behavioral ratings since puberty in order to determine the extent to which he or she has changed over time, the number and nature of the sexual partnerships involved, whatever factors might have accounted for the ebb and flow of homosexual experience, and the various meanings which the individual or others attached to that experience. . . .

The same inquiry should be made with regard to the patient's feelings rating on the Kinsey Scale. Very often the clinician will find that there is not a perfect fit between the two ratings. For example, theoretically it is possible for a person to be exclusively heterosexual in behavior but exclusively homosexual in feeling. Such a person might be married and sexually engaged only with his wife, all the while fantasizing a male partner. The fact that one has less control over one's thoughts and feelings than one's behaviors may be why behavior ratings tend to crowd around the ends of the homosexual-heterosexual continuum, while feelings ratings are spread out more along the scale. Some experts believe that a person's sexual *behavior*, either in the past or at the present time, is a poor indicator of his or her true sexual orientation. They maintain that much more important clues in that regard are provided by a detailed history of a person's sexual *feelings*. . . . The majority of homosexual males, and even larger numbers of homosexual females, report extensive heterosexual experience. Many can perform heterosexually, even as adults, but it is a performance frequently bereft of either deep emotional satisfactions or intense sexual arousal.

Out of this inquiry should come an awareness of the extent to which the label "homosexual" is arbitrary. There are females who are multiorgastic with a variety of male sexual partners, but who define themselves as "homosexual" because they find it easier to become emotionally involved with a sexual partner of the same sex. A growing number of females, very much into women's liberation and resentful of their female status, can be found defining themselves as "homosexual," a definition which amounts to more of a political statement than a "true" indication of their sexual orientation. Some adolescents think of themselves as "homosexual" because of sexual explorations involving members of the same sex or because they have no particular or exaggerated interest in persons of the opposite sex. . . . There are other males who can be engaged in a variety of homosexual behaviors but who do not define themselves as "homosexual" as long as they do the penile inserting.

"To put it another way, there are as many different kinds of homosexuals as heterosexuals, and thus it is impossible to predict the nature of any patient's personality, social adjustment, or sexual functioning on the basis of his or her sexual orientation."

. . . There is [also] a growing number of young persons, sometimes termed "bisexual" or "ambisexual," who refuse to define themselves sexually in highly restrictive ways. They find that they are able to respond sexually, in different ways and on different bases, to a variety of persons, regardless of their sex, and they are unwilling to deny themselves opportunities for sexual exchange out of regard for highly restrictive cultural expectations. . . . The bisexual's experience certainly belies the notion that homosexuality and heterosexuality are mutually exclusive. It has challenged a growing number of people—homosexual and heterosexual—to enlarge their capacities for sexual responsiveness. And, of course, in certain circles the person who reports himself or herself to be bisexual is viewed with alarm, often with disbelief. Heterosexuals are apt to conclude that the bisexual is simply on his or her way to an exclusive homosexual orientation, while politicized gays are apt to characterize the bisexual as a "cop-out," giving in to the pressures of a straight society.

In summary, how one defines one's sexual orientation and the basis on which that definition is made differ from one individual to the next, and deserve a great deal of attention before moving into other dimensions of the patient's sexual experience.

LEVEL OF SEXUAL INTEREST

Despite the assumption by the "man-on-the-street" that all homosexuals are constantly preoccupied with sexual thoughts, impulses, and behaviors, the fact is that homosexuals, like heterosexuals, differ in the attention they give to the sexual aspects of their lives. Some eroticize all of their social contacts, and often their sexual engagements become a substitute for genuine intimacy with another human being. Others, probably the majority, go on about their business—of seeking an education or making a living or engaging in various avocational pursuits—with hardly an awareness of their sexual interests. Males, whether they be predominantly homosexual or heterosexual, are more apt to report higher levels of sexual interest than their female counterparts. Homosexuals of either sex who have just "come out," who are in the process of defining their homosexual potential and crystallizing their sexual repertoire, are much more apt to consider sex a very important aspect of their lives or to think about sexual things frequently during the course of a day. . . . A continuing sexual preoccupation can often reflect a lack of suitable sexual outlets or else a dearth of satisfactions from other corners of one's life. On the other hand, the absence of sexual interest may denote a depressive episode, very often triggered off by the disruption of a lover relationship. In the case of the homosexual, categorized on the basis of his or her sexual proclivities, it would not be difficult to understand whatever inclination there is to define the self and others chiefly in sexual terms. And it would be important for the clinician to broaden the homosexual's self-definition as well as the range of his or her interpersonal experience.

SEXUAL STIMULATION

Any appraisal of a person's homosexuality should include a consideration of the kinds of stimuli which are found sexually arousing. . . . More homosexual males than females are apt to report high levels of sexual attraction to persons of the same sex, and it would appear that the less explicitly sexual characteristics of another person (i.e., a good-looking stranger, the bare chest) have a greater stimulus value than those aspects directly associated with sexual activity (i.e., the genitals or buttocks). . . .

It would be important for the clinician to explore the nature of the patient's sexual stimulation, particularly with regard to how restrictive are his or her preferences. The exploration should also include a consideration of the patient's body image as well as whatever remedial steps could be taken to make himself or herself more sexually appealing. . . .

SEXUAL REPERTOIRE

Again we find that homosexuals can be differentiated with regard to how locked in they are to certain sexual roles and techniques. Some insist on being the penile inserters, others on being the insertees, but clearly this polarization is not characteristic of most homosexuals. . . . To be sure, there are preferences, but they are often modified on the basis of the partner's expectations or the individual's sexual interest or arousal. . . .

The number of different sexual roles and activities which homosexuals are willing to engage in is often related to their age, to how long they have been involved homosexually with others, and to whether or not they have been involved with other persons who are capable of or interested in sexual experimentation. Frequently their range of sexual behaviors will reflect the degree to which they accept their sexual impulses and/or homosexual orientation. Sometimes a rigid repertoire will indicate a continuing remoteness from their sexual partners; those homosexuals who risk emotional closeness are more apt to perform sexually in ways that are pleasing to their partners, even if the behaviors do not coincide perfectly with their own special preferences.

The clinician who happens upon a homosexual patient whose sexual repertoire is severely limited would do well to explore the reasons for and consequences of the patient's restrictiveness. It may reflect dominance-submission issues or concerns about being in control of oneself and of one's sexual partner or various erotophobic features in the patient which make a wholehearted and spontaneous sexual experience well-nigh impossible.

LEVEL OF SEXUAL ACTIVITY

In addition to differences in technical preferences, homosexuals differ in the degree to which they are sexually active. Some are satisfied with the frequency of their sexual outlets, while others are not. The latter are apt not to be involved in a relatively permanent sexual partnership and are forced to squander their time and energy in "cruising" (i.e., going out to look for a sexual partner) where successful "scoring" is often not as frequent as many have been led to believe. Some of those who are dissatisfied find it difficult to act in the role of sexual pursuer; they wait to be approached and wooed in a splendid indifference with which they would hide their fears and uncertainty. . . . Some actually enjoy the "chase" more than the sexual outcome and will sabotage whatever attempts are made to effect sexual closure. The helpful clinician will explore, with his patient, whatever there is about the patient's attitudes or life style that is preventing him from fulfilling his sexual potential.

"The clinician who happens upon a homosexual patient whose sexual repertoire is severely limited would do well to explore the reasons for and consequences of the patient's restrictiveness. It may reflect dominance-submission issues or concerns about being in control of oneself and of one's sexual partner or various erotophobic features in the patient which make a wholehearted and spontaneous sexual experience well-nigh impossible."

SEXUAL PROBLEMS

Many homosexuals report that finding a suitable sexual partner is a problem for a variety of reasons: their age, physical attractiveness, their social inhibitions. Some have difficulty maintaining affection for their partners or responding to their partners' sexual requests. Some are concerned with their sexual adequacy: males who have problems maintaining an erection or who cannot ejaculate, females who cannot reach orgasm.

In our society—which does all it can to drive homosexuals underground and to instill fear in those who seek out sexual partners, which endows furtive, impersonal sexual encounters with survival value, and which attempts to inculcate negative views of homosexual behaviors to which homosexuals themselves are frequently not immune—the kinds of sexual problems which many homosexuals report are not at all surprising. Homosexuals for whom their sexual orientation is no longer ego-alien, who have managed to integrate their affectional and sexual needs, and whose sexual partnerships are relatively stable, are apt to report fewer sexual difficulties than those who continue to experience them-selves as "odd man out." Regardless, the sensitive clinician should be mindful of these potential difficulties and be prepared to discuss their psychological and social ramifications as well as their possible remedies. He should not conclude that reports of sexual difficulties by homosexuals amount to a general dissatisfaction with their sexual orientation, any more than he would reach such a conclusion on the basis of reports from heterosexuals that they are experiencing sexual problems.

SEXUAL CRUISING AND PARTNERSHIPS

The number and nature of a person's sexual partnerships, as well as the conditions under which they are sought, are extremely important vari-ables within the homosexual experience. Most have experienced at least one "affair" of a relatively long duration, many having lived with the person to whom they were romantically attached and with whom they were erotically involved. For both homosexual males and females such a relationship represents a considerable emotional investment, and its breakdown can have a traumatic effect. For some, and this is more likely to be true of females than males, a permanent relationship of this kind serves as the "be all and end all" of their lives. The first such relationship is sometimes experienced as the first opportunity they have ever had to draw close to another human being, to be accepted for what they are, including their homosexuality. . . . However, only a small minority ever experience the fulfillment of their original hopes and dreams. More often than not the highly charged sexual atmosphere of the gay world conspires against sexual monogamy. Homosexual males, like their het-erosexual counterparts, are apt to seek out opportunities for sexual ad-venture and conquest. In those relationships which preclude sexual free-dom for the partners involved, such temptations or activities can provoke a great deal of rancor, guilt, and jealousy. What may be more problem-atic for the homosexual female is an attachment to a person whose sexual orientation is an unsettled state. . . . Other factors which tend to make homosexual partnerships so tenuous are their lack of institutional supports and the fact that a successful relationship makes one's homosexual orientation more obvious to family, friends, and employers. In our society, long-standing homosexual partnerships can become as much a liability as an asset.

Given such circumstances, the fact that many male homosexuals report having had literally hundreds of sexual partners should come as no surprise, nor should the facts that most of these partners became known to them for the first and last time in connection with one sexual episode, and most of their sexual encounters involve little care or affection between them and their partners. . . .

". . . the sensitive clinician . . . should not conclude that reports of sexual difficulties by homosexuals amount to a general dissatisfaction with their sexual orientation, any more than he would reach such a conclusion on the basis of reports from heterosexuals that they are experiencing sexual problems."

Sometimes such casual and anonymous encounters are a function of a person's inability to relate comfortably to others and a paucity of social contacts. Some who limit their sexual pursuits to a single locale do so because of a long-standing association between sexual arousal and a particular setting. For others it may simply indicate a novice's unfamiliarity with a particular gay community. Again we find that the homosexual experience can mean quite different things to different people.

Any clinician who would be an influence for good in the life of a homosexual patient would be well advised to become familiar with the social setting of his or her clientele, well-versed in the argot of the gay world, and acquainted with a variety of homosexual life styles, some of which are far more productive than others. He should help his patient examine the realism of his expectations vis-à-vis a lover relationship and be in a position to help homosexual couples work through the special difficulties of their relationships. Above all, he should help the homosexual to realize that norms or standards which may be feasible and appropriate for the heterosexual are not necessarily so for the homosexual. Finally, it would be profitable to review the patient's cruising patterns, either in an effort to make them more effective or to reduce the likelihood of harmful social consequences.

OVERTNESS-COVERTNESS

An important area for the clinician to explore with his homosexual patient is the extent to which he or she is open or secretive about his or her homosexuality. Some homosexuals remain "in the closet," a term used to denote those who lead highly secretive lives. Others reveal their homosexuality only to their closest friends. A growing number of homosexuals are becoming politicized in consciousness-raising groups sponsored by various gay liberation organizations and find themselves on picket lines or zapping politicians or various meetings of the American Psychiatric Association. Needless to say, where one stands on the continuum which extends from the "closet queen" to the gay radical will have a profound effect upon a person's experience of homosexuality.

The most covert individual, sometimes married and often of high socio-economic status, will frequently limit himself to highly casual sexual encounters in situations where anonymity will be preserved. Such persons will tend to compartmentalize their sexual lives in ways that do them little good. They frequently experience a great deal of tension in pretending to be what they are not, a profound disparity between their inner and outer selves. . . . On the other hand, there are homosexuals whose openness is inappropriate and self-defeating, the motivations for which deserve exploration and understanding. Still others feel ashamed that they have not "laid it on the line" and view themselves as moral cowards. Such persons should be led to an understanding that their life situation is unique and that, in fact, on a very deep level their homosexuality is no one else's business. Perhaps only after that becomes their realization will they be in a position to make themselves known to others in ways and on levels which promote their personal growth and sense of well-being.

ATTITUDES TOWARD HOMOSEXUALITY

One's clinical contact with a homosexual is especially important because of the opportunity it provides for the patient to examine his or her attitudes toward homosexuality, either in self or others. The clinician who can communicate a genuine interest, understanding, and acceptance—attitudes which will go far in diminishing the patient's initial defensiveness—is apt to find that the patient has not entirely accepted homosexuality. The possible reasons for such negative attitudes deserve exploration. Sometimes it is because the patient feels that he or she has let down parents, has not lived up to their expectations, and fears their rejection. For some, homosexuality conjures up a host of unacceptable images . . . which leads them to false conclusions about themselves and about how life will be for them in the future. . . . Sometimes negative attitudes toward homosexuality among homosexuals themselves are the result of social difficulties they have encountered (i.e., arrests, loss of job, blackmail) or of their social isolation within the gay community. Often negative attitudes will amount to no more than a momentary reaction to the loss of a lover or to a transitory lack of sexual relationships. Frequently such attitudes will reflect more general feelings of worthlessness which have little to do with homosexuality *per se*.

It is important that the clinician help his patient gain insight into his or her attitudes, first determining whether they are of short or long standing, and then identifying their various sources and the conditions under which such negative attitudes have emerged. . . . This might involve encouraging the patient to read the more recent (and positive) literature on homosexuality . . . or to participate in a consciousness-raising group sponsored by a gay liberation organization. Usually it will be accompanied by the insight that homosexuality should not be used as the scapegoat for other, even more important, issues in the patient's life which need to be met head on.

PSYCHOLOGICAL AND SOCIAL ADJUSTMENT

For a long time, and for a variety of reasons, many people have supposed that homosexuality is *ipso facto* pathological. The fact is, almost without exception, whenever nonclinical samples of homosexuals are compared with equivalent heterosexual samples, very few if any differences are found in their psychological functioning. . . . Whenever differences are found, they usually do not stand up in other studies, or . . . the kinds of analyses that are done make it difficult to conclude that the differences are a function of a person's sexual orientation *per se*.

Perhaps more homosexuals than heterosexuals seek professional help or have attempted suicide, but it is as easy to interpret these behaviors as the consequence of being homosexual in a society which is hostile to homosexuality as it is to conclude that homosexuality necessarily involves or is caused by psychological maladjustment. . . .

With regard to their social adjustment, again we find occupational, religious, and political differences among homosexuals, as well as differences in the ways they spend their leisure time, the number of friends they have, where they live, and how involved they are in the gay subculture. Very few homosexuals have ever been rolled, robbed, arrested, or fired from their jobs. Much larger numbers report wide circles of friends and a variety of rewards which they believe to be absent in most "straight" life styles. . . .

CONCLUSION

. . . What I have tried to do is indicate that homosexuality involves a large number of divergent experiences. . . . Homosexuals are found to differ with respect to . . . dimensions which are themselves related to a homosexual's psychological and social adjustment. Very clearly, there is no such thing as *the* homosexual, and little can be predicted about an individual on the basis of that label.

Only the clinician with this sense of the matter is in a position to help the homosexual client take stock of where he or she is sexually and of where he or she wants or needs to be. . . .

WEINBERG AND WILLIAMS 7
Social Reactions to Sexual Deviance

Colin Williams and I came to the Institute in 1968, which could be described as the beginning of the fourth stage in the Institute's history. This stage is characterized by two features. First, the aim of gathering empirical data to answer more general questions in sociological and psychological theory becomes crystallized. Second, there is a change in the social organization of research projects. In its early years, the Institute had been characterized by single research projects on which all the staff collaborated. In the third stage, this tradition began to break down. For example, the third period includes think-pieces done by one or two individuals, but research projects of the period usually involved all the research staff. In the fourth stage, multiple research projects, with only a segment of the staff working on each project, became the norm. In addition, the studies generally continue to be smaller in scope than the early Institute studies.

Williams and I, for example, are sociologists interested in the meanings people attach to various facets and forms of sexuality. We link our sex research to general theoretical interests in sociology, and we often work together as one research team at the Institute.

The first selection in this chapter illustrates my interest in the meanings surrounding human sexuality and in how these meanings are socially constructed. It is from a paper on nudists that I published in 1970.

The second excerpt is from Williams and my *Homosexuals and the Military: A Study of Less than Honorable Discharge.* In this excerpt, we look at which homosexuals are most likely to be discovered and expelled from the armed forces and the events associated with their discovery. In the book, we also investigate the long-range effects of getting a less than honorable discharge.

The third selection is from our latest book, *Male Homosexuals: Their Problems and Adaptations.* This study describes the homosexual's situation in the United States, the Netherlands, and Denmark, and it examines questionnaire data from over 2400 American, Dutch, and Danish homosexual males. This excerpt provides an overview of the findings of the questionnaire study.

17. Gebhard. *Dellenback*   18. Weinberg. *Dellenback*

EXECUTIVE COMMITTEE, 1975

19. Williams. *Dellenback*   20. Bell. *Dellenback*

THE NUDIST MANAGEMENT
OF RESPECTABILITY

Martin S. Weinberg

Public nudity is taboo in our society. Yet there is a group who breach this moral rule. They call themselves "social nudists."

A number of questions may be asked about these people. For example, how can they see their behavior as morally appropriate? Have they constructed their own morality? If so, what characterizes this morality and what are its consequences? [1]

This article will attempt to answer these questions through a study of social interaction in nudist camps. The data come from three sources: two summers of participant observation in nudist camps; 101 interviews with nudists in the Chicago area; and 617 mailed questionnaires completed by nudists in the United States and Canada. [2]

THE CONSTRUCTION OF SITUATED MORAL MEANINGS:
THE NUDIST MORALITY

The construction of morality in nudist camps is based on the official interpretations that camps provide regarding the moral meanings of public heterosexual nudity. These are (1) that nudity and sexuality are unrelated, (2) that there is nothing shameful about the human body, (3) that nudity promotes a feeling of freedom and natural pleasure, and (4) that

From *Deviance and Respectability*, edited by Jack D. Douglas. Copyright © 1970, Basic Books, Inc. Reprinted by permission. Revised version.

nude exposure to the sun promotes physical, mental, and spiritual well-being.

This official perspective is sustained in nudist camps to an extraordinary degree, illustrating the extent to which adult socialization can affect traditional moral meanings. (This is especially true with regard to the first two points of the nudist perspective, which will be our primary concern since these are its "deviant" aspects.) The assumption in the larger society that nudity and sexuality are related, and the resulting emphasis on covering the sexual organs, make the nudist perspective a specifically situated morality. My field work, interview, and questionnaire research show that nudists routinely use a special system of rules to create, sustain, and enforce this situated morality.

STRATEGIES FOR SUSTAINING A SITUATED MORALITY

The first strategy used by the nudist camp to anesthetize any relationship between nudity and sexuality [3] involves a system of organizational precautions regarding who can come into the camp. Most camps, for example, regard unmarried people, especially single men, as a threat to the nudist morality. They suspect that singles may indeed see nudity as something sexual. Thus, most camps either exclude unmarried people (especially men), or allow only a small quota of them. Camps that do allow single men may charge them up to 35 per cent more than they charge families. (This is intended to discourage single men, but since the cost is still relatively low compared with other resorts, this measure is not very effective. It seems to do little more than create resentment among the singles, and by giving formal organizational backing to the definition that singles are not especially desirable, it may contribute to the segregation of single and married members in nudist camps.)

Certification by the camp owner is another requirement for admission to camp grounds, and three letters of recommendation regarding the applicant's character are sometimes required. These regulations help preclude people whom members regard as a threat to the nudist morality.

[The camp owner] invited us over to see if we were *desirable* people. Then after we did this, he invited us to camp on probation; then they voted us into camp. [Q: Could you tell me what you mean by desirable people?]

Well, not people who are inclined to drink, or people who go there for a peep show. Then they don't want you there. They feel you out in conversation. They want people for mental and physical health reasons.

Whom to admit [is the biggest problem of the camp]. [Q] [4] Because the world is so full of people whose attitudes on nudity are hopelessly warped. [Q: Has this always been the biggest problem in camp?] Yes. Every time anybody comes, a decision has to be made. [Q] . . . The lady sitting at the gate decides about admittance. The director decides on membership.

A limit is sometimes set on the number of trial visits a non-member may make to camp. In addition, there is usually a limit on how long a person can remain clothed. This is a strategy to mark guests who may not sincerely accept the nudist perspective.

The second strategy for sustaining the nudist morality involves norms of interpersonal behavior. These norms are as follows:

"I try very hard to look at them from the jaw up—even more than you would normally."

No Staring. This rule controls overt signs of overinvolvement. As the publisher of one nudist magazine said, "They all look up to the heavens and never look below." Such studied inattention is most exaggerated among women, who usually show no recognition that the male is unclothed. Women also recount that they had expected men to look at their nude bodies, only to find, when they finally did get up the courage to undress, that no one seemed to notice. As one woman states: "I got so mad because my husband wanted me to undress in front of other men that I just pulled my clothes right off thinking everyone would look at me." She was amazed (and appeared somewhat disappointed) when no one did.

The following statements illustrate the constraints that result:

[Q: Have you ever observed or heard about anyone staring at someone's body while at camp?] I've heard stories, particularly about men that stare. Since I heard these stories, I tried not to, and have even done away with my sunglasses after someone said, half-joking, that I hide behind sunglasses to stare. Toward the end of the summer I stopped wearing sunglasses. And you know what, it was a child who told me this.

[Q: Would you stare. . . ?] Probably not, cause you can get in trouble and get thrown out. If I thought I could stare unobserved I might. They might not throw you out, but it wouldn't do you any good. [Q] The girl might tell others and they might not want to talk to me. . . . [Q] They disapprove by not talking to you, ignoring you, etc.

[Someone who stares] wouldn't belong there. [Q] If he does that he is just going to camp to see the opposite sex. [Q] He is just coming to stare. [Q] You go there to swim and relax.

I try very hard to look at them from the jaw up—even more than you would normally.[5]

No Sex Talk.   Sex talk, or telling "dirty jokes," is uncommon in camp. The owner of a large camp in the Midwest stated: "It is usually expected that members of a nudist camp will not talk about sex, politics, or religion." Or as one single male explained: "It is taboo to make sexual remarks here." During my field work, it was rare to hear "sexual" joking such as one hears at most other types of resort. Interview respondents who mentioned that they had talked about sex qualified this by explaining that such talk was restricted to close friends, was of a "scientific nature," or, if a joke, was of a "cute sort."

Asked what they would think of someone who breached this rule, respondents indicated that such behavior would cast doubt on the situated morality of the nudist camp:

One would expect to hear less of that at camp than at other places. [Q] Because you expect that the members are screened in their attitude for nudism—and this isn't one who prefers sexual jokes.

I've never heard anyone swear or tell a dirty joke out there.

No. Not at camp. You're not supposed to. You bend over backwards not to.

They probably don't belong there. They're there to see what they can find to observe. [Q] Well, their mind isn't on being a nudist, but to see so and so nude.

No Body Contact.   Although the extent to which this is enforced varies from camp to camp, there is at least some degree of informal enforcement in nearly every camp. Nudists mention that they are particularly careful not to brush against anyone or have any body contact for fear of how it might be interpreted:

I stay clear of the opposite sex. They're so sensitive, they imagine things.

People don't get too close to you. Even when they talk. They sit close to you, but they don't get close enough to touch you.

We have a minimum of contact. There are more restrictions [at a nudist camp]. [Q] Just a feeling I had. I would openly show my affection more readily someplace else.

And when asked to conceptualize a breach of this rule, the following response is typical:

They are in the wrong place. [Q] That's not part of nudism. [Q] I think they are there for some sort of sex thrill. They are certainly not there to enjoy the sun.

Also, in photographs taken for nudist magazines, the subjects usually have only limited body contact. One female nudist explained: "We don't want anyone to think we're immoral." Outsiders' interpretations, then, can also constitute a threat.

Associated with the body contact taboo is a prohibition of nude dancing. Nudists cite this as a separate rule. This rule is often talked about by members in a way that indicates organizational strain—that is, the rule itself makes evident that a strategy is in operation to sustain their situated morality.

This reflects a contradiction in our beliefs. But it's self-protection. One incident and we'd be closed.

No Alcoholic Beverages in American Camps. This rule guards against breakdowns in inhibition, and even respondents who admitted that they had "snuck a beer" before going to bed went on to say that they fully favor the rule.

Yes. We have [drunk at camp]. We keep a can of beer in the refrigerator since we're out of the main area. We're not young people or carousers. . . . I still most generally approve of it as a camp rule and would disapprove of anyone going to extremes. [Q] For common-sense reasons. People who overindulge lose their inhibitions, and there is no denying that the atmosphere of a nudist camp makes one bend over backwards to keep people who are so inclined from going beyond the bounds of propriety.

Anyone who drinks in camp is jeopardizing their membership and they shouldn't. Anyone who drinks in camp could get reckless. [Q] Well, when guys and girls drink they're a lot bolder—they might get fresh with someone else's girl. That's why it isn't permitted, I guess.

Rules Regarding Photography.   Photography in a nudist camp is controlled by the camp management. Unless the photographer works for a nudist magazine, his (or her) moral perspective is sometimes suspect. One photographer's remark to a woman that led to his being so typed was, "Do you think you could open your legs a little more?"

Aside from a general restriction on the use of cameras, when cameras are allowed, it is expected that no pictures will be taken without the subject's permission. Members blame the misuse of cameras especially on single men. As one nudist said: "You always see the singles poppin' around out of nowhere snappin' pictures." In general, control is maintained, and any infractions that take place are not blatant or obvious. Overindulgence in picture-taking communicates an overinvolvement in the subjects' nudity and casts doubt on the assumption that nudity and sexuality are unrelated.

> Photographers dressed only in cameras and light exposure meters. I don't like them. I think they only go out for pictures. Their motives should be questioned.

Photographers for nudist magazines recognize the signs that strain the situated morality that characterizes nudist camps. As one such photographer commented:

> I never let a girl look straight at the camera. It looks too suggestive. I always have her look off to the side.

Similarly, a nudist model showed the writer a pin-up magazine to point out how a model could make a nude picture "sexy"—through the use of various stagings, props, and expressions—and in contrast, how the nudist model eliminates these techniques to make her pictures "natural." Although it may be questionable that a nudist model completely eliminates a sexual perspective for the non-nudist, the model discussed how she attempts to do this.

> It depends on the way you look. Your eyes and your smile can make you look sexy. The way they're looking at you. Here, she's on a bed. It wouldn't be sexy if she were on a beach with kids running around. They always have

some clothes on too. See how she's "looking sexy"? Like an "oh dear!" look. A different look can change the whole picture.

Now here's a decent pose. . . . Outdoors makes it "nature." Here she's giving you "the eye," or is undressing. It's cheesecake. It depends on the expression on her face. Having nature behind it makes it better. Don't smile like "come on honey!" It's that look and the lace thing she has on. . . . Like when you half-close your eyes, like "oh baby," a Marilyn Monroe look. Art is when you don't look like you're hiding it halfway.

The element of trust plays a particularly strong role in socializing women to the nudist perspective. Consider this in the following statements made by another model for nudist magazines. She and her husband had been indoctrinated in the nudist ideology by friends. At the time of the interview, however, the couple had not yet been to camp, although they had posed indoors for nudist magazines.

[Three months ago, before I was married] I never knew a man had any pubic hairs. I was shocked when I was married. . . . I wouldn't think of getting undressed in front of my husband. I wouldn't make love with a light on, or in the daytime.

With regard to being a nudist model, this woman commented:

None of the pictures are sexually seductive. [Q] The pose, the look—you can have a pose that's completely nothing, till you get a look that's not too hard to do. [Q: How do you do that?] I've never tried. By putting on a certain air about a person; a picture that couldn't be submitted to a nudist magazine—using _____ [the nudist photographer's] language. . . . [Q: Will your parents see your pictures in the magazine?] Possibly. I don't really care. . . . My mother might take it all right. But they've been married twenty years and she's never seen my dad undressed.[6]

No Accentuation of the Body. Accentuating the body is regarded as incongruent with the nudist morality. Thus, a woman who had shaved her pubic area was labeled "disgusting" by other members. There was a similar reaction to women who sat in a blatantly "unladylike" manner.

I'd think she was inviting remarks. [Q] I don't know. It seems strange to think of it. It's strange you ask it. Out there, they're not unconscious about their posture. Most women there are very circumspect even though in the nude.

For a girl, . . . [sitting with your legs open] is just not feminine or ladylike. The hair doesn't always cover it. [Q] Men get away with so many things. But, it would look dirty for a girl, like she was waiting for something. When I'm in a secluded area I've spread my legs to sun, but I kept an eye open and if anyone came I'd close my legs and sit up a little. It's just not ladylike.

You can lay on your back or side, or with your knees under your chin. But not with your legs spread apart. It would look to other people like you're there for other reasons. [Q: What other reasons?] . . . To stare and get an eyeful. . . . not to enjoy the sun and people.

No Unnatural Attempts at Covering the Body. "Unnatural attempts" at covering the body are ridiculed since they call into question the assumption that there is no shame in exposing any area of the body. If such behavior occurs early in one's nudist career, however, members usually have more compassion, assuming that the person just has not yet fully assimilated the new morality.

It is how members interpret the behavior, however, rather than the behavior per se, that determines whether covering up is disapproved.

If they're cold or sunburned, it's understandable. If it's because they don't agree with the philosophy, they don't belong there.

I would feel their motives for becoming nudists were not well founded. That they were not true nudists, not idealistic enough.

A third strategy that is sometimes employed to sustain the nudist reality is the use of communal toilets. Not all the camps have communal toilets, but the large camp where I did most of my field work did have such a facility, which was marked, "Little Girls Room and Little Boys Too." Although the stalls had three-quarter-length doors, this combined facility still helped to provide an element of consistency; as the owner said, "If you are not ashamed of any part of your body or any of its natural functions, men and women do not need separate toilets." Thus, even the physical ecology of the nudist camp was designed to be consistent with the nudist morality. For some, however, communal toilets were going too far.

I think they should be separated. For myself it's all right. But there are varied opinions, and for the satisfaction of all, I think they should separate them. There are niceties of life we often like to maintain, and for some people this is embarrassing. . . . [Q] You know, in a bowel movement it always isn't silent.

THE ROUTINIZATION OF NUDITY

In the nudist camp, nudity becomes routinized; its attention-provoking quality recedes, and nudity becomes a taken-for-granted state of affairs. Thus, when asked questions about staring ("While at camp, have you ever stared at anyone's body? Do you think you would stare at anyone's body?"), nudists indicate that nudity generally does not invoke their attention.

Nudists don't care what bodies are like. They're out there for themselves. It's a matter-of-fact thing. After a while you feel like you're sitting with a full suit of clothes on.

To nudists the body becomes so matter-of-fact, whether clothed or unclothed, when you make it an undue point of interest it becomes an abnormal thing.

[Q: What would you think of someone staring?] I would feel bad and let down. [Q] I have it set up on a high standard. I have never seen it happen. . . . [Q] Because it's not done there. It's above that; you don't stare. . . . If I saw it happen, I'd be startled. There's no inclination to do that. Why would they?

There are two types—male and female. I couldn't see why they were staring. I wouldn't understand it.

In fact, these questions about staring elicit from nudists a frame of possibilities in which what is relevant to staring is ordinarily not nudity itself. Rather, what evokes attention is something unusual, something the observer seldom sees and thus is not routinized to.[7]

There was a red-haired man. He had red pubic hair. I had never seen this before. . . . He didn't see me. If anyone did, I would turn the other way.

Well, once I was staring at a pregnant woman. It was the first time I ever saw this. I was curious, her stomach stretched, the shape. . . . I also have stared at extremely obese people, cripples. All this is due to curiosity, just a novel sight. [Q] . . . I was discreet. [Q] I didn't look at them when their eyes were fixed in a direction so they could tell I was.

[Q: While at camp have you ever stared at someone's body?] Yes. [Q] A little girl. She has a birthmark on her back, at the base of her spine.

[Q: Do you think you would ever stare at someone's body while at camp?] No. I don't like that. I think it's silly. . . . What people are is not their fault if they are deformed.

I don't think it would be very nice, very polite. [Q] I can't see anything to stare at, whether it's a scar or anything else. [Q] It just isn't done.

I've looked, but not stared. I'm careful about that, because you could get in bad about that. [Q] Get thrown out by the owner. I was curious when I once had a perfect view of a girl's sex organs, because her legs were spread when she was sitting on a chair. I sat in the chair across from her in perfect view of her organs. [Q] For about ten or fifteen minutes. [Q] Nobody noticed. [Q] It's not often you get that opportunity.[8]

[Q: How would you feel if you were alone in a secluded area of camp sunning yourself, and then noticed that other nudists were staring at your body?] I would think I had some mud on me. [Q] . . . I would just ask them why they were staring at me. Probably I was getting sunburn and they wanted to tell me to turn over, or maybe I had a speck of mud on me. [Q] These are the only two reasons I can think of why they were staring.

In the nudist camp, the arousal of attention by nudity is usually regarded as *unnatural*. Thus, staring is unnatural, especially after a period of grace in which to adjust to the new meanings.

If he did it when he was first there, I'd figure he's normal. If he kept it up I'd stay away from him, or suggest to the owner that he be thrown out. [Q] At first it's a new experience, so he might be staring. [Q] He wouldn't know how to react to it. [Q] The first time seeing nudes of the opposite sex. [Q] I'd think if he kept staring, that he's thinking of something, like grabbing someone, running to the bushes and raping them. [Q] Maybe he's mentally unbalanced.

He just sat there watching the women. You can forgive it the first time, because of curiosity. But not every weekend. [Q] The owner asked him to leave.

These women made comments on some men's shapes. They said, "He has a hairy body or ugly bones," or "Boy his wife must like him because he's hung big." That was embarrassing. . . . I thought they were terrible. [Q] Because I realized they were walking around looking. I can't see that.

ORGANIZATIONS AND THE CONSTITUTION OF NORMALITY

The rules-in-use of an organization *and the reality they sustain* form the basis on which behaviors are interpreted as "unnatural." [9] Overinvolvement in nudity, for example, is interpreted by nudists as unnatural (and not simply immoral). Similarly, erotic stimuli or responses, which breach the nudist morality, are defined as unnatural.

> They let one single in. He acted peculiar. . . . He got up and had a big erection. I didn't know what he'd do at night. He might molest a child or anybody. . . . My husband went and told the owner.

> I told you about this one on the sundeck with her legs spread. She made no bones about closing up. Maybe it was an error, but I doubt it. It wasn't a normal position. Normally you wouldn't lay like this. It's like standing on your head. She had sufficient time and there were people around.

> She sat there with her legs like they were straddling a horse. I don't know how else to describe it. [Q] She was just sitting on the ground. [Q] I think she's a dirty pig. [Q] If you sit that way, everyone don't want to know what she had for breakfast. [Q] It's just the wrong way to sit. You keep your legs together even with clothes on.

> [Q: Do you think it is possible for a person to be modest in a nudist camp?] I think so. [Q] If a person acts natural. . . . An immodest person would be an exhibitionist, and you find them in nudism too. . . . Most people's conduct is all right.

When behaviors are constituted as *unnatural*, attempts to understand them are usually suspended, and reciprocity of perspectives is called into question. (The "reciprocity of perspectives" involves the assumption that if one changed places with the other, one would, for all practical purposes, see the world as the other sees it.[10])

"When behaviors occur that reflect other forms of 'immodesty,' . . . nudists often fear a voiding of the nonsexual meaning that they impose on nudity."

> [Q: What would you think of a man who had an erection at camp?] Maybe they can't control themselves. [Q] Better watch out for him. [Q] I would tell the camp director to keep an eye on him. And the children would question that. [Q: What would you tell them?] I'd tell them the man is sick or something.

> [Q: What would you think of a Peeping Tom—a non-nudist trespasser?] They should be reported and sent out. [Q] I think they shouldn't be there. They're sick. [Q] Mentally. [Q] Because anyone who wants to look at someone else's body; well, is a Peeping Tom, is sick in the first place. He looks at you differently than a normal person would. [Q] With ideas of sex.

[A trespasser] . . . is sick. He probably uses this as a source of sexual stimulation.

Such occurrences call into question the taken-for-granted character of nudity in the nudist camp and the situated morality that is officially set forth.

INHIBITING BREAKDOWNS IN THE NUDIST MORALITY

Organized nudism promulgates a nonsexual perspective toward nudity, and breakdowns in that perspective are inhibited by (1) controlling erotic actions and (2) controlling erotic reactions. Nudity is partitioned off from other forms of "immodesty" (e.g., verbal immodesty, erotic overtures). In this way, a person can learn more easily to attribute a new meaning to nudity.[11] When behaviors occur that reflect other forms of "immodesty," however, nudists often fear a voiding of the nonsexual meaning that they impose on nudity.

This woman with a sexy walk would shake her hips and try to arouse the men. . . . [Q] These men went to the camp director to complain that the woman had purposely tried to arouse them. The camp director told this woman to leave.

Nudists are sensitive to the possibility of a breakdown in the nudist morality. Thus, they have a low threshold for interpreting acts as "sexual."

Playing badminton, this teenager was hitting the birdie up and down and she said, "What do you think of that?" I said, "Kind of sexy." _____ [the president of the camp] said I shouldn't talk like that, but I was only kidding.

Note the following description of "mauling":

I don't like to see a man and a girl mauling each other in the nude before others. . . . [Q: Did you ever see this at camp?] I saw it once. . . . [Q: What do you mean by mauling?] Just, well, I never saw him put his hands on her breast, but he was running his hands along her arms.

This sensitivity to "sexual" signs also sensitizes nudists to the possibility that certain of their own acts, although not intended as "sexual," might nonetheless be interpreted that way.

Sometimes you're resting and you spread your legs unknowingly. [Q] My husband just told me not to sit that way. [Q] I put my legs together.

Since "immodesty" is defined as an unnatural manner of behavior, such behaviors are easily interpreted as being motivated by "dishonorable" intent. When the individual is thought to be in physical control of the "immodest" behavior and to know the behavior's meaning within the nudist scheme of interpretation, sexual intentions are assigned. Referring to a quotation that was presented earlier, one man said that a woman who was lying with her legs spread may have been doing so unintentionally, "but I doubt it. [Q] It wasn't a normal position. Normally you wouldn't lay like this. It's like standing on your head."

Erotic reactions, as well as erotic actions, are controlled in camp. Thus, even when erotic stimuli come into play, erotic responses may be inhibited.

When lying on the grass already hiding my penis, I got erotic thoughts. And then one realizes it can't happen here. With fear there isn't much erection.

Yes, once I started to have an erection. Once. [Q] A friend told me how he was invited by some young lady to go to bed. [Q] I started to picture the situation and I felt the erection coming on; so I immediately jumped in the pool. It went away.

I was once in the woods alone and ran into a woman. I felt myself getting excited. A secluded spot in the bushes which was an ideal place for procreation. [Q] Nothing happened, though.

When breaches of the nudist morality do occur, other nudists' sense of modesty may inhibit sanctioning. The immediate breach may go unsanctioned. The observers may feign inattention or withdraw from the scene. The occurrence is usually communicated, however, via the grapevine, and it may reach the camp director.

We were shooting a series of pictures and my wife was getting out of her clothes. _____ [the photographer] had an erection but went ahead like nothing was happening. [Q] It was over kind of fast. . . . [Q] Nothing. We tried to avoid the issue. . . . Later we went to see _____ [the camp director] and _____ [the photographer] denied it.

[If a man had an erection] people would probably pretend they didn't see it.

[Q: What do you think of someone this happens to?] They should try to get rid of it fast. It don't look nice. Nudists are prudists. They are more prudish. Because they take their clothes off they are more careful. [Q] They become more prudish than people with clothes. They won't let anything out of the way happen.

As indicated in the remark, "nudists are prudists," nudists may at times become aware of the fragility of their situated moral meanings.

> At _____ [camp], this family had a small boy no more than ten years old who had an erection. Mrs. _____ [the owner's wife] saw him and told his parents that they should keep him in check, and tell him what had happened to him and to watch himself. This was silly, for such a little kid who didn't know what happened.

"Thus, what are 'deviant' occurrences in nudist camps probably would be regarded by members of the clothed society as natural and understandable rather than unnatural and difficult to understand."

DEVIANCE AND MULTIPLE REALITIES

There are basic social processes that underlie responses to deviance. Collectivities control thresholds of response to various behaviors, determining the relevance, meaning, and importance of the behavior. In the nudist camp, as pointed out previously, erotic overtures and erotic responses are regarded as unnatural, and reciprocity of perspectives is called into question by such behaviors.

> We thought this single was all right, until others clued us in that he had brought girls up to camp. [Then we recalled that] . . . he was kind of weird. The way he'd look at you. He had glassy eyes, like he could see through you.[12]

Such a response to deviance in the nudist camp is a result of effective socialization to the new system of moral meanings. The deviant's behavior, on the other hand, can be construed as reflecting an ineffective socialization to the new system of meanings.

> I think it's impossible [to have an erection in a nudist camp]. [Q] In a nudist camp you must have some physical contact and a desire to have one.

He isn't thinking like a nudist. [Q] The body is wholesome, not . . . a sex object. He'd have to do that—think of sex.

Sex isn't supposed to be in your mind, as far as the body. He doesn't belong there. [Q] If you go in thinking about sex, naturally it's going to happen. . . . You're not supposed to think about going to bed with anyone, not even your wife.

As these quotes illustrate, the unnaturalness or deviance of a behavior is ordinarily determined by relating it to an institutionalized scheme of interpretation. Occurrences that are "not understandable" in the reality of one collectivity may, however, be quite understandable in the reality of another collectivity.[13] Thus, what are "deviant" occurrences in nudist camps probably would be regarded by members of the clothed society as natural and understandable rather than unnatural and difficult to understand.

Finally, a group of people may subscribe to different and conflicting interpretive schemes. Thus, the low threshold of nudists to anything "sexual" is a function of their marginality; the fact that they have not completely suspended the moral meanings of the clothed society is what leads them to constitute many events as "sexual" in purpose.

NOTES

1. In my previous papers, I have dealt with other questions that are commonly asked about nudists. How persons become nudists is discussed in my "Becoming a Nudist," *Psychiatry*, XXIX (February, 1966), 15–24. A report on the nudist way of life and social structure can be found in my article in *Human Organization*, XXVI (Fall, 1967), 91–99.

2. Approximately one hundred camps were represented in the interviews and questionnaires. Interviews were conducted in the homes of nudists during the off season. Arrangements for the interviews were initially made with these nudists during the first summer of participant observation; selection of respondents was limited to those living within a one-hundred-mile radius of Chicago. The questionnaires were sent to all members of the National Nudist Council. The different techniques of data collection provided a test of convergent validation.

3. For a discussion of the essence of such relationships, see Alfred Schutz, *Collected Papers: The Problem of Social Reality*, Maurice Natanson, ed. (The Hague: Nijhoff, 1962), I, 287 ff.

4. [Q] is used to signify a neutral probe by the interviewer that follows the course of the

last reply, such as "Could you tell me some more about that?" or "How is that?" or "What do you mean?" Other questions by the interviewer are given in full.

5. The King and Queen contest, which takes place at conventions, allows for a patterned evasion of the staring rule. Applicants stand before the crowd in front of the royal platform, and applause is used for selecting the winners. Photography is also allowed during the contest, and no one is permitted to enter the contest unless willing to be photographed. The major reason for this is that this is a major camp event, and contest pictures are used in nudist magazines. At the same time, the large number of photographs sometimes taken by lay photographers (that is, not working for the magazines), makes many nudists uncomfortable by calling into question a nonsexual definition of the situation.

6. I was amazed at how many young female nudists described a similar pattern of extreme clothing modesty among their parents and in their own married life. Included in this group was another nudist model, one of the most photographed of nudist models. Perhaps there are some fruitful data here for cognitive-dissonance psychologists.

7. Cf. Schutz, *op. cit.*, p. 74.

8. For some respondents, the female genitals, because of their hidden character, never become a routinized part of camp nudity; thus their visible exposure does not lose an attention-provoking quality.

9. Compare Harold Garfinkel, "A Conception of, and Experiments with, 'Trust' as a Condition of Stable Concerted Actions," in O. J. Harvey, ed., *Motivation and Social Interaction* (New York: Ronald, 1963).

10. See: Schutz, *op. cit.*, I, 11, for his definition of reciprocity of perspectives.

11. This corresponds with the findings of learning-theory psychologists.

12. For a study of the process of doublethink, see James L. Wilkins, "Doublethink: A Study of Erasure of the Social Past," unpublished doctoral dissertation, Northwestern University, 1964.

13. Cf. Schutz, *op. cit.*, pp. 229 ff.

HOMOSEXUALS AND THE MILITARY

Colin J. Williams and Martin S. Weinberg

Current among sociological conceptions of deviance is an approach that concerns itself less with the attributes of the person or persons said to have violated a social rule than with the character of the reactions of other persons to these attributes and events. This approach, sometimes called the "labeling" approach to deviance, sees the deviant as a social product, the outcome of interaction sequences between labelers and labeled (cf. Becker, 1964a). The questions that are raised by this approach thus concern the behaviors that are labeled as deviant, what the processes are by which the labels are successfully applied or avoided, and what the consequences of such processes are for both labelers and labeled. . . .[1]

"It is important to note that the great majority of homosexuals in the armed forces do complete their service without incident and leave with an honorable discharge."

This paper examines in one particular situation, what the effects of the *deviant's behavior* are on the application of the deviant label. Our focus is the contribution made by the deviant himself to his discovery. To what

From "Being Discovered: A Study of Homosexuals in the Military." *Social Problems*, vol. 18, no. 2, 1970. Copyright © 1971, Colin J. Williams and Martin S. Weinberg. Tables omitted. Reprinted by permission. For the larger study, see *Homosexuals and the Military: A Study of Less than Honorable Discharge* (New York: Harper & Row, 1971). Revised version.

extent is he an active participant in the process? Are there any factors in his behavior which place him more or less "at risk" as regards the scanning operations of control agencies?

The particular situation in question concerns irregular discharge from the military for reasons of homosexual conduct. We shall examine the role played by the individual serviceman in having his sexual status called into question by military authorities. We are aware that the type and extent of surveillance and differential sanctioning activities on the part of these authorities are an important factor in this process.[2] For this study, however, this subject is . . . [suspended]; we propose that it is still possible to get some notion of the deviant's role in the labeling process.

It is important to note that the great majority of homosexuals in the armed forces do complete their service without incident and leave with an honorable discharge. Over 90 percent of all servicemen receive honorable discharges and many homosexuals are included in the majority. In a study done by the Institute for Sex Research in 1967, of some 458 male homosexuals, 214 had served in the military of whom 77 percent had received honorable discharges. Earlier data reported by Simon and Gagnon (1967) indicate that only one-fifth of 550 homosexual males reported any difficulties in the military. Finally, in the present study, of 136 male homosexuals who had served in the military, 76 percent received honorable discharges.[3]

"Most homosexuals, not unlike heterosexuals, pursue sex according to rules which reduce visibility and potential risk."

These should not be considered remarkable findings; to define them as such suggests a stereotyped view of the homosexual as a person having uncontrollable sex drives that demand constant and indiscriminate satisfaction (a view implicitly held by military authorities). Most homosexuals, not unlike most heterosexuals, pursue sex according to rules which reduce visibility and potential risk. The homosexual realizes the consequences of homosexual behavior in the military; as the consequences have similarities to discovery in civilian settings, he is likely to apply the same type of operative rules that he had learned before.

What of those who are discovered? It is our contention that such eventualities are mainly determined by transgressions from those rules, either to their not being learned in the first place or to situational conditions making them difficult to follow.

We considered the following to be possible contributing factors as to whether a homosexual comes to the attention of military authorities.

Homosexual Frequency Prior to Induction into the Military

If a person is frequently engaging in homosexual behavior before he enters the military, then it is reasonable to expect that he is likely to perceive and evaluate the military situation in terms of the opportunities open to a homosexual to a greater degree than do those persons whose homosexual behavior is less frequent prior to their induction. For this reason we expected discovery to be positively related to frequency of homosexual sex before induction.

The Nature of Homosexual Conduct while in the Military

The way in which the homosexual manages his sex in the military was also expected to be related to discovery. We anticipated a positive relationship between discovery and (a) frequency of homosexual sex while in service and (b) the degree to which such sex is engaged in with other military personnel. Those homosexuals who frequently engage in sex while in the military place themselves more at risk than those who have little sex. Having other servicemen as partners also increases the risk of discovery. (For example, in prosecuting these cases, military authorities endeavor to find out the names of all partners of the accused who are also servicemen; this is often done by threats and promises to the accused, or through the inspection of personal effects—letters, diaries, and the like. Also, homosexuals who want to get out of the service and so admit their homosexuality often agree to provide the names of other homosexual servicemen. Cf. Williams and Weinberg 1970.)

The manner in which a homosexual is discovered is also of interest. It is our contention, which we examine later, that manner of discovery is closely associated with the variables that determine discovery in the first place.

METHOD

The research design . . . involved comparing male homosexuals who had been less than honorably discharged from the military with homosexuals who received honorable discharges.

Two sample sources were utilized: the Mattachine Society of New York and the Society for Individual Rights in San Francisco. Both are homophile organizations with large memberships. Using their mailing lists those persons who lived in the New York or San Francisco metropolitan areas were respectively selected out. . . .

A short questionnaire was sent to each of these persons. . . .

From the responses to this questionnaire it was possible to separate out those who received a less than honorable discharge due to homosexuality (hereinafter referred to as the LHD group) and a comparison group of homosexuals who had served in the military but who had received honorable discharges (the HD group). It was also possible to estimate the equivalence of both groups as to the stage of their homosexual careers at the time of their induction into the military. . . . [Of the 136 respondents who had served in the military and who agreed to be interviewed, we interviewed 31 who had received less than honorable discharges (LHD) due to their homosexuality and 32 who had received honorable discharges (HD).]

Included in the personal interview were questions designed to tap the following: the stage of the respondent's homosexual career prior to induction into the military . . . ; his homosexual behavior in the military (how often and with whom); and how his homosexuality was discovered (LHD group only). On both the initial questionnaire and in the interview a large number of other questions that had nothing to do with the military were also included. These were asked to gather data on other aspects of the homosexual's sociopsychological situation.[4] These other questions concealed the fact that military experiences were the main focus of interest and thereby limited some of the bias that could appear, for example, through the creation of a "sad tale." Thus questions on the military were the last questions to be asked.

RESULTS

Manner of Discovery

The homosexuality of those respondents who were discovered came to the attention of military authorities in three main ways. . . .

The most common manner of discovery involved *discovery through another person*. Seventeen of the respondents were discovered in this way (54 percent of the LHD group). This mode of discovery is sometimes related to jealousy, a lovers' tiff, or blackmail.

(R 28 year old salesman. Served in the Navy for almost three years before receiving an Undesirable Discharge. Exclusively homosexual before service.)
I was turned in by a civilian—he was a bartender. The ship came to Monterey and he fell in love with me. I couldn't stand him. . . . He said if I didn't become his lover he'd turn me in. I ignored him. He called ONI (Office of Naval Intelligence) and turned me in.

There were also cases where another serviceman was discovered and persuaded to reveal his previous sexual partners or whoever else he knew in the service to be homosexual. Through threats or promises or through a search of personal effects names are discovered.

(R 45 year old policeman. Served in both the Army and the Navy for a period of about six years receiving an Undesirable Discharge from each service. R exclusively homosexual before entering service.)
I was having an affair with a serviceman on a ship, who kept a diary. He was apprehended with another fellow and through this they got the diary and I was apprehended along with several other people.

This mode of discovery is often linked to many *voluntary admissions*. . . . To get out through voluntary admission the military requires proof of homosexuality. The best proof is to provide the name of a partner who is also a serviceman. Not only can he be interrogated at length by military authorities, but there is the further possibility that he will supply additional names. Six of the 17 cases who were discovered through another person were victims of servicemen who were onetime sexual partners and wished to get out of the service. An example of one such case is as follows:

(R 31 year old male nurse. In the Navy seven years before receiving an Undesirable Discharge. No homosexual experience prior to service.)
A drag queen asked if 'she' could stay in my apartment. I said yes, but don't hustle and don't bring tricks back. But she didn't listen to me. She brought two sailors back and we got into an orgy. They both wanted out of the service and used me as a reference. . . . I denied I was in the Navy but they went ahead and used my name.

Twenty-nine percent of the LHD group (nine cases) were voluntary admissions. The most frequent reason given for seeking discharge was dissatisfaction with military life. Generally absent from such accounts were any pressures that the homosexual might undergo such as fear of exposure or the inability to control sexual tendencies. Such reasoning seems more an influence of stereotypical views of homosexuals, held especially by the military. Also . . . few were unduly bothered by the potential stigma of a less than honorable discharge. Note the following case:

(R 50 year old dress designer-manufacturer. Served in the Army for two and a half years before receiving an Undesirable Discharge. Exclusively homosexual before service.)
I felt I was just wasting time. . . . I wanted out because I was bored to death. . . . I had the advantage of being able to get out as a homosexual. . . . If I had been doing something of value I would have stayed.

The final manner of discovery was through the *homosexual's own indiscretion*. There were five cases (16 percent of the LHD group) where discovery was due to imprudent action on the part of the respondent.

(R 30 years old, hydraulic engineer. After serving two years in the Navy he was released with a General Discharge. No homosexual experience before service.)
It's not a very good story. I was turning gay and one feels he's the only one in that category. It was coming to the surface and I didn't want to control it and had sex and was caught in the locker room.

It is obvious from these cases that the serviceman runs a risk in engaging in homosexual behavior. Not only may he be directly discovered but there is even more of a chance of indirect discovery due to being the "fall guy" in connection with another serviceman or through his name arising in connection with the other's case.

Having discussed the manner in which the homosexual serviceman is

discovered, we turn to the factors associated with the probability of discovery and whether these factors are related to the particular manner of
discovery.

Two sets of variables were conceptualized as related to discovery.
These were: how "homosexual" . . . the respondent was at the time of
his induction and the nature of his homosexual behavior while in the military.

Prior Homosexual Frequency and Discharge Status

In an attempt to reconstruct the comparability of the HD and LHD
groups when they entered the service the respondents were asked on the
initial questionnaire how often they had been engaging in homosexual
sex at the time of their induction. . . . Of those who before induction
were having homosexual sex once a week or more, 69 percent received
less than honorable discharges. Of those who were having homosexual
sex less than once a week, 43 percent received less than honorable discharges. . . .

Other data regarding the stage of the respondent's homosexual career
at the time of induction support the conclusion that those who eventually
received less than honorable discharges were more likely to be further
advanced than were those who eventually received honorable discharges.
[They differed in terms of] . . . the exclusiveness of [their] homosexuality, . . . associating with other homosexuals, . . . and extent of [their]
social activity with other homosexuals. . . .

Sexual Behavior in the Military and Discharge Status

Frequency of sex. . . . Of those engaging in homosexual sex [once a
month or more while in the military,] . . . 61 percent received less than
honorable discharges. Of those engaging in homosexual sex less
frequently, 38 percent received less than honorable discharges. . . .

Type of partner. . . . Respondents were asked whether they had sex
predominantly with military personnel while they were in the armed
forces. . . .

Of those who engaged in homosexual sex predominantly with other servicemen, 82 percent received less than honorable discharges. Of those who did not have predominantly military partners, 35 percent received less than honorable discharges. . . .

In summary, we have seen thus far that not only are those who have more frequent homosexual sex before they enter the military less likely to receive honorable discharges, but that those who have more homosexual sex while in the military and who restrict this sex mostly to other servicemen are also less likely to receive honorable discharges.

There is thus a relationship between discharge status and the character of the respondent's homosexual career at induction as well as his sexual behavior in the military. . . . Goodman's (1964) test for analyzing interaction in contingency tables showed no significant interactions [between these factors].

"Their [homosexuals caught through their own indiscretion] low frequency of sex while in the military is at variance with a frequency-probability model of risk, which would suggest that those discovered this way would be engaging most in the behavior. *All* such cases did, however, report that their frequency was greater than it had been prior to induction. As these respondents were *all* engaging in sex primarily with other military personnel, and were not high in sexual frequency *prior* to induction, it seems reasonable to say that their discovery was mainly due to inexperience in a deviant role. . . ."

The data support out hypotheses regarding factors involved in the probability of discovery. The relationships . . . turned out, however, to be more complex when the *manner of discovery* was considered.

Prior Sexual Frequency and Manner of Discovery

Among those who received less than honorable discharges, what is the relationship between their homosexual frequency at induction and the manner of their discovery? . . . Those who had higher frequencies at induction were more likely to come to the attention of military authorities by their own wish; those who were lower in frequency at induction were more likely to come to the attention of the authorities due to being caught through their own indiscretion. Sexual frequency at induction was not related to discovery through another person. . . .

Sexual Behavior in the Military and Manner of Discovery

Sexual frequency in the military. . . . Those whose in-service activity was high were more likely to be discovered through another person. Those whose sexual behavior in the military was relatively infrequent were more likely to be caught through their own indiscretion or to voluntarily admit to their homosexuality. . . .

Usual type of sex partner while in the military. . . . Those whose sexual partners were predominantly other servicemen were more likely to have been discovered through their own indiscretion, whereas those whose sexual partners were not predominantly other servicemen were more likely to have been discovered through another person. . . .

It is evident that of all variables considered, sexual frequency while in the military shows the strongest relationship to *manner of discovery*. . . . There are three main patterns that led to the discovery of homosexuals by military authorities.

Two groups of LHD respondents had low frequency of sex while in the military. The first of these are those homosexuals caught through their own indiscretion. Their low frequency of sex while in the military is at variance with a frequency-probability model of risk, which would suggest that those discovered this way would be engaging most in the behavior. *All* such cases did, however, report that their frequency was greater than it had been prior to induction. As these respondents were *all* engaging in sex primarily with other military personnel, and were not high in sexual frequency *prior* to induction, it seems reasonable to say that their discovery was mainly due to inexperience in a deviant role; i.e., their indiscretion was not due to the extensity of their behavior but to ignorance of, or disregard for, the safest ways in which to engage in the behavior.

The second group of respondents who had low frequency of sex while in the military provide us with another pattern of discovery. These were those respondents who voluntarily admitted their homosexuality. Contrary to the above group, they tended to score high on sex frequency prior to induction [5] . . . [and were broader] in their choice of partners while in the military. From the interviews it was apparent that their disclosure was motivated by a desire to leave the service, the stigma of the discharge not being the major concern. Being further advanced in their homosexual career at induction seems to have made them less afraid to use their homosexuality to get out of the service.

The final pattern of discovery involves those respondents who differ from the above by having high frequencies of sex while in the military. This group was primarily discovered through another person. Nothing was specified by sexual frequency prior to induction and, as regards type of sex partner, they were represented somewhat less among those having sex primarily with other servicemen. This pattern of discovery was most common to our respondents and represents those who put themselves more at risk regarding involuntary discovery by military authorities.

CONCLUSION

The data reveal the deviant's role in his discovery. On the part of those who vouluntarily admit their deviance, this influence is directly seen; in this case the homosexual uses a self label to gain a social label which can serve him. For those whose discovery is not voluntary, discovery involves placing one's self more at risk due to the frequency of the behavior and imprudent choice of sexual partners. With our respondents there were no cases of a "bum rap." All had engaged in a form of behavior proscribed by the organization in which they were involved.[6] . . .

In this study, official labeling was found to be related to the frequency and character of the deviant's acts. As such, labeling theorists should perhaps make more precise the character of their "unconventional sentimentality."[7] Such a stance does not preclude a recognition of the deviant's role in his own plight; on the other hand, this need not imply the sociologist's endorsement of the policies or processes of control agencies.[8]

NOTES

1. [Editor's note] The original article from which this excerpt is taken includes an extensive theoretical discussion of the "labeling" approach to the study of deviance and the model of the deviant which characterizes this approach.

2. For an indication of some of the variability across time and the influence of other factors, cf. West and Glass (1965).

3. We are aware, of course, that a proportion of homosexuals do not serve at all because they either avoid induction or are rejected at induction. How large this proportion is we do not know for sure. Kinsey (1948) *et al.*, report some figures from the Second World War which state that less than one percent were turned down at induction centers or rejected by draft boards for being "homosexual."

   The only other estimate we could find as to the proportion of those persons who avoid the draft comes from a reported statement by Col. Robert A. Bier, Chief Medical Officer for the National Selective Service System, who in a study of 1,500,000 men called for examination between 1960 and 1962, found that 382,000 (25.4 percent) were granted medical deferments. Psychiatric disorders including homosexuality accounted for 11 percent of the latter. What proportion homosexuality was of psychiatric disorders was not mentioned (*Time Magazine* 1968, p. 15). Estimates after this date must be read with caution as homosexuality apparently has been increasingly used as an excuse to avoid the draft by some of those opposed to the Vietnam War (cf. Anonymous, 1968).

4. These . . . [are] evaluated in terms of the effects of receiving a less than honorable discharge in . . . [other sections of the book].

5. Also, all but one of the voluntary admissions had labeled themselves as homosexual before induction into the military.

6. This is not to say that "bum raps" do not occur. For a description of such cases cf. West and Glass (1965).

7. This is Becker's (1964b:5) phrase, used to describe those who assume, ". . . that the underdog is always right and those in authority always wrong."

8. Conversely, it should be mentioned that attributing a recognition of the role of control agencies in the labeling process by no means implies their moral condemnation.

BIBLIOGRAPHY

Anonymous
   1968 "How Faked Faggotry Can Lead to Your Honorable Discharge." *The Realist* 76(January): 11–14.
Becker, Howard S.
   1964a *Outsiders: Studies in the Sociology of Deviance.* New York: The Free Press of Glencoe.
   1964b *The Other Side: Perspectives on Deviance.* New York: The Free Press of Glencoe.
Goodman, Leo
   1964 "Simple Methods for Analyzing Three Factor Interaction in Contingency Tables." *Journal of the American Statistical Association* 59 (June): 319–362.
Kinsey, Alfred C., Wardell B. Pòmeroy, and Clyde Martin
   1948 *Sexual Behavior in the Human Male.* Philadelphia: W. B. Saunders.
Simon, William and John H. Gagnon
   1967 "Homosexuality: The Formation of a Sociological Perspective." *Journal of Health and Social Behavior* 8(September): 177–185.

Time Magazine
   1968   91(March 15): 15.
West, Louis Jolyon and Albert J. Glass
   1965   "Sexual Behavior and the Military Law." Pp. 250–272 in Ralph Slovenko (ed.), *Sexual Behavior and the Law.* Springfield, Illinois: Charles C Thomas.
Williams, Colin J. and Martin S. Weinberg
   1970   "The Military: Its Processing of Accused Homosexuals." *American Behavioral Scientist* 14(November/December): 203–217.

21. Gebhard lecturing at the Institute's Summer Program in Human Sexuality. 1974. *Dellenback*

22. Bell meeting with group facilitators before the attitude reassessment workshop. *Dellenback*

23–26. Institute staff (Gebhard, Weinberg, Williams, Bell) who, along with invited guest speakers, provided the summer program lectures. *Dellenback*

MALE HOMOSEXUALS:
THEIR PROBLEMS AND ADAPTATIONS

Martin S. Weinberg and Colin J. Williams

We are interested in studying the social correlates of the adaptations the homosexual makes to the heterosexual world, to the homosexual world, and to potential psychological problems. We conceptualize such relationships through the utilization of the societal reaction perspective as formulated in contemporary sociology.

Three societies—the United States, the Netherlands, and Denmark— were chosen so as to provide variation in societal reaction. The United States, in terms of its laws and public opinions, is one of the most anti-homosexual of modern Western societies. The Netherlands and Denmark, on the other hand, are relatively liberal in this regard.

[In our book,] we provide ethnographies of the homosexual's situation in these societies and, more specifically, his situation in New York, San Francisco, Amsterdam, and Copenhagen. For each locale we describe the social institutions which surround the homosexual. Following these descriptions, we present an account of the method and the manner in which respondents were obtained for a questionnaire study. Data on the characteristics of the samples are given as well as an analysis of the types of homosexual obtained from each of our sample sources—homophile mail organizations, homosexual bars, and homosexual clubs.

[In this excerpt, we go directly to] . . . the results of our questionnaire study, looking first at the differences found between homosexuals from the American and the European locales. After examining the locale differences, . . . [we] examine similarities. Here our cross-cultural data provide replications for the United States findings. First, we compare our homosexual samples with general population samples from the same locales. Next, we examine the correlates of self-other processes and of passing and being known about. We then examine the relationship between the respondents' adaptations and their degree of social involvement with other homosexuals, exclusiveness of homosexual orientation, age, occupation, living arrangements, religious background, religiosity, and race. In these comparisons the data are organized in the tripartite manner outlined . . . [above]: patterns of relating to the heterosexual world, the homosexual world, and psychological problems.

LOCALE

. . . [We] compared American, Dutch, and Danish homosexuals in order to determine the effects of locale [and corresponding variations in societal reactions toward homosexuality] on social and psychological dimensions. We compared homosexuals in the four major cities that we studied—New York, San Francisco, Amsterdam, and Copenhagen—and those in outlying areas as well. We found European homosexuals to be more at ease with, and less threatened by, the heterosexual world than are American homosexuals. The European homosexuals are less secretive about their homosexuality and more known about, and they anticipate less discrimination and rejection from heterosexuals.

European homosexuals are also more involved in the public aspects of homosexual life, for example, in attending homosexual clubs and bars, and are higher in acculturation. . . . Moreover, more European homosexuals neutralize any responsibility for their homosexuality. This is perhaps best viewed as a cultural phenomenon, reflecting European theories of human behavior rather than being specifically related to the homosexual milieu.

The most unexpected result is that, contrary to the widely held belief that greater societal rejection leads to greater psychological problems, virtually no such differences appeared between American and European homosexuals. The only exception was that homosexuals living outside the major cities feel somewhat less guilt, shame, or anxiety regarding their homosexuality in Europe than in America. . . .

. . . Perhaps the societal reaction model we have employed is too simple to do justice to the complexity of the situation. We argue (and the data suggest) that there are no major differences among the three societies with regard to our respondents' psychological problems, despite differences in the socio-cultural reactions to homosexuals. (Differences between our homosexual and general population samples within each society—which are meaningful with respect to this question—are examined . . . [next]; these results also support the present argument.)

We offer four points with regard to this model and our research. First, this model implies that societal rejection and psychological problems are related in a linear manner, with increasing "amounts" of rejection followed by a similar monotonic increase in psychological problems. It may be, instead, that after a certain degree of rejection is reached—be it official reactions in the United States or the . . . [tolerance, without] acceptance in Europe—further increments of rejection may not increase the number or severity of noticeable negative effects. (Of course, we exclude the most extreme forms of persecution of homosexuals, for example, as practiced in Nazi Germany where homosexuals were placed in concentration camps.) . . .

Second, perhaps rejection itself is not *directly* the major cause of the homosexual's stress. . . . The social features of homosexual . . . [life styles], as practiced in . . . [all] three societies, [and not rejection per se, may be the major factor in producing stress]. . . .

Third, even if negative societal reactions do produce stress, it may also be that in each country homosexuals have worked out ways of adapting to these problems, perhaps with equal success, which again would account for a lack of difference in psychological problems. Homosexuals in the United States, due to a broad-based rejection, make more use of subcultural solutions. Homosexuals in Europe, due to a less pervasive rejection, rely perhaps on other modes of solution, for example, official intervention. Both modes may be effective . . . , given the particular problem; the results . . . could be a lack of cross-cultural differences in psychological problems.

Finally, the character of our samples might preclude a fair test of the model. The samples are, most likely, not representative of those homosexuals who are the most covert and who are inactive in the subculture.

And it could be precisely among these homosexuals that the greatest cross-cultural differences in psychological problems exist. These are the homosexuals who are perhaps the most affected by societal reactions, since they lack the mitigating elements the homosexual subculture might provide. With our own respondents we reran indices of psychological problems by country holding constant the extent of involvement with other homosexuals. We still find no differences among countries, however. . . .

". . . social scientists often seem to forget the tremendous human potential for adaptation, even to the most strained situations. People commonly use techniques such as compartmentalization to divert attention from conflicts and thus to facilitate adaptation. Homosexuals are no exception. The evidence presented . . . suggests that many homosexuals do become routinized to 'being homosexual' so that occupying a 'deviant status' need not necessarily intrude upon their day-to-day functioning."

HOMOSEXUAL-GENERAL POPULATION COMPARISONS

To further examine societal reaction theory, samples of homosexuals and of the general male population were compared in terms of psychological problems. Our expectation was that the former would have more problems, but that the magnitude of the differences between the two groups would be less in Europe, where there is more tolerance of homosexuality. Generally, these notions were not supported. On the basis of these findings, even though they are only suggestive (due to the small size of our European general samples), we propose that societal reaction theory be further amplified to [include the following.] . . .

First, sexual orientation is not necessarily strongly correlated with psychological problems, even in a society generally rejecting of homosexuality. Both heterosexuals and homosexuals engage in a nonsexual, daily round of life and face a multitude of nonsexual situations that affect their psychological well-being. For example, the extent to which a man has psychological problems may be affected by job frustrations. Moreover, even in the sexual realm, there are heterosexual behaviors—for example, extramarital sex—that may be as guilt- and anxiety-producing as being homosexual.

Second, social scientists often seem to forget the tremendous human potential for adaptation, even to the most strained situations. People commonly use techniques such as compartmentalization to divert attention from conflicts and thus to facilitate adaptation.[1] Homosexuals are no exception. The evidence . . . suggests that many homosexuals do become routinized to "being homosexual" so that occupying a "deviant status" need not necessarily intrude upon their day-to-day functioning.

Finally, the whole question of the homosexual's psychological status is typically raised from a heterosexual point of view. Commentators on homosexuals' psychological problems usually attribute powers to both sexual orientation and societal reaction that are universalized and exaggerated.[2] Oversimplifying and thus dehumanizing the homosexual, they deny him the recuperative strategies that most people use in dealing with "problems." In terms of this logic, then, it follows that the homosexual *must* be psychologically maladjusted. (Here we are talking about those commentators who naïvely employ the societal reaction perspective; for those employing a "pathology perspective," such maladjustment is, of course, antecedent to and inherent in homosexuality. . . .)

Also, such commentators treat homosexuals as a unitary and homogeneous type. We believe, instead, that there are some types of male homosexuals who are on the average better adjusted than the general male population as well as some who are less well adjusted.[3]

In all three countries homosexuals do score lower in happiness and faith in others. This . . . [may be] interpreted as being congruent with societal reaction theory without invalidating our points about the abilities of humans to adjust. . . .

SELF-OTHER PROCESSES

Focusing on the social psychological aspects of societal reaction theory, . . . [we] examined the relationships between various aspects of the homosexual's looking glass self and his psychological well-being. First, we considered how the homosexual perceives others as appraising him. We found that the more negative the perceived appraisal of others, the greater the homosexual's psychological problems. These relationships hold regardless of the significance of the appraiser to the homosexual, perhaps because rejection from anyone symbolizes society's more global rejection of the homosexual. Also, feeling accepted by either heterosexuals or homosexuals, regardless of their significance, is correlated with psychological well-being.

Second, we looked at various situations and experiences less directly reflecting the perceived appraisals of others, and which also can augment or diminish a homosexual's sense of social competence. Thus, infrequent sex, never having had an exclusive relationship, and loneliness are related to psychological problems. Furthermore, interpersonal awkwardness and effeminacy are also related to psychological problems.

Finally, we evaluated more direct forms of self-labeling, especially those that signify the respondent's acceptance of the homosexual label. Acculturation (the routinization of secondary homosexual behaviors), normalization (viewing homosexuality from an acceptable interpretive framework), and commitment (a reluctance to give up homosexuality) all are . . . [positively] related to psychological . . . [well-being].

PASSING AS HETEROSEXUAL

. . . [With regard to societal reactions, we also] explored the problematic relationships between passing, being known about, and psychological well-being. Passing [as heterosexual] seems to be a more complex phenomenon than is generally assumed. Although homosexuals who behave in a secretive manner do show greater psychological problems than those who do not, it does not seem that passing per se leads to great psychological strain. Instead, those psychological problems which appear seem to be, by and large, more directly associated with the factors which lead to passing. Thus, worry about exposure and anticipated discrimination against the known homosexual are associated with psychological problems and with certain aspects of relating to the homosexual world. . . .

Compared with less known about homosexuals, the more known about are not found to have greater psychological problems, as many would expect. Thus, being known about is not the "end of the world," as many homosexuals fear. In fact, the more known about homosexuals seem to experience less stress with regard to the heterosexual world, indicating that the covert homosexual's fears of exposure may be exaggerated. . . .

SOCIAL INVOLVEMENT WITH OTHER HOMOSEXUALS

. . . [We] examined the effect of social involvement with other homosexuals on the way the homosexual manages his homosexuality. Compared with those low in involvement, those who are higher are less threatened by the heterosexual world. They anticipate less rejection and discrimination from heterosexuals and are less likely to impute negative feelings to them. This . . . [may be] explained in terms of the learning experiences from other homosexuals whereby stereotypes of a universally hostile heterosexual world are replaced by a more subtle, less generalized, and more realistic appreciation of the situation. Such social involvement also provides models of homosexuals who successfully manage a deviant public identity as well as provide a cushion or retreat to fall back on if heterosexual relationships prove problematic. Thus, homosexuals who are more socially involved with other homosexuals are less concerned with passing, less fearful of exposure, and less bothered by labeling. In addition, they are more known about.

With regard to the homosexual world, homosexuals with greater social involvement are more likely to have had an exclusive homosexual relationship and to have higher frequencies of sex. This . . . [may be] explained by seeing social involvement as providing opportunities for meeting potential partners.

". . . those higher in social involvement [with other homosexuals] report fewer psychological problems. This . . . [may be] seen as a function of the social psychological support coming from other homosexuals and the effect of this support on self-image."

Those higher in such involvement are also more acculturated. Again, association . . . [may be] viewed as providing a socializing situation whereby, for example, certain practices could be learned and their meaning reinterpreted. The greater homosexual commitment of those higher in social involvement with other homosexuals . . . .[is] further seen as a product of the rewards that such association can bring.

Finally, those higher in social involvement report fewer psychological problems. This . . . [may be] seen as a function of the social psychological support coming from other homosexuals and the effect of this support on self-image. . . .

BISEXUALITY

. . . Respondents who view themselves as bisexual were compared with those who consider themselves as more homosexual. Bisexuals were found to be more likely to associate with heterosexuals and less likely to associate with homosexuals and to score lower in acculturation. Furthermore, they report themselves to be more concerned with passing and to be less known about as homosexual. However, the preponderance of psychological problems which many commentators attribute to bisexuals is not supported by our data. On only one psychological measure did we find a difference—bisexuals report more guilt, shame, or anxiety over being homosexual. Thus, they do not appear to be a "product of abject confusion," as Cory and LeRoy suggest.[4] Homosexuality may be somewhat peripheral to their general existence, and the various social features of homosexual life may simply hold little interest for them. Thus, their sexual orientation may be of little concern or cause few problems in their everyday life. . . .

AGE

As a whole, our older homosexuals are less involved in the homosexual world, have homosexual sex less frequently, and are more likely to be living alone. These findings . . . [may be] interpreted as reflecting the social, psychological, and sexual changes that accompany aging among homosexuals.

Contrary to popular beliefs, however, our older homosexuals are no worse off than our younger homosexuals on various psychological dimensions, and are, on some dimensions, better off. This finding is in accord with trends found in the general population.

The stereotype which portrays the homosexual as decreasing in psychological well-being as he gets older results, we believe, from incorrectly attributing or overgeneralizing meanings to the socio-sexual situation of the older homosexual which he himself does not experience. . . .

OCCUPATIONAL STATUS

. . . We considered the way in which the homosexual's . . . [occupational status] affects the management of his homosexuality. Being homosexual is a potential threat to the investments and rewards associated with a higher-status occupation. Thus, it was expected that homosexuals in higher-status occupations would be more discreet in their homosexuality, pass more, and be less involved in the overt homosexual world than would homosexuals in lower-status occupations. Our results were as expected. Homosexuals in higher-status occupations are less known about, more worried about exposure, and more concerned with passing. . . . Homosexuals in high-status occupations also report more social involvement with heterosexuals and feel more accepted by them. Finally, homosexuals in higher-status occupations more often report that they feel closer to a heterosexual of the same class than to a homosexual from a lower class, indicating that for them class identification may override identification based on sexual orientation.

With respect to relating to the homosexual world, homosexuals from higher-status occupations are less willing to associate with known homosexuals, which we interpret as indicative of their greater discretion.

Finally, with regard to most psychological problems, we found no difference between homosexuals in higher-status occupations and those in lower-status occupations. However, homosexuals in high-status occupations report more self-acceptance and faith in others. These results contradict notions that homosexuals in high-status occupations experience greater psychological maladjustment [due to their greater fear of societal reactions]. They seemingly reflect the self-esteem and other social psychological advantages that accrue from a high-status occupation, regardless of one's sexual orientation. . . .

LIVING ARRANGEMENTS

. . . The relationships of homosexuals' living arrangements to their life styles and problems were examined.

Homosexuals with homosexual roommates were found to be the most open about their homosexuality and the least socially involved with heterosexuals. They are the most integrated into the homosexual world and show the greatest psychological well-being. Homosexuals with homosexual roommates seem to be the most effectively insulated from negative responses by heterosexuals and from psychological stress.

Homosexuals who live alone are not outstanding on any of our measures, generally scoring between those with homosexual roommates and those with other living arrangements.

Homosexuals who live with their parents are the youngest, high in worry about their homosexuality being exposed, and the least likely to have close friends. They also show the most psychological problems.

Homosexuals living with wives are the most integrated into the heterosexual world and the least integrated into the homosexual world, especially the social aspects of the homosexual world. They report the most guilt, shame, or anxiety regarding their homosexuality but do not stand out in terms of other psychological problems. . . .

RELIGION

We found no general relationship between the life styles or psychological problems of homosexuals and their religious backgrounds. . . .

Kinsey and his associates found that religious affiliation is not so strongly correlated with sexual behavior as is religiosity. They note that

> [the] differences between religiously devout persons and religiously inactive persons of the same faith are much greater than the differences between two equally devout groups of different faiths.[5]

In the next . . . [section], we examine religiosity and its relationship to the respondent's management of his homosexuality.

RELIGIOSITY

Because the Judeo-Christian tradition condemns homosexuality, homosexuals who ascribe importance to religion face a dilemma. . . . We examined the situation of the religious homosexual and the success of accommodations between his religious beliefs and his homosexuality. Measuring religiosity as the personal importance attributed to formal religion, we found that religious homosexuals are less known about, more concerned with passing, more worried about exposure, and more likely to attribute importance to the opinion of others. Homosexuals for whom religion is more important are also less socially involved with other homosexuals and less likely to have experienced all the sexual practices common among homosexuals, are more likely to believe they were born homosexual, and are the least committed to their homosexuality.

"The stereotype which portrays the homosexual as decreasing in psychological well-being as he gets older results, we believe, from incorrectly attributing or overgeneralizing meanings to the socio-sexual situation of the older homosexual which he himself does not experience."

It was expected that the conflict between religiosity and sexuality would result in greater psychological problems for religious homosexuals. Other than showing greater guilt, shame, or anxiety after their first homosexual experience, however, this is not the case. We found that many religious homosexuals reinterpret religion as *not* violated by homosexuality. And among the most religious homosexuals, whom we had expected to show the greatest psychological problems, such an interpretation can neutralize the negative psychological effects of their dilemma. Thus, we found that some psychological problems are correlated with the perception that homosexuality violates religion, but that this relationship holds only among the most religious respondents. . . .

RACE

Comparisons between black and white homosexuals in the United States showed that blacks expect less negative reaction to their homosexuality and anticipate less discrimination from other people on account of it. In addition, blacks are more known as homosexual and less concerned with passing as heterosexual. . . . [We] suggest that this is related to the less puritanical attitudes of blacks and the greater tolerance of homosexuals by the black community.

Blacks in our sample more often had their first homosexual experience at an early age, are more likely to be having an exclusive homosexual relationship, and, when living with another homosexual, are more likely to be lovers with their roommate.

Finally, with regard to psychological measures, we found only one difference—that black homosexuals are somewhat more self-accepting. It seems to be the case, however, that among our homosexuals, race is generally uncorrelated with our psychological measures. . . .

NOTES

1. Cf., for example, William J. Goode, "A Theory of Role Strain," *American Sociological Review* 25 (August 1960), p. 486.

2. Regarding the actual nature of societal reactions to homosexuals, which are often very mild, see John I. Kitsuse, "Societal Reaction to Deviant Behavior," *Social Problems* 9 (Winter 1962), pp. 247–56.

3. Such typological delineations are beyond the scope of this work but will be investigated in a future Institute for Sex Research volume. Alan P. Bell and Martin S. Weinberg, *The Development and Management of Homosexuality* (tentative title).

4. Donald Webster Cory and John P. LeRoy, *The Homosexual and His Society* (New York: Citadel, 1963), p. 61.

5. Alfred C. Kinsey, Wardell B. Pomeroy, and Clyde E. Martin, *Sexual Behavior in the Human Male* (Philadelphia: W. B. Saunders Company, 1948), p. 486.

OUR MONOGRAPH SERIES 8
The Spectrum of Human Sexuality

The Institute also sponsors a monograph series, *Studies in Sex and Society*, consisting of works done by authors who are not Institute staff members. Originally designed for works based on Institute materials, the series has been expanded to include other important studies of sex as well.

This chapter includes selections from three books in the monograph series. The first is from *The Other Victorians: A Study of Sexuality and Pornography in Mid-Nineteenth-Century England* by Steven Marcus. A former professor of English and comparative literature at Columbia University, Marcus draws on writings from the Victorian period to highlight the discrepancies between private sexual practices and official views of sexuality. In addition, Marcus looks at the structure of pornographic writing and the role of pornography in supplementing social history.

Next is an excerpt from a book of articles edited by Donald Marshall and Robert Suggs, *Human Sexual Behavior: Variations in the Ethnographic Spectrum*. In this selection, John Messenger, an anthropologist and folklorist at Ohio State University, examines sexual attitudes in a repressive rural Irish community.

Finally, Picasso's sexual imagery is analyzed by Robert Rosenblum of the Institute of Fine Arts at New York University. Rosenblum's analysis comes from *Studies in Erotic Art*, edited by Theodore Bowie and Cornelia Christenson. Reflecting Kinsey's conviction that art provides important insights into human sexuality, this book brings together papers presented in 1967 at the Indiana University Conference on Erotic Art.

THE OTHER VICTORIANS

Steven Marcus

THE SECRET LIFE

My Secret Life consists of eleven uniform volumes, the whole coming to some 4,200 pages. It is in small crown octavo and is printed on hand-made ribbed paper. The title page of each volume bears the imprint, "Amsterdam. Not for publication." There is no date, but we can be reasonably certain that it was printed over a period of time in which 1890 can stand as a midpoint. . . .

The eleven volumes of *My Secret Life* are a unique document. They are the sexual memoirs of a Victorian gentleman who began to memorialize himself at a very early age and who continued to do so for more than forty years. . . .

Since *My Secret Life* is the most important document of its kind about Victorian England, we might use it to test the thesis which holds that writings of a sexual nature are of a unique value or importance as social history. In other words, what in the way of social history do we learn from such a work? Does it contain matters of general importance that have been suppressed, overlooked, or forgotten by historians? [1] In the first place, a work of more than 4,000 pages which concentrates remorselessly on one image, the human body—its organs, functions, and operations—is bound to provide a host of details about how that image, or

From "The Secret Life-I" and "The Secret Life-II" in *The Other Victorians: A Study of Sexuality and Pornography in Mid-Nineteenth-Century England.* Copyright © 1964, 1965, 1966, by Steven Marcus. Reprinted by permission of Basic Books and Weidenfeld & Nicolson Ltd.

body, is managed, how its biology is dealt with. *My Secret Life* tells us a good deal about the excremental functions, and about the conduct of personal hygiene in Victorian England. For example, we learn that, before the middle of the century, in such places of public resort as Hampton Court Park there were no toilets. Men and women, including gentlemen and ladies, would go off into the bushes, to "some vacant place on which dead leaves and sweepings were shot down," and relieve themselves. . . . Similarly, we learn that until fairly late in the [nineteenth] century the London streets were a veritable barnyard. . . .

"The first thing we learn, . . . is what did *not* get into the Victorian novel, what was by common consent and convention left out or suppressed."

Since the author describes literally hundreds of his experiences with prostitutes, *My Secret Life* provides us with a good deal of information about how part of sexual life in Victorian England was organized or institutionalized.[2] . . . If one wanted to take a prostitute—or any woman—to some place indoors, "accommodation houses" of various degrees of costliness were to be found in every part of London. . . . The author is extremely knowledgeable about the economics of sexuality in the England of his time and is as precise—and as interested—in his notations of costs as he is in his descriptions of physiology.

. . . *My Secret Life* shows us that amid and underneath the world of Victorian England as we know it—and as it tended to represent itself to itself—a real, secret social life was being conducted, the secret life of sexuality. Every day, everywhere, people were meeting, encountering one another, coming together, and moving on. And although it is true that the Victorians could not help but know of this, almost no one was reporting on it; the social history of their own sexual experiences was not part of the Victorians' official consciousness of themselves or of their society.

. . . As simple social history, then, the facts and details of *My Secret Life* are interesting and useful, and there can be no question that we should know them. They add to and thicken our sense of the Victorian reality, and they move it further ahead in the direction toward which much modern historical research has already tended. Taken by themselves, however, the details and revelations of *My Secret Life* do not immediately or automatically fall into new patterns of generalization. Something must be done to them before their meanings can emerge.

In this connection, *My Secret Life* is perhaps most interesting if we consider it in relation to the Victorian novel. Its material bears directly on both the concerns or interests of the great Victorian novelists and on their ways of representing those interests.

. . . The first thing we learn, . . . is what did *not* get into the Victorian novel, what was by common consent and convention left out or suppressed. . . .

There is no doubt that the Victorian conventions of censorship had a severely limiting effect on the range of the novel. Having accepted censorship on explicit sexual statements, however, the Victorian novelists had to find less direct means of communicating the sexual component in the situations they described. . . . The first use to which *My Secret Life* can be put, therefore, is as an additional context for the study of Victorian literature. To which we must add the proviso that *My Secret Life* is itself a piece of literature. Like a novel, it is the product of the mind of a single man, and whatever authority we wish to ascribe to it must be exercised within the framework of that definition.

. . . Another way of putting the matter is to say that a work such as *My Secret Life* falls within the scope of G. M. Young's statement that "the real, central theme of History is not what happened, but what people felt about it when it was happening." That is to say, *My Secret Life* is important by virtue of its authenticity. It is the authentic record of what one man perceived, felt, saw, believed, and wanted to believe. Regarding it within the context of social history, we understand it as being informed at all points by a consciousness which is subjective and historical.

. . . One of the central interests of *My Secret Life* is to be found in the way it embodies and presents certain social attitudes. Chief among these attitudes are those which make up the nexus of sex, class, and money. They form an inseparable matrix in the author's mind and provide, in an external way, the unifying theme of this document. The vast majority of the author's experiences are had with three kinds of women—domestic servants, girls from the working or lower classes, and prostitutes of varying degrees of expensiveness. . . . Most of the women whom he knows sexually, therefore, come from a single and fairly homogeneous population, since it is safe to say that both servants and prostitutes were by and large recruited from the same parts of society, the agricultural and urban laboring or working classes.

. . . For him the absolute reality of class, its "naturalness," is as self-evident, inevitable, and unquestionable as his own sexual drives.[3] The two are inextricably joined, and he experiences his own sexuality, as well as the sexuality of women, in class terms. . . .

The author's accounts of his experiences with servants are only special instances of a general case. The nexus formed by his attitudes toward sex, class, and money constitutes the very tissue of his sensibility and is actively present in almost every story he tells.

. . . The author of *My Secret Life* underwent a development in his sexual beliefs and attitudes that can be called revolutionary; at the same time, and contrary to what one might expect, these developments seemed to find no corollary or further consequences in other and adjacent areas of social and moral belief and behavior. In this experience, he was anticipating in a significant way the future development of his own and our society. We have in our own time been witness to a sexual revolution which has also been split off from what might have been expected to accompany it—impulses of a social revolutionary kind. The reasons for this occurrence are of the profoundest kind, and have to do with such immense matters as the economic structure and history of our society, with the course of development that the Industrial Revolution pursued in the West, with the development of our forms of parliamentary and social democracy, and even with the confrontation of communist and capitalist systems of society. . . . It is still necessary to note, however, that the structure and history of modern Western society made possible, or legitimized, the revolution in sexual beliefs and behavior through which we are now living; conversely, those same forces have steadily worked to reduce both the possibility and the legitimacy of those impulses that have historically found expression in thought and action of a socially radical nature. . . .

The third component in the nexus, money, is much easier to understand. Like class, it has become fused with almost all the author's sexual responses. Since most of his experiences are with prostitutes or poor women, money is actively present throughout the work and is in fact one of its principal characters. Money in *My Secret Life* is what money is in the nineteenth-century novel or in *Das Kapital*. It is the universal commodity that has the power of converting all other things into commodities, or that all other things can be converted into. The author is uncommonly careful and precise in his accounts, and never fails to put down how much he did or did not pay or to record the nature of the transaction that went on between himself and a woman. In the course of these descriptions, we learn a good deal of casual social history—which mostly amounts to the conclusion that the price of sex, like the price of most other commodities, underwent a gradual but steady inflation as the century advanced. . . .

The author's attitude toward the relation of money to sex is not different from his attitude toward the relation of class to sex. He accepts its existence as part of the order of nature and happily makes use of it.

"One of the central interests of *My Secret Life* is to be found in the way it embodies and presents certain social attitudes."

. . . The author asserts that the connection between sex and money was a normative one, an assumed value, among all classes in Victorian England. This is generally in accord with what we know from Victorian literature and other sources. . . . Although the author serenely accepts this norm, his attitude . . . presents an interesting combination of qualities. It is . . . both brutal and humane at once. It is brutal in its unwavering acceptance of such a moral system and in the cynicism that such an acceptance entails. It is humane in its sympathy for the poor and its sense of the difficulties involved in matters of sexual choice. This tone which combines brutality and humaneness is the characteristic tone of the entire document and is, I think, unique to it.

. . . One of the principal components in male sexuality is the desire for power, the desire to dominate. In modern society, money is one of the two or three most important instruments of personal power, and the association of sex and money through the medium of power is an inevitable one. Money operates in still another way to further the author's sense of power. It interposes itself between the author and the women whose bodies he is both paying for and seeking to enter. It creates an even further distance—in both a social and psychic sense—between the two partners to this transaction, and turns the women into commodities, objects—to use the classic term once more, a process of "objectification" occurs. The dehumanization which such an experience incurs is always evident, on both sides of the transaction. It is only one of the many paradoxes inherent in this relation that a man seeking the most intimate union with another person should do so by creating the maximum possible distance between them, or that the fullest expression of his inmost humanity should be achieved only through circumstances which are bound to depersonalize both himself and his partner. We begin to unpack the paradox when we realize that the author is not actually seeking union with another person. He is seeking to fulfill or act out certain fantasies; and the success of such a project depends on the degree to which he can dominate or control his sexual partners, the degree to which he can turn them into objects. . . .

The chief conscious or explicit intention of *My Secret Life* is to be honest. The author tells us at the outset that it was his determination "to write my private life freely as to fact, and in the spirit of the lustful acts done by me, or witnessed; it is written therefore with absolute truth, and without any regard for what the world calls decency. Decency and voluptuousness in its fullest acceptance cannot exist together; one would kill the other. . . ." There can be no doubt that the author does make a considerable effort of honesty—in reporting on thoughts and attitudes as well as in recording behavior.

. . . We tend to think of honesty as invigorating; we forget that often it can be depressing. The literature of sex, in all its branches, is not a particularly joyful or happy literature. It is on the whole rather grim and sad; even at its most intense moments there is something defeated in it. Something in the nature of its subject, one may reflect, dictates this prevailing tone. . . .

"There is . . . the ubiquitous projection of the male sexual fantasy onto the female response—the female response being imagined as identical with the male. In this fantasy, women have orgasms as quickly, easily, and spontaneously as men, and tend to be ready for sexual activity at almost any time."

Surrounded by darkness and ignorance, and living amid what he took to be a conspiracy of silence in regard to sexual matters, the author often wonders about his own oddness or singularity. . . .

. . . There is little doubt that, however puzzled he may often be by

his own behavior, he is unwilling to think about it beyond a certain
point. It is as if he had somehow correctly surmised that reasoning about
himself, inquiring into his motives, pursuing explanations would tend to
deprive him of pleasure or endanger his equilibrium. That is to say, the
exposure of his behavior and the fantasies embodied in it to the processes
of reason would be tantamount either to a questioning of their validity or
justification, or to a renunciation. We should also observe that he shares
this disinclination for inquiring into reasons and motives with . . . almost all the literature of sexuality and with pornography itself—and that
we can now conclude that this attitude is characteristic of the last pre-
psychological epoch of modern culture. Conscious of psychology, and
even regarding his own work as a "contribution" to it, he is yet afraid
and unable to psychologize.

    . . . He himself is acutely aware of the limitations imposed by such
conditions. Late in the work . . . he goes on to say, in what seems to me
the crowning sentence of the book, that although he has written at endless length about "love's mysteries . . . there is nothing mysterious
about it excepting in the psychology." In addition to much insight, there
is much merit in such a statement, in the author's being able to make it.
Bound within the world of the physiological, the world of organs and actions, and having lived his life as if the mystery existed there and could
be discovered there, he is yet able to see that the mystery exists somewhere else. And he enables us to see a further truth about his own writing and about pornography in general, a truth which helps us to understand why it is such a cheerless, frustrated, and defeated kind of
literature. Where it seeks mystery, none exists. Where it seeks to discover, nothing is to be discovered. What it looks for cannot be found.
The mystery is that there is no mystery.

    . . . The author conceives of his own sexuality, and of male sexuality
in general, as almost pure aggression. In this conception, woman is an
object who must be dominated; she must be made by the male "to sub-
mit to his will in copulation." She should at first resist, and her resistance must be overcome by the impulsive power of the male, by that
power itself and by the communication and installation of that lust in
herself. The author also experiences his own sexual drive as a kind of
direct demonic possession. When he is overtaken by his desires, he says,
he is almost deranged, out of control. . . .

In attesting to the demonic power of his sexual drives, the author is doing more than making a confession of weakness or depravity. He describes his lust as "strong, unreflecting, unconscious, and unmanageable," and, after rehearsing an episode in which this series of "lewd and sequential impulses" carried him very far indeed, he reflects that the whole thing seems to him now "a psychological phenomenon, and nothing more." This is his way of saying that he doesn't understand what has happened to him or what he did, and we can sympathize with his bewilderment.

. . . Although it is true that the author is able to abandon himself to his instinctual drives in a demonic and archaic way, it is equally true that he must pay a price for this liberty. This price is exacted in the severe limitation of the emotions that he is able to feel, in the restricted range of his responses to other persons, in his extremely weak capacities for establishing relations with others. His emotional anesthesia is never more apparent than it is immediately after he has successfully seduced a woman. . . .

"The form of a pornographic work . . . has only an excuse for a beginning, but once having begun it goes on and on and on and ends nowhere. . . ."

It should . . . be noted that the general style, tone, and method of *My Secret Life* share certain properties in common with the style, tone, and method of pornography itself. And we must finally conclude that in *My Secret Life* we are confronted with a document that is an authentic account of experience that is also at the same time in certain ways pornography. At this stage in history the two modes overlap and are sometimes identical. Certain of the similarities between the writing of *My Secret Life* and pornographic writing are worth considering. There is first the ubiquitous projection of the male sexual fantasy onto the female response—the female response being imagined as identical with the male. In this fantasy, women have orgasms as quickly, easily, and spontaneously as men, and tend to be ready for sexual activity at almost any time. Their sexual needs are as impetuous as men's, if not more so, and there is the usual accompanying fantasy that they ejaculate during orgasm. These fantasies are connected with the focus or concentration upon organs, particularly the genital organs, although no area of the body is excluded from sexualization—indeed the whole fantasy of the highly excited woman has as one of its meanings that the woman herself is an organ; with the penis in her she becomes an extension of it, an expansion of it, a reassurance of its continued existence, and a witness to its supreme power. Regarding women as bodies and then finally as organs results in their abstraction and depersonalization. In both *My Secret Life* and pornography, it is often extremely difficult to distinguish one woman from another; finally they are all the same, although the search for variety and the quantitative accumulation of experiences mechanically persists. And there is also in both the final absence of almost all emotions except the aggressive ones.

Both kinds of writing tend to regard the world as a pornotopia. Reality is conceived as the scene of exclusively sexual activities and human and social institutions are understood to exist only insofar as they are conducive to further sexual play. It makes sense, then, that the form taken by the life of the author resembles the form of a typical piece of pornographic literature. Beginning rather simply, it goes on to gradually increasing elaboration and freedom and to a considerable mechanical complexity of combinations. This development is accompanied by the steady emergence of the forbidden and the systematic violation of prohibitions and taboos. The whole process culminates in the desire for totality and the effort to achieve it, either in action or fantasy; in this culminating expression of infantile megalomania, we have the beginning, and the desire to return to the beginning, making itself felt at the very end.

But it is not only the form of the author's life that resembles the form often taken by pornography; the form of his book as well resembles the form of a pornographic work of fiction. It has only an excuse for a beginning, but once having begun it goes on and on and on and ends nowhere; it really has no ending, since one of its cardinal principles of existence is repetition. This endless repetition, this repetition without a real termination, indicates to us again that, on at least one of its sides, this kind of fantasy is both a sad and frustrating mode of either experience or expression. Obsessed with the idea of infinite pleasure, the author does not permit the counter-idea of genuine gratification, and of an end to pleasure, to develop. And this absence helps us further to understand why it is that pornography is so profoundly, and by nature, anti-literature and anti-art. One of the few useful literary definitions is that form consists in the arousal in the reader of certain expectations and the fulfillment of those expectations. But the idea of fulfillment inevitably carries in its train the ideas of completion, of gratification, of an ending—and the pornographic fantasy resists such notions. The ideal pornographic novel, as everyone knows, would go on forever—it would have no ending. If it has no ending in the sense of completion or gratification, then it can have no form; and it is this confinement to the kind of form that art or literature must by nature take which is noxious to the idea of pornography. We see here one more reason for the opposition of pornography to literature.

Nevertheless, we must also observe that in this one sense at least pornography is closer to certain existential realities than art or literature can usually be. For life itself does not end in the way that a work of literature does. It ends in the meaninglessness of non-existence, of nothing (only very rarely does a life occur whose end can be thought of as a completion).[4] And if one takes a work such as My Secret Life and strips away the superstructure of sexual fantasies, one discovers directly beneath them the meaningless void, the sense that life is founded on nothing and that there is nothing to hold on to. If it were not for the fact that the activities we are discussing are of a compulsive nature, one would be tempted to regard them as in their way courageous—it takes some courage, after all, to live constantly on the brink of the meaningless. And indeed certain kinds of what we ordinarily think of as free choices appear to take the form of compulsion; it seems that one can be driven to choose certain paths or courses of action. (The contradictory logic of experience here exceeds the logic of rationality.) Among the many extraordinary—and even admirable—qualities of the author of My Secret Life is the fact that he had the courage of his compulsions. The considerable achievement of this document, if not of the life that it records, is founded in such paradoxical circumstances.

What we have, therefore, in My Secret Life is the record of a real life in which the pornographic, sexual fantasy was acted out. That the writing is both authentic and pornographic at the same time tells us something again about the stage of intellectual and sexual development that Victorian culture had reached.

NOTES

1. I am aware that . . . [elsewhere] I argued against the value of this notion and that this may seem a contradiction of that argument. I trust that the reader will see that I am not following the line of reasoning pursued by Ashbee—and others—and that my arguments tend in an altogether different direction. Furthermore, *My Secret Life* is the only work from the period that I know of which can even pretend to offer this kind of material for analysis.

2. One of the author's counterparts by analogy was William Ewart Gladstone. He too regularly walked the London streets at night, accosted prostitutes, and then tried to help them—to offer them aid or even take them home to tea. One fancifully imagines a meeting between these two Victorians—what an abyss would have opened between these two representatives of a single culture. See Philip Magnus, *Gladstone: A Biography* (New York, 1954), *passim*.

3. The attitude is omnipresent in him and in the language he uses. He speaks, for example, of his "class in life." What this conventional phrase implies is that social class was thought of as a fact of nature and that society and nature were in all ways congruent, not to say identical.

4. For an extremely cogent discussion of these and related matters, see K. R. Eissler, *The Psychiatrist and the Dying Patient* (New York, 1955).

SEX AND REPRESSION
IN AN IRISH FOLK COMMUNITY

John C. Messenger[1]

. . . I will discuss sexual repression . . . in a small island community of the Gaeltacht that I will call Inis Beag.[2]

. . . [This community has] a money economy, but barter still persists; a low standard of living prevails, and the birth rate is high; the family is of central importance, and marriage figures prominently as a provision of economic welfare. . . .

The island boasts a post office with radio-telephone facilities, a "national school" in which three teachers instruct ninety pupils in the seven "standards," two provision shops with attached "pubs," a former coast guard station now housing the nurse and a knitting industry which employs local girls, a lighthouse, and a chapel served by a curate who resides nearby. Inis Beag lacks electricity and running water . . . [and] has experienced far less cultural change than other island communities in Ireland.

. . . Crime is rare in Inis Beag, and there are no "guards" stationed there. The island is seldom visited by politicians, and many inhabitants are either apathetic or antagonistic toward the county and national governments.

. . . Anticlerical sentiment . . . is as strong as, or stronger than, its antigovernment counterpart. . . .

Inis Beag lacks a class system, and the status symbols which affect human relationships are few. There is, in fact, little difference in the style of life between the most and the least prosperous of the islanders. The web of kinship rather than the possession of status attributes, for the most part, determines who will interact with whom and in what manner.

. . . Courtship is almost nonexistent, and most marriages are arranged with little concern for the desires of the young people involved. Late marriage and celibacy are as prevalent in Inis Beag as elsewhere in Ireland.

. . . The average marriage age for males is thirty-six and for females twenty-five. My wife and I isolated almost two dozen interrelated causes of late marriage and the prevalence of bachelor and spinsterhood. . . .

To the man in his late twenties and thirties who is secure in his home and has established regularized patterns of conduct (and has a mother who acts in most ways as a wife surrogate), the general responsibilities of marriage, and specifically its sexual responsibility, are factors militating against his seeking a spouse. Some men who have land, the consent of their parents, and willing "sweethearts" will balk at a match because they are too happy "running with the lads," and if persuaded to marry, they will try to retain as much of their bachelor role as possible within marriage.

. . . Reflected in this . . . is the male age-grading conceptualized by the folk: a man is a "boy" or "lad" until forty, an adult until sixty, middle-aged until eighty, and aged after that (exhilarating to the American anthropologist approaching forty who comes from a society obsessed with the "cult of youth"). . . . [Another] cause, often articulated by the islanders, is the fact that divorce is impossible in Ireland, therefore the choice of a spouse must be well considered. It appears, however, that this argument is usually used as a rationalization for late marriage, when other causal factors are, in reality, responsible—certainly when "considering" covers two or more decades!

. . . The functions of the family are mainly economic and reproductive, and conjugal love is extremely rare. A sharp dichotomy exists between the sexes. . . . The average family has seven offspring. . . .

The island folk are devout Catholics, despite the fact that they are critical of their priests and hold pagan religious beliefs. . . . Elders cling to traditional pagan beliefs and practices (many of which are Druidic in origin) about which they are extremely secretive for fear of being ridiculed by outsiders and their more skeptical neighbors. The non-Christian array of spiritual beings includes various spirits and demons, ghosts, witches, phantom ships, and animals and material objects possessing human attributes and volitions. . . .

"Both lack of sexual knowledge and misconceptions about sex among adults combine to brand Inis Beag as one of the most sexually naive of the world's societies."

SEXUAL REPRESSION: ITS MANIFESTATIONS

Both lack of sexual knowledge and misconceptions about sex among adults combine to brand Inis Beag as one of the most sexually naive of the world's societies. Sex never is discussed in the home when children are about. . . .

Menstruation and menopause arouse profound misgivings among women of the island, because few of them comprehend their physiological significance. . . . It is commonly believed that the menopause can induce "madness." . . . Yet the harbingers of "insanity" are simply the physical symptoms announcing the onset of menopause. . . . Mental illness is also held to be inherited or caused by inbreeding (or by the Devil, by God punishing a sinner, or by malignant pagan beings) and stigmatizes the family of the afflicted. One old man came close to revealing what is probably the major cause of neuroses and psychoses in Ireland, when he explained the incarceration of an Inis Beag curate in a mental institution for clerics as caused by his constant association with a pretty housekeeper, who "drove him mad from frustration."

. . . The islanders share with most Western peoples the belief that men by nature are far more libidinous than women. The latter have been taught by some curates and in the home that sexual relations with their husbands are a "duty" which must be "endured," for to refuse coitus is a mortal sin. A frequently encountered assertion affixes the guilt for male sexual strivings on the enormous intake of potatoes of the Inis Beag male. . . . There is much evidence to indicate that the female orgasm is unknown—or at least doubted, or considered a deviant response. . . .

Inis Beag men feel that sexual intercourse is debilitating. . . . They will desist from sex the night before they are to perform a job which will require the expenditure of great energy.

. . . Our study revealed that male masturbation in Inis Beag seems to be common, premarital coitus unknown, and marital copulation limited as to foreplay and the manner of consummation. . . .

. . . Nudity and physiological evacuation are considered sexual in Inis Beag. Nudity is abhorred by the islanders. . . . Only infants have their entire bodies sponged once a week, on Saturday night; children, adolescents, and adults, on the same night, wash only their faces, necks, lower arms, hands, lower legs, and feet. . . .

"The inculcation of sexual puritanism in Inis Beag must be examined in four contexts: the role of the curate, the influence of visiting missions, enculturation in the home, and what I will term 'secular social control'—the behavioral regulations imposed on themselves by Inis Beag adolescents and adults. It is through these agencies that Jansenism, masochism, the Oedipus complex, male solidarity, and other inextricably linked factors shape the severe sexual repression which gives rise to the cultural manifestations discussed. . . ."

Despite the fact that Inis Beag men spend much of their time at sea in their canoes, as far as we could determine none of them can swim. . . . They have never dared to bare their bodies in order to learn the skill. Some women claim to have "bathed" at the back of the island during the heat of summer, but this means wading in small pools with skirts held knee-high, in complete privacy. Even the nudity of household pets can arouse anxiety. . . . In some homes, dogs are whipped for licking their genitals. . . .

The drowning of seamen, who might have saved themselves had they been able to swim, is not the only result of the sexual symbolism of nudity; men who were unwilling to face the nurse when ill, because it might have meant baring their bodies to her, were beyond help when finally treated. . . .

Other major manifestations of sexual repression in Inis Beag are the lack of a "dirty joke" tradition . . . and the style of dancing, which allows little bodily contact among participants. I have heard men use various verbal devices—innuendoes, puns, and asides—that they believed bore sexual connotations; relatively speaking, they were pallid. In a song that I composed, one line of a verse refers to an island bachelor . . . "dreaming perhaps of a beautiful mate"; this is regarded as a highly suggestive phrase, and I have seen it redden cheeks and lower glances in a pub. . . .

SEXUAL REPRESSION: ITS INCULCATION

The inculcation of sexual puritanism in Inis Beag must be examined in four contexts: the role of the curate, the influence of visiting missions, enculturation in the home, and what I will term "secular social control"—the behavioral regulations imposed on themselves by Inis Beag adolescents and adults. It is through these agencies that Jansenism, masochism, the Oedipus complex, male solidarity, and other inextricably linked factors shape the severe sexual repression which gives rise to the cultural manifestations discussed. . . .

Priests of Jansenist persuasion have had subtle means of repressing the sexual instincts of the islanders in addition to the more extreme methods of controlling behavior—"clerical social control," such as employing informers, allocating indulgences, and refusing the sacraments to, and placing curses on, miscreants. . . . Some curates have suppressed courting, dancing, visiting, and other behavior either directly or "indirectly" (widely interpreted in Ireland) sexual in nature by physical action: that is, roaming the trails and fields at night seeking out young lovers and halting dancing by their threatening presence. . . .

Church influence is also exerted through missions which visit Inis Beag every three to five years. . . . [Their] most common theme is "controlling one's passions." . . .

The seeds of repression are planted early in childhood by parents and kin through instruction supplemented by rewards and punishments. . . . Although mothers bestow considerable affection and attention on their offspring, especially on their sons, physical love as manifested in intimate handling and kissing is rare in Inis Beag. Even breast feeding is uncommon because of its sexual connotation, and verbal affection comes to replace contact affection by late infancy. Any form of direct or indirect sexual expression—such as masturbation, mutual exploration of bodies, use of either standard or slang words relating to sex, and open urination and defecation—is severely punished by word or deed. Care is taken to cover the bodies of infants in the presence of siblings and outsiders, and sex is never discussed before children. Several times my wife inadvertently inquired as to whether particular women were pregnant, using that word before youths, only to be "hushed" or to have the conversation postponed until the young people could be herded outside. The adults were so embarrassed by the term that they found it difficult to communicate with her after the children had departed. . . .

"Despite the fact that Inis Beag men spend much of their time at sea in their canoes, as far as we could determine none of them can swim. . . . They have never dared to bare their bodies in order to learn the skill."

Inis Beag people are ambivalent about gossip; they welcome every opportunity to engage in it, yet detest the practice when they are its victims. When asked to cite the major deficiencies of their way of life, islanders usually place the prevalence of malicious gossiping near the top of their list. Boys and men hide themselves in the darkness or behind fences to overhear the conversations of passersby; they maintain close scrutiny of visitors during the summer, both day and night, in order to discover them in "compromising" situations. Parties are organized at the last moment and persons will leave the island without any previous announcement—often to emigrate or enter the hospital or join a religious order—in order to circumvent gossip. Rumors run rife in Inis Beag, especially when they concern, for example, the "nude" sun bathing of a visiting actress (bared shoulders and lower thighs) or the "attack" on a Dublin girl late at night by an island youth (an effort to hold her hand while under the influence of stout). Over a dozen efforts on our part to determine the truth behind the most pernicious rumors of this genre revealed sexual fantasy at their core in every case. . . .

It is sometimes heard in Ireland, from those aware of, and willing to admit, the fact, that the inability of most Irish to "share themselves" with one another, even husbands and wives, is a heritage of the fear of gossip—a fear that one's intimate revelations will become common knowledge and lead to censure and "loss of face." A more likely explanation, according to those of Freudian bent, is the Oedipus configuration, which numbers among its many effects the following: the prevalence of romantic attachments and the rarity of conjugal love; the lack of sexual foreplay, marked by little or no concern with the female breast; the brevity of the coital act and the frequent spurning of the woman following it; the need to degrade the woman in the sexual encounter and the belief that the "good" woman does not like sex, and, conversely, that the sexually disposed woman is by virtue of the fact "bad." All of these widely reported phenomena bespeak the overwhelming influence of the mother image.

NOTES

1. A grant from the Indiana University Ford International Program enabled me to write this chapter.

2. For other reports on Inis Beag, consult Messenger 1962, 1968, and 1969.

BIBLIOGRAPHY

Messenger, J. C.
  1962. "A Critical Reexamination of the Concept of Spirits," *American Anthropologist*, 64, No. 2: 267–272.
  1968. "Types and Causes of Disputes in an Irish Community." *Eire-Ireland*, 3, No. 3: 27–37.
  1969. *Inis Beag: Isle of Ireland*. New York: Holt, Rinehart and Winston, Inc.

PICASSO
AND THE ANATOMY OF EROTICISM

Robert Rosenblum

No other great artist of our century has explored so wide a variety of human experience as Pablo Picasso; nor has any other modern artist considered the diversity of human behavior from so many different and even contradictory viewpoints. Within Picasso's vast scope, sexual themes are recurrent, and are subjected, in general, to interpretations consonant with the artist's preoccupations of the moment. Thus, in the early, pre-Cubist years, Picasso's occasional excursions into erotic art reflect, on the one hand, the libertine ambiance of an artist's Bohemia [1] or, on the other, the passive desperation of the ascetic figures who populate the works of the "Blue Period." [2] In the Cubist years, the rare references to sexual themes are, expectedly, intellectualized in the form of witty and risqué verbal puns concealed within a complex formal structure; [3] and in the Neoclassic years of the late teens and early 1920's, sexual motifs are generally interpreted in the guise of classical erotic mythologies. [4]

Such motifs, however, are relatively peripheral to Picasso's art until the mid-1920's. Then, for nearly a decade, the multiple aspects of sexual experience become a major obsession in his imagery, a phenomenon that may be explained, in part, by both public and private reasons. In public terms, this surge of interest in sexuality is a direct parallel to the official launching of the Surrealist movement in 1924, with its willful efforts to create an art and a literature that could release those suppressed well-

From *Studies in Erotic Art*, edited by Theodore Bowie and Cornelia V. Christenson. Copyright © 1970, Institute for Sex Research, Inc., and Basic Books, Inc. Reprinted by permission.

springs of erotic impulse which Freud had found basic to an explanation of human behavior.[5] And in private terms, this new fascination with the erotic may also reflect the particular tensions of Picasso's own life during these years, a period in which a growing hostility toward his wife, Olga Koklova, in the late 1920's was followed, in the early 1930's, by a period of erotic harmony in the person of a new mistress, Marie-Thérèse Walter.[6] Whatever the value of such speculations (and it should be cautioned that an art as complex as Picasso's can seldom be explained satisfactorily by a single, one-to-one correlation with the events of his personal life), there is no doubt that during the years that concern us here, from about 1927 to 1933, Picasso devoted much of his energy to the creation of images corresponding to the psychological and physiological realities of sexual experience.

"Within Picasso's vast scope, sexual themes are recurrent, and are subjected, in general, to interpretations consonant with the artist's preoccupations of the moment."

These realities, as interpreted by Picasso, cover an enormous range. At times, sexual impulses, particularly those of women, are seen as menacing, brutal, and destructive; in other cases, these forces are viewed as almost Rabelaisian jokes that turn man into a clumsy, comical creature; and elsewhere, eroticism is celebrated as a lyrical, tender experience saturated with the magic of love and the miracle of procreation. Needless to say, these interpretative possibilities are by no means mutually exclusive, but form, rather, only some of the major leitmotifs which Picasso explores and combines in the rich, multi-leveled visual metaphors of these years.

The image of female sexuality as a monstrous threat dominates the work of the late 1920's, especially in paintings that juxtapose a male profile of classical beauty with a female head of grotesque ugliness. Characteristically, these works may be read on many levels, both public and private, aesthetic and psychoanalytic. . . . In all of these works, the rationally ordered artist's world of rectilinear framing elements and of timeless serenity is shrilly assaulted by female heads of nightmare horror and violence. In one (Fig. 1), the female head almost seems to be an internal, psychological menace, a gaping maw with savage teeth and red barbed tongue that assails the profile from behind and from within its contours. In another (Fig. 2), this succubus is momentarily caged, squirming, within a frame, although a spearlike tongue form protrudes to assault the male profile's open mouth. And in another (Fig. 3), an amoeboid head, with a stitched mouth, swells toward the artist and threatens the space between him and the T-shaped form suggestive of picture frames, stretchers, and easels.

In such female heads, humanity is reduced to a subrational, bestial level, almost a pictorial equivalent of Freud's concept of the id. Indeed, in their descent down the ladder of evolution to primitive biological forms and functions, these heads can often take on strong sexual connotations, even to the point where human physiognomy is related, in visual puns, to sexual organs. . . .

Such preoccupations with Freudian sexual metaphors were not unique in Picasso, but were shared by much Surrealist imagery of the 1920's and 1930's, not only in the work of Miró but in that of the more photographic double and triple images invented by masters such as Dali and Magritte. . . . Yet Picasso's art, freed from the realist premises of Dali's or Magritte's Surrealism (which permit only a finite number of readings of a multiple image), could create infinitely more evocative puns and metaphors. Thus, in his treatment of the human head alone, the sexual analogies invented are prodigious. In one case, that of a harlequin head (Fig. 4), the mouth is aligned vertically to produce a vulva shape; in another, a fantastically scaled dream monument (Fig. 5), the vertical slit of the mouth is armed with tiny sharp teeth which evoke that Freudian metaphor of psychosexual castration fear, the *vagina dentata*. At times, the metamorphosis of a head into sexual organs is associated with a sleeping female figure, as if the relaxation of consciousness exposed the sleeper's repressed sexuality. Thus, in two paintings of 1927 (Figs. 6 and 7), a nap in an armchair permits the female sitter's mouth to open in sphincteral forms, round and oval, whose inherent savagery is emphasized by the continuous rings of teeth and, in one case, by the upward projection of a pointed red tongue. . . .

The sexual creatures Picasso invented range from sadistic monsters, armed with fanged teeth, barbed tongues, and cutting carapaces, to unicellular blobs, whose tumescence transforms them into ludicrously clumsy shapes barely capable of performing their urgent functions. Such is the case in a drawing of 1927 (Fig. 8), in which the setting is a seaside resort, a locale that often creates in Picasso's work of these years an ambiance where the human species can cavort, far from civilization, in a maximum of animal abandon. Here, a grotesquely swollen female nude, composed entirely of the same erectile tissue, attempts, with a fingerless hand, to manipulate a key in the lock of a beach cabana.[7] This action, recurrent in Picasso's seaside paintings and drawings of the late 1920's, introduces yet another metaphor whose sexuality would be apparent even without knowledge of Freud.[8]

Even more androgynous and tumescent is the sexual monster in another drawing of 1927 (Fig. 9), whose pneumatic plasm has expanded to a gravity-defiant stiffness that stands with momentary monumental grandeur in a hideous yet comical parody of the distorting protuberances produced by sexual excitement. . . .

"The image of female sexuality as a monstrous threat dominates the work of the late 1920's, especially in paintings that juxtapose a male profile of classical beauty with a female head of grotesque ugliness."

In most works of these years, diverse sexual behavior is conveyed through single figures, almost always female or androgynous, rather than through sexually active couples. Nevertheless, some works of this period do represent sexual couplings, interpreted with a comparably amazing variety that can swiftly change from the tragic to the comic, the sadistic to the gentle, the grotesque to the beautiful. In a pair of kissing heads of 1931 (Fig. 10), one finds a whimsical statement of the discrepancy between sexual passion and modern manners. Man and woman assault each other with a familiar animal savagery of bristling hair, gnashing teeth, and barbed tongue, yet the lady closes her eyes demurely and the pair modestly conceal their bodies under what would appear to be a sheet. The juxtaposition of brute sexual instinct with the constraints of modern civilization recalls the irony of many of Picasso's other works in which the orderly trappings of modern man—beach cabanas, armchairs, middle-class interiors—are startlingly contrasted with the revelation of a monstrously primal sexual force. . . .

Although the representation of a copulating couple is relatively rare in Picasso's work, in one year, 1933, he did execute a number of astonishingly imaginative variations upon this theme. At times, the motif was seen in classical guise, with one of Picasso's recurrent mythological symbols, the minotaur, as a male assailant who rapes his partner (Fig. 11).[9] Half-bull and half-man, the minotaur is particularly appropriate to Picasso's frequent association of sexual desire with the eruption of bestial forces, . . . But, characteristically, Picasso explored this theme down to its biological roots in a series of brilliant metamorphoses.[10] In one drawing (Fig. 12), the locked limbs and torsos still seem as human as in the minotaur drawing, but the heads of the sexual partners are transformed into images of more basic sexual instinct—that of the male becomes phallic, that of the supine female becomes a multiple organic form that suggests buttocks, vulva, and leaf. The equation of sexual passion with the unleashing of primal animal urges is seen even more fantastically in a drawing of a couple copulating on a beach near a cabana (Fig. 13). Here, the intricate maneuvering of limbs and torsos is geared solely to the brutal plunge of a gigantic penis into the female, an act whose inexorable force reduces the partners to a pair of brontosaurus-like monsters, whose tiny, reptilian heads look pitifully helpless and exhausted. Even lower on the biological ladder than these love-making fossils is another copulating couple who now pertain far more to a submarine species of crustaceans or mollusks than to the human race (Fig. 14). Their male and female hair flowing like antennae in aquatic currents, they lock shells in an armored sexual embrace. Other copulation drawings of 1933 introduce more comical elements. In one, the sexual encounter takes place on what appears to be a bed, a civilized intrusion that makes the couple's animal metamorphoses all the more bizarre (Fig. 15). Both male and female fingers turn into clumsily outstretched doglike claws, whereas the heads descend to even lower biological realms. Once again, the female head turns into buttocks, vulva, and leaf, whereas the phallic shaft of the male neck blossoms into a kind of sea anemone, its antennae alertly extended. In another pure line drawing of a copulating couple, sexual activity is confounded not only with organic but with mechanical metaphors (Fig. 16). Here, above the serene horizon of the sea, the male, from the waist up, is miraculously airborne, a fantastic Freudian flying machine. His head becomes a steering wheel that permits him to locate and to drop his mechanistic genitals just above their female goal, the rotund womb of a fertility goddess, whose round head and buttocks are merged in generative harmony with the circular plant growth of the earth below. . . .

. . . In his exploration of sexual imagery, Miró at times may . . . have preceded Picasso, especially in his conception of the female figure as a wellspring of procreative forces, a conception which Picasso investigated intensively only in the early 1930's. . . . Such veneration of female sexuality as a positive, life-giving force contradicted the pessimistic mood of Picasso's female monsters of the late 1920's, whose sexual attributes and functions are usually destructive, like those of a female praying mantis.[11] But soon after, in the early 1930's,[12] Picasso adapted this alternate interpretation at a time when his wife Olga was replaced by a new mistress, Marie-Thérèse Walter, who seems to have inspired a series of works that view the female form as a passive, fecund vessel of biological mystery rather than as an aggressive, menacing trap.[13]

". . . In his exploration of sexual imagery, Miró at times may . . . have preceded Picasso, especially in his conception of the female figure as a wellspring of procreative forces, a conception which Picasso investigated intensively only in the early 1930's."

In *Woman with a Flower* of 1932 (Fig. 17), the Miró-like head and hair became a pun on a sprouting seed, a germinal image which is further elaborated in the vigorous, tendril-like arms that pinwheel outward from the fruitlike breasts, and the curling stem and flower that likewise seem to grow from the fingers themselves. Generative metaphors are even richer in a series of reclining or sleeping nudes of 1931–1932 that may reflect the penchant of the blond, voluptuous, and placid Marie-Thérèse for napping and slumbering. In one of these works of 1931 (Fig. 18), the relaxation of consciousness induced by sleep turns the figure into a human still life. A green leaf sprouts from the extended fingers; two pears in the right foreground are echoed by the two ripening breasts; the lunar and seedlike head, enclosed in a dark, uterine cushion, matures with the solar heat of dawn, whose warm rays are echoed in the fiery, radiant patterns of the wallpaper. Similarly, in another sleeping nude of 1932 (Fig. 19), human and vegetal images are again confounded. Here, a philodendron plant, nurtured by the orange-red heat of the rising sun, virtually grows from the loins of the nude sleeper, just as a white flower blossoms from her fingers, and her blond hair becomes a pun upon a seed that appears to be fertilizing an ovarian breast. . . .

These metaphors of procreative magic and energy attain their richest form in two paintings of 1932 that introduce a mirror as yet another motif that may generate sexual imagery. In the earlier of the two, *The Mirror*, a sleeping blonde is seen before a mirror whose circular shape is warped into a more spiraling organic form of uterine connotations (Fig. 20). Indeed, the image reflected in the mirror is not that of the sleeper's head, but that of her buttocks and groin, from which curls forth, along the reflection of the yellow seedlike hair, a green stem, as if from a fertilized seed. . . .

In Picasso's art, these meditations reached their summit in the great painting of 1932, the *Girl before a Mirror* (Fig. 21), whose imagery, like that of another masterpiece completed in the 1930's, James Joyce's *Finnegans Wake*, is so dense and metamorphic in its constantly fluid evocations of human and biological archetypes that only a few of its multileveled metaphors may be suggested here.[14] However, it can at least be said that this work synthesizes many of the sexual themes that preoccupied Picasso at this time. For one, female sexual impulses are conveyed in a series of transformations that evoke these welling biological forces and that contrast virginity and consummation. Thus, the lavender profile view of the girl, enclosed by a white veil-halo, suggests an overt innocence that opposes the more covert frontal view of a roughed cheek and lipsticked mouth upon a glowing, golden face; moreover, the ripening forms of breasts, womb, and buttocks are temporarily constrained by the rectilinear armature of the corseted, skeletal form which holds the figure taut from behind and by the angular frontal silhouette which suppresses the organs of generation that swell toward fulfillment. Furthermore, this tense ambiance of the awakening of sexual desire is underlined by the androgynous puns so common to Picasso's work of these years. . . . Thus, the anatomies of both the girl and the mirror image that she embraces and contemplates evoke their male counterparts. In particular, the upraised left arm of the girl becomes, especially in conjunction with the testicular pair of breasts directly below it, an ithyphallic form whose sprouting fingers, in turn, metamorphose it into an image of generation, a kind of Aaron's rod. . . .

Once more, as in the sleeping nudes of 1931–1932, the *Girl before a Mirror* conveys the procreative attributes of sexual desire by a kind of vegetal imagery. The hair that adorns the girl's virginal profile is again seedlike; its mirror reflection is of a green tendril. Indeed, the anatomical zones of sexual function are generally verdant; and the breasts are like ripening fruits that exert organic, burgeoning pressures upon the concentric arcs and circles that surround them. Perhaps most telling is the black, nipple-like spot on the breast reflected at the right of the mirror. As if newly fertilized, this egg shape blossoms forth with a green sprout that in turn is continued above in the green protective layer which surrounds a half-formed head of strange, primitive mystery, both embryo and death mask. Uterus and shroud, the oval enclosure of the mirror image carries within it the wonder and terror of the ultimates of human experience. For Picasso in the *Girl before a Mirror*, these ultimates meant primarily the biological cycle of life, death, and rebirth, a cycle perpetuated by those sexual tensions which, from 1927 to 1933, also created a reigning muse, alternately monstrous and lyrical, for his art.

NOTES

1. As in the bedroom scene of the artist himself and a nude woman in the act of fellation; illustrated in Ove Brusendorff and Poul Henningsen, *Love's Picture Book* (Copenhagen, 1960), II, 112.

2. For example, the 1904 drawing of a lean and bony couple who copulate in a joyless grip; illustrated in David Douglas Duncan, *Picasso's Picassos* (New York, 1956), p. 204.

3. As in the clipping that spells out TROU ICI and is pasted under a lingerie advertisement in a Cubist collage of 1912; illustrated in Christian Zervos, *Picasso: oeuvre catalogue* (Paris, 1932 ff.), II (2), 378 (hereafter abbreviated as *Zervos*).

4. For example, in a series of drawings of a centaur abducting a woman (1920), probably to be identified as the myth of Nessus and Dejanira. For illustrations, see the exhibition catalogues *Hommage à Picasso* (Paris, Petit Palais, 1966–1967) (dessins, No. 66) and *Picasso: 75th Anniversary Exhibition* (New York, Museum of Modern Art, 1957), p. 51, where three of these drawings are reproduced.

5. I have elaborated the problematic relationship of Picasso to Surrealism in a short essay, "Picasso as a Surrealist," in the exhibition catalogue *Picasso and Man* (The Art Gallery of Toronto, 1964), pp. 15–17; reprinted in *Artforum*, V (September, 1966), 21–25.

6. The importance of Picasso's amorous life to the sexual character of his work of these years is stressed in the important study by Jan Runnqvist, *Minotaurus: en studie i förhallandet mellan ikonografi och form; Picassos konst 1900–1937* (Stockholm, 1959); and in John Berger, *The Success and Failure of Picasso* (Harmondsworth, 1965).

7. Picasso himself has referred to his fascination for keys and to their appearance in these scenes of bathers. See Antonina Vallentin, *Picasso* (Paris, 1957), p. 90.

8. It may be noted that the sexual connotation of inserting a key in a lock is so basic that the Italian slang word for copulate is *chiavare*.

9. For another version of this minotaur rape, see *Zervos*, VIII, 12.

10. These metamorphic copulation drawings, oddly enough, seem to be ignored in the Picasso literature, with the exception of Runnqvist, who briefly mentions them and illustrates one of them (*op. cit.*, p. 122).

11. The simile of a praying mantis is borne out, in particular, in such insectile heads, complete with vertical mandibles, as found in the *Seated Bather* of 1930 (*Zervos*, VII, 306).

12. The date of the beginning of Picasso's relationship with Marie-Thérèse is frequently given as 1932, but Berger (*op. cit.*, p. 154) gives it as 1931. That Picasso did, in fact, know her in 1931 is suggested by the appearance in paintings of that year of the blond, lunar head associated with Marie-Thérèse. See, for example, the 1931 Cecil Beaton photograph of Picasso before such a painting; illustrated in Ronald Penrose, *Portrait of Picasso* (New York, 1957), p. 56.

13. The profound impact of Marie-Thérèse on Picasso's art is particularly emphasized in Runnqvist, *op. cit.*, pp. 108–117, and in Berger, *op. cit.*, pp. 154 ff.

14. The only close study of this painting is that by Carla Gottlieb, "Picasso's *Girl before a Mirror*," *Journal of Aesthetics and Art Criticism*, XXIV (Summer, 1966), 509–518. Some highly suggestive comments about its multiple symbolism are found in Wylie Sypher, *Rococo to Cubism in Art and Literature* (New York, 1960), p. 280.

PLATES

Fig. 1.   Picasso, *Woman's Head and Profile*, 1929. *(Philadelphia, Collection of Mrs. J. Wintersteen.)*

Fig. 2.   Picasso, *Woman's Head and Profile*, 1927–1928.

Fig. 3. Picasso, *Woman's Head and Profile*, 1928.

Fig. 4.   Picasso, *Harlequin*, 1927.

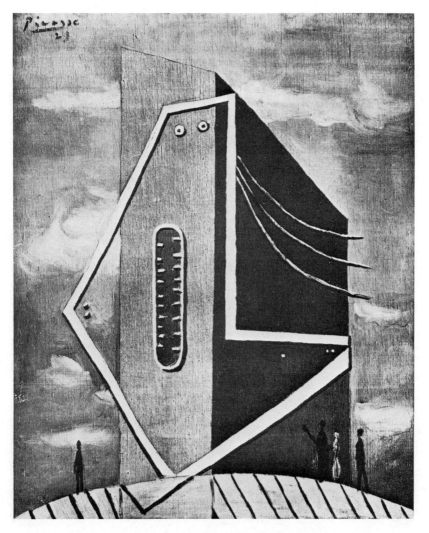

Fig. 5.   Picasso, *Monument: Woman's Head*, 1929.

Fig. 6. Picasso, *Sleeping Woman in Armchair*, 1927. (*New York, Collection of Samuel A. Berger.*)

Fig. 7. Picasso, *Sleeping Woman in Armchair*, 1927. (*Brussels, Collection of Betty Barman.*)

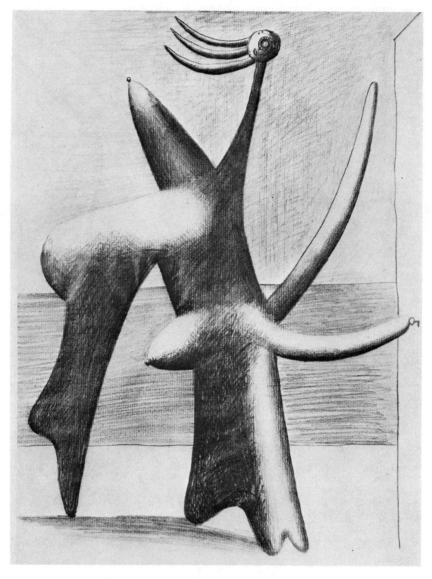

Fig. 8.   Picasso, *Drawing*, Summer, 1927.

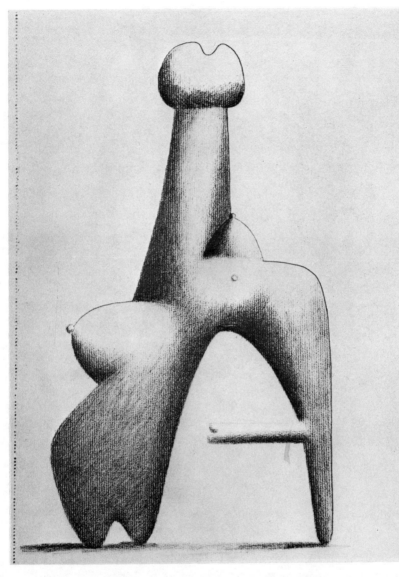

Fig. 9.   Picasso, *Drawing*, Summer, 1927.

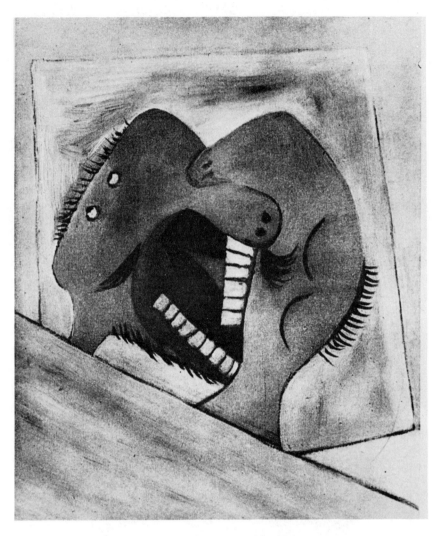

Fig. 10.   Picasso, *Two Heads*, 1931.

Fig. 11. Picasso, *Minotaur* (drawing), June 28, 1933.

Fig. 12.   Picasso, *Two Figures* (drawing), April 20, 1933.

Fig. 13.   Picasso, *Two Figures* (drawing), April 18, 1933.

Fig. 14.   Picasso, *Two Figures* (drawing), November 19, 1933.

Fig. 15.   Picasso, *Two Figures* (drawing), April 21, 1933.

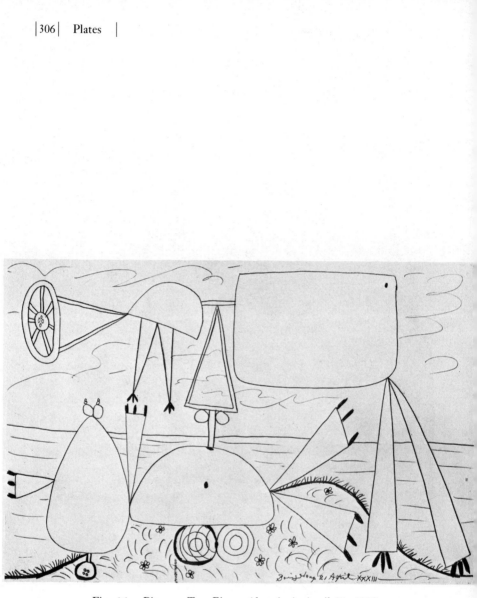

Fig. 16. Picasso, *Two Figures* (drawing), April 21, 1933.

Fig. 17. Picasso, *Woman with a Flower*, April 10, 1932.

Fig. 18. Picasso, *Sleeping Nude*, 1931.

Fig. 19. Picasso, *Sleeping Nude*, March 9, 1932.

Fig. 20. Picasso, *The Mirror*, March 14, 1932. (*Gustav Stern Foundation.*)

Fig. 21. Picasso, *Girl before a Mirror*, March 14, 1932. Oil on canvas, 64 x 51¼".
(*New York, Collection of the Museum of Modern Art, gift of Mrs. Simon Guggenheim.*)

BIBLIOGRAPHY
OF INSTITUTE WORK

BOOKS

Kinsey, Alfred C., Wardell B. Pomeroy, and Clyde E. Martin. *Sexual Behavior in the Human Male.* Philadelphia: W. B. Saunders, 1948.

Kinsey, Alfred C., Wardell B. Pomeroy, Clyde E. Martin, and Paul H. Gebhard. *Sexual Behavior in the Human Female.* Philadelphia: W. B. Saunders, 1953. (Paperback—New York: Pocket Books, Inc., 1965.)

Gebhard, Paul H., Wardell B. Pomeroy, Clyde E. Martin, and Cornelia V. Christenson. *Pregnancy, Birth and Abortion.* New York: Harper-Hoeber, 1958. (Paperback—New York: John Wiley and Sons, Inc., 1966.)

Gebhard, Paul H., John H. Gagnon, Wardell B. Pomeroy, and Cornelia V. Christenson. *Sex Offenders: An Analysis of Types.* New York: Harper-Hoeber, 1965. (Paperback—New York: Bantam Books, Inc., 1967.)

Gagnon, John H., and William Simon (eds.). *Sexual Deviance.* New York: Harper and Row, 1967.

Gebhard, Paul H., J. Raboch, and H. Giese. *Die Sexualität der Frau.* Reinbeck bei Hamburg, Germany: Rowohlt Verlag, 1968.

Bell, Alan P., and Calvin S. Hall. *The Personality of a Child Molester: An Analysis of Dreams.* Chicago: Aldine, 1971.

Christenson, Cornelia V. *Kinsey: A Biography.* Bloomington, Ind.: Indiana University Press, 1971.

Williams, Colin J., and Martin S. Weinberg. *Homosexuals and the Military: A Study of Less than Honorable Discharge.* New York: Harper and Row, 1971.

Weinberg, Martin S., and Alan P. Bell (eds.). *Homosexuality: An Annotated Bibliography.* New York: Harper and Row, 1972.

Weinberg, Martin S., and Colin J. Williams. *Male Homosexuals: Their Problems and Adaptations.* New York: Oxford University Press, 1974. (Paperback—New York: Penguin Books, 1975.)

JOURNAL ARTICLES, BOOK CHAPTERS, AND PAMPHLETS

Kinsey, Alfred C. "Criteria for a Hormonal Explanation of the Homosexual," *Journal of Clinical Endocrinology.* 1941, 1:424–428.

Ramsey, Glenn V. "The Sexual Development of Boys," *American Journal of Psychology.* 1943, 56:217–234.

Ramsey, Glenn V. "The Sex Information of Younger Boys," *American Journal of Orthopsychiatry.* 1943, 13:347–353.

Kinsey, Alfred C. "Sex Behavior in the Human Male." In S. Bernard Wortis et al., "Physiological and Psychological Factors in Sex Behavior," *Annals of the New York Academy of Sciences.* 1947, 47:603–664.

Kinsey, Alfred C., Wardell B. Pomeroy, Clyde E. Martin, and Paul H. Gebhard. "Concepts of Normality and Abnormality in Sexual Behavior." In P. H. Hock and J. Zubin (eds.), *Psychosexual Development in Health and Disease.* New York: Grune and Stratton, 1949.

Pomeroy, Wardell B. "Psychosurgery and Sexual Behavior." In N. D. C. Lewis, C. Landis, and H. E. King (eds.), *Studies in Topectomy.* New York: Grune and Stratton, 1956.

Kinsey, Alfred C., Paul H. Gebhard, and Cornelia V. Christenson. "Hormonal Faktorers

Betydning for den Seksuelle Adfaerd." In H. Hoffmeyer (ed.), *Samliv og Samfund.* Copenhagen: Hassings Forlag, 1957.

Tietze, Christopher, and Clyde E. Martin. "Foetal Deaths, Spontaneous and Induced in the Urban White Population of the United States," *Population Studies.* 1957, 11:2:170–176.

Pomeroy, Wardell B. "An Analysis of Questions on Sex," *Psychological Record.* 1960, 10:3:191–201.

Leser, Hedwig. "The Hirschfeld Institute for Sexology." In A. Ellis and A. R. Abarbanel (eds.), *Encyclopedia of Sexual Behavior.* New York: Hawthorne Books, 1961.

Pomeroy, Wardell B. "The Institute for Sex Research." In A. Ellis and A. R. Abarbanel (eds.), *Encyclopedia of Sexual Behavior.* New York: Hawthorne Books, 1961.

Pomeroy, Wardell B. "Masturbation: Attitudes and Incidence." In E. Duvall and S. M. Duvall (eds.), *Sex Ways—In Fact and Faith.* New York: Association Press, 1961.

Gagnon, John H. "Wonder Drugs, Fear of Venereal Disease, Infection and Sexual Contact." In *Proceedings of the World Forum on Syphilis and other Trepenamotoses.* (Washington, D. C., September 4–12, 1962), U.S. Government Printing Office, PHS Publication 997, 1964.

Christenson, Cornelia V. "Premarital Pregnancies and Their Outcome," *Journal of the National Association of Women Deans and Counselors.* 1963, 26:29–33.

Pomeroy, Wardell B. "Human Sexual Behavior," In Norman L. Faberow (ed.), *Taboo Topics.* New York: Atherton Press, 1963.

Pomeroy, Wardell B. "Reluctant Respondent," *Public Opinion Quarterly.* Summer 1963, vol. 27.

Gebhard, Paul H., and John H. Gagnon. "Male Sex Offenders Against Very Young Children," *American Journal of Psychiatry.* 1964, 121:6:576–579.

Gebhard, Paul H. "Sex Education," *News and Views of NABT.* 1964, 8:2.

Christenson, Cornelia V. and John H. Gagnon. "Sexual Behavior in a Group of Older Women, *Journal of Gerontology.* 1965, 20:3:351–356.

Gagnon, John H. "Female Child Victims of Sex Offenses," *Social Problems.* 1965, 13:2:176–192.

Gebhard, Paul H. "Situational Factors Affecting Human Sexual Behavior." In F. Beach (ed.), *Sex and Behavior.* New York: John Wiley, 1965.

Gagnon, John H. "Sexuality and Sexual Learning in the Child," *Psychiatry.* 1965, 28:3:212–228.

Pomeroy, Wardell B., and Paul H. Gebhard. "Sexual Behavior," *Encyclopedia Britannica.* 1965.

Weinberg, Martin S. "Sexual Modesty, Social Meaning, and the Nudist Camp," *Social Problems.* 1965, 12:3:311–318.

Gebhard, Paul H. "Factors in Marital Orgasm," *Journal of Social Issues.* (Special issue: "The Sexual Renaissance in America," ed. Ira L. Reiss.) 1966, 22:2:88–95.

Weinberg, Martin S. "Becoming a Nudist," *Psychiatry: Journal for the Study of Interpersonal Processes.* 1966, 29:1:240–251.

Gagnon, John H., and William Simon. "The Sociological Perspective on Homosexuality," *Dublin Review.* 1967, 510:96–114.

Gagnon, John J., and William Simon. "Pornography—Raging Menace or Paper Tiger," *Trans-Action.* July-August 1967, pp. 41–48.

Gebhard, Paul H. "Normal and Criminal Sexual Behavior at Older Ages," *Beitrage zur Sexualforschung.* 1967, 41:2:83–87.

Pomeroy, Wardell B., and Paul H. Gebhard. "Human Sexual Behavior," *Encyclopedia Britannica.* 1967.

Simon, William, and John H. Gagnon. "Femininity in the Lesbian Community," *Social Problems*. 1967, 15:2:212–221.

Simon, William, and John H. Gagnon. "Homosexuality: The Formulation of a Sociological Perspective," *Journal of Health and Social Behavior*. 1967, 8:3:177–185.

Simon, William, and John H. Gagnon. "The Lesbians: A Preliminary Overview." In John H. Gagnon and William Simon (eds.), *Sexual Deviance*. New York: Harper and Row, 1967.

Simon, William, and John H. Gagnon. "The Pedagogy of Sex," *Saturday Review*. 1967, 91:74–76.

Pomeroy, Wardell B., and Cornelia V. Christenson. "Characteristics of Male and Female Sexual Responses." SIECUS Discussion Guide No. 4. New York: Sex Information and Education Council of the United States, 1967.

Weinberg, Martin S. "The Nudist Camp: Way of Life and Social Structure," *Human Organization*. 1967, 26:3:91–99.

Bell, Alan P., Roy M. Whitman (Moderator), J. L. Titshoner, and S. Hornstein. "Foreplay" (Roundtable discussions at University of Cincinnati College of Medicine), *Medical Aspects of Human Sexuality*. 1968, 2:6:9, 11–13.

Christenson, Cornelia V. "Kinsey, Alfred C.," *The International Encyclopedia of the Social Sciences*. New York: Crowell-Collier, 1968.

Elias, James E. "Current Research—Sexual Patterns and Attitudes on Campus," *Proceedings of the Illinois State Deans Meeting*. Southern Illinois University Press, April 1968.

Gagnon, John H. "Prostitution," *International Encyclopedia of the Social Sciences*. New York: Crowell-Collier, 1968.

Gagnon, John H., and William Simon. "The Social Meaning of Prison Homosexuality," *Federal Probation*. np., March 1968.

Gagnon, John H., and William Simon. "Sexual Deviance in Contemporary America," *The Annals of the American Academy of Political and Social Sciences*. Philadelphia, 1968, 376:106–122.

Gagnon, John H., and William Simon. "Sex Education and Human Development." In P. J. Fink (ed.), *Human Sexual Function and Dysfunction*. Philadelphia: F. A. Davis, 1968.

Gagnon, John H., and William Simon. "Sex Talk—Public and Private," *ETC: A Review of General Semantics*. 1968, 25:2:173.

Gebhard, Paul H. "Human Sex Behavior Research." In Milton Diamond (ed.), *Perspectives in Reproduction and Sexual Behavior*. Bloomington, Ind.: Indiana University Press, 1968.

Gebhard, Paul H. "Homosexual Socialization." In J. Ibor (ed.), *Proceedings of the World Congress of Psychiatry*. Excerpta Medica International Congress Series No. 150, 1968.

Gebhard, Paul H. "Projects Since the Kinsey Reports," *Medical Aspects of Human Sexuality*. 1968, 2:4:51–55.

Gagnon, John H. "Sexual Behavior: Deviation: Social Aspects," *The International Encyclopedia of the Social Sciences*. New York: Crowell-Collier, 1968.

Simon, William, and John H. Gagnon. "On Psychosexual Development." In D. A. Goslin (ed.), *Handbook of Socialization Theory and Research*. New York: McGraw-Hill, 1968.

Sonenschein, David. "The Ethnography of Male Homosexual Relationships," *Journal of Sex Research*. 1968, 4:2:69–83.

Weinberg, Martin S. "Embarrassment: Its Variable and Invariable Aspects," *Social Forces*. 1968, 46:3:382–388.

Bell, Alan P. "Adolescent Sexuality and the Schools," *North Central Association Quarterly*. 1969, 43:4:342–347.

Bell, Alan P. "The Scylla and Charybdis of Psychosexual Development," *Journal of Sex Research*. 1969, 5:2:86–89.

Bell, Alan P. "Attitudes towards Nudity by Social Class," *Medical Aspects of Human Sexuality.* 1969, 3:9:101, 105–108.

Bell, Alan P. "Viewpoints: At What Age Should a Parent Tell His Child About Homosexuality?" *Medical Aspects of Human Sexuality.* 1969, 3:11:8–9, 13, 15.

Christenson, Cornelia V. "The Museum Dilemma: To Hang or Not to Hang," *Proceedings, 77th Annual Convention of American Psychological Association.* 1969, pp. 467–468.

Elias, James E., and Paul H. Gebhard. "Sexuality and Sexual Learning in Childhood: Research and Possible Implications for Education," *Phi Delta Kappan.* 1969, 1:7:401–405.

Gebhard, Paul H. "Misconceptions about Female Prostitutes," *Medical Aspects of Human Sexuality.* 1969, 3:3:24, 28–30.

Gebhard, Paul H. "Why Chant d'Amour Was Banned," *Censorship Today.* 1969, 2:4:17–19.

Gebhard, Paul H. "Fetishism and Sadomasochism," *Science and Psychoanalysis.* 1969, 15:71–80.

Weinberg, Martin S. "The Aging Male Homosexual," *Medical Aspects of Human Sexuality.* 1969, 3:12:66–67, 72.

Gebhard, Paul H. "Sexual Motifs in Prehistoric Peruvian Ceramics." In Theodore Bowie and Cornelia V. Christenson (eds.), *Studies in Erotic Art.* New York: Basic Books, 1970.

Gebhard, Paul H. "Personlichkeitstypen bei Sittlichkeitsverbrechern im Hinblick auf die Therapie." In *Triebtäter, Menschen oder Unmenschen.* A special magazine issue by *Stern* magazine. Hamburg, Germany: 1970.

Gebhard, Paul H. "Postmarital Coitus Among Widows and Divorcees." In Paul Bohannon (ed.), *Divorce and After.* New York: Doubleday, 1970.

Gebhard, Paul H. "Preface." In A. Shiloh (ed.), *Studies in Human Sexual Behavior: The American Scene.* Springfield, Ill.: Charles C Thomas, 1970.

Weinberg, Martin S. "The Nudist Management of Respectability: Strategy for, and Consequences of, the Construction of a Situated Morality." In Jack Douglas (ed.), *Deviance and Respectability: The Social Construction of Moral Meanings.* New York: Basic Books, 1970.

Weinberg, Martin S. "The Male Homosexual: Age Related Variations in Social and Psychological Characteristics," *Social Problems.* 1970, 17:4:529–537.

Weinberg, Martin S. "Homosexual Samples: Differences and Similarities," *Journal of Sex Research.* 1970, 6:4:312–325.

Williams, Colin J., and Martin S. Weinberg. "Being Discovered: A Study of Homosexuals in the Military," *Social Problems.* 1970, 18:2.

Williams, Colin J., and Martin S. Weinberg. "The Military: Its Processing of Accused Homosexuals," *American Behavioral Scientist.* 1970, 14:2:203–217.

Gebhard, Paul H. "The Exposure Factor." In *The V. D. Crisis. Proceedings of the International Venereal Disease Symposium,* St. Louis, April 14–16, 1971.

Gebhard, Paul H. "Human Sexual Behavior" (also Preface and Appendix). In Donald S. Marshall and Robert C. Suggs (eds.), *Human Sexual Behavior: Variations in the Ethnographic Spectrum.* New York: Basic Books, 1971.

Gebhard, Paul H. "Prostitution," *Encyclopedia Britannica.* 1971.

Weinberg, Martin S. "Nudists," *Sexual Behavior.* August 1971, 1:5:51–55.

Bell, Alan P. "Human Sexuality—A Response," *International Journal of Psychiatry.* March 1972, 10:1:99–102.

Christenson, Cornelia V. "Kinsey—A Biography," *Medical Aspects of Human Sexuality.* May 1972, 6:5:136–173.

Christenson, Cornelia V. "Kinsey Revisited," *The Review.* Indiana University Alumni Association of the College of Arts and Sciences. Spring 1972, 14:3:11–18.

Gebhard, Paul H. "A Comparison of White-Black Offender Groups." In H. L. P. Resnik and Marvin E. Wolfgang (eds.), *Sexual Behavior: Social, Clinical and Legal Aspects.* Boston: Little, Brown and Co., 1972.

Gebhard, Paul H. "Human Sexual Behavior." In *Biology Today.* Del Mar, California: CRM Books, 1972.

Gebhard, Paul H. "Incidence of Overt Homosexuality in the United States and Western Europe." In John M. Livingood (ed.), *National Institute of Mental Health Task Force on Homosexuality: Final Report and Background Papers.* Washington, D.C.: U.S. Government Printing Office, 1972.

Gebhard, Paul H. "Securing Sensitive Personal Information by Interviewing." In Peter Olch and Forrest C. Pogue (eds.), *Selections from the Fifth and Sixth National Colloquia on Oral History.* New York: Oral History Association, 1972.

Weinberg, Martin S., and Colin J. Williams. "Fieldwork Among Deviants: Social Relations with Subjects and Others." In Jack Douglas (ed.), *Research on Deviance.* New York: Random House, 1972.

Williams, Colin J. "Opinion: Is There a Relationship Between Homosexuality and Creativity?" *Sexual Behavior.* February 1972, 2:2:47–48.

Bell, Alan P. *SIECUS Study Guide No. 2: Homosexuality.* Revised edition. New York: Sex Information and Education Council of the U.S., 1973.

Christenson, Cornelia V., and Alan B. Johnson. "Sexual Patterns in a Group of Older Never-Married Women," *Journal of Geriatric Psychiatry.* 1973, 6:1:80–98.

Gebhard, Paul H. "Sex Differences in Sexual Response," *Archives of Sexual Behavior.* 1973, 2:3:201–203.

Gebhard, Paul H. "Sexual Behavior of the Mentally Retarded." In Felix de la Crux and Gerald D. LaVeck (eds.), *Human Sexuality and the Mentally Retarded.* New York: Brunner/Mazel, 1973.

Hammersmith, Sue K., and Martin S. Weinberg. "Homosexual Identity: Commitment, Adjustment and Significant Others," *Sociometry,* March 1973, 36:1:56–79.

Weinberg, Martin S., and Colin J. Williams. "Neutralizing the Homosexual Label." In Martin S. Weinberg and Earl Rubington (eds.), *The Solution of Social Problems: Five Perspectives.* New York: Oxford University Press, 1973.

Bell, Alan P. "Homosexualities: Their Range and Character." In James K. Cole and Richard Dienstbier (eds.), *Nebraska Symposium on Motivation, 1973.* Lincoln: University of Nebraska Press, 1974.

Gebhard, Paul H. "Prostitution." *Encyclopaedia Britannica, Macropaedia:* 75–81. Fifteenth edition, 1974.

Gebhard, Paul H. "Sexual Behavior, Human." *Encyclopaedia Britannica, Macropaedia:* 593–601. Fifteenth edition, 1974.

Levitt, Eugene E., and Albert D. Klassen, Jr. "Public Attitudes toward Homosexuality: Part of the 1970 National Survey by the Institute for Sex Research," *Journal of Homosexuality.* Fall 1974, 1:1:29–43.

Williams, Colin J. "Comment on 'The Africaine Courts-Martial'," *Journal of Homosexuality.* Fall 1974, 1:1:123.

Bell, Alan P. "The Homosexual as Patient." In Richard Green (ed.), *Human Sexuality: A Health Practitioner's Text.* Baltimore: Williams & Wilkins, 1975.

Bell, Alan P. "Research in Homosexuality: Back to the Drawing Board." In Eli Rubinstein, Richard Green, and Edward Brecher (ed.), *Future Directions for Sex Research.* New York: Plenum Press, in press.

Dixon, Rebecca D. "Bibliographical Control of Erotica." In Charles Busha (ed.), *An Intellectual Freedom Primer.* Littleton, Colorado: Libraries Unlimited, in press.

Gebhard, Paul H. "Comprehensive Sex Research Centers: Design and Operation Needs for Effective Functioning." In Eli Rubinstein, Richard Green, and Edward Brecher (eds.), *Future Directions for Sex Research*. New York: Plenum Press, in press.

Gebhard, Paul H. "Marital Stress" and "Stressor Aspects of Societal Attitudes toward Sex Roles and Relationships." In Lennart Levi (ed.), *Society, Stress and Disease: Male and Female Roles and Relationships*. Oxford University Press, in press.

Beasley, Ruth A. "Current Status of Sex Research." *Journal of Sex Research*, in press.

Weinberg, Martin S., and Colin J. Williams. "Gay Baths and the Social Organization of Impersonal Sex," *Social Problems*, in press.

MONOGRAPH SERIES

Marcus, Steven. *The Other Victorians: A Study of Sexuality and Pornography in Mid-Nineteenth-Century England*. New York: Basic Books, 1966.

Peckham, Morse. *Art and Pornography*. New York: Basic Books, 1969.

Bowie, Theodore, and Cornelia V. Christenson (eds.). *Studies in Erotic Art*. New York: Basic Books, 1970.

Marshall, Donald S., and Robert C. Suggs (eds.). *Human Sexual Behavior: Variations in the Ethnographic Spectrum*. New York: Basic Books, 1971